£7

The
Quest for
Frank Wild

The Quest for Frank Wild

Angie Butler

Jackleberry
Press
June 2011

First published in Great Britain 2011

Published by Jackleberry Press

Jackleberry Press
Radway
Warwick CV35 0UJ

angie.butler@dsl.pipex.com

ISBN 978-0-9569272-0-0

Designed by Lodge Graphics
Printed in Great Britain by MPG Biddles Ltd.

British Library Cataloguing in Publication Data
A catalogue for this book is available from the British Library

For my siblings Adrian, Pippa
and twin brother Mark

He was the man who had been to them as a hiding place from the wind, and a covert from the tempest; as rivers of water in a dry place, as a shadow of a great rock in a weary land.

For many men will always have courage so long as the man who leads them has courage. When a great man dies, we weep not so much for what he was, as for what we thought him to be and are therefore all the more deeply bereft.

South African Tragedy: Life and Times of Jan Hofmeyr
Alan Paton

CONTENTS

Robert Falcon Scott

Ernest Shackleton

Douglas Mawson

Roald Amundsen

PROLOGUE

"He was short in inches but he had the heart of a lion and his intensely blue eyes were set stedfastly towards what is right"

Eight years ago I read *The Worst Journey in the World* by Apsley Cherry-Garrard, one of the definitive books on the 'Heroic Age' of polar exploration and one that has fired up many people's interest in polar history. It was not long before I began to devour bookshelves of literature on the subject. Robert Falcon Scott, Ernest Shackleton, Douglas Mawson and Roald Amundsen. In the face of terrible hardship they wrote about their ordeals in beautifully succinct prose with a modesty not often found today. But one man in particular caught my attention: he was much less known than the others, yet he had more experience of the Antarctic than any of the famous four. His tally of five expeditions to Antarctica was without equal for which he was awarded the Polar Medal with four bars – a unique achievement. He spent more than 10 years in the frozen wastes of Antarctica and ended his days in the sun-baked land of South Africa. He was John Robert Francis Wild - known as Frank.

Frank Wild's quiet good manners, sound education, humour and spirit for adventure was shaped in childhood. He came from a solid, hard-working middle-class Yorkshire family. At the age of 16 he joined the merchant navy, a school of hard knocks that prepared him for his life on the ice fields. He had all the attributes needed to make a first-class explorer, an inexhaustible reserve to bear hardship, a willingness for laborious backbreaking work and an exceptionally level head.

He died in 1939 at the age of 66 working as a storekeeper on a mine in the small Transvaal town of Klerksdorp. Over the years it has been reported he was an alcoholic and a drifter, forgotten by his comrades and disregarded by his adopted country. This description of his later life has often even eclipsed his brilliant career in polar exploration. There was also something utterly bewildering in the story: no one knew where he was buried. How had one of the greatest explorers of the 'Heroic Age' become lost in life and seemingly in death too?

I realized that practically nothing was known of Wild's life in Africa and the little that was known was a truly damning account of his time spent there. I have felt an affinity for this story because I was born and brought up in South Africa and have a passionate love for the country, and also because Wild's exceptional character as an explorer did not tie up with the man who ended his days in that country.

However, I did not set out to write a book – I merely set out to discover how he had spent those years between the wars, why he had fallen on hard times and more than anything I wanted to find his grave. I always told myself once I had discovered what I was looking for, I would hand my research over to those better qualified to deal with it: polar historians, institutes and societies.

I had but one lead, the name Rowbotham. Wild's second wife was a South African called Beatrice Lydia Rys Rowbotham, known generally as Trix. During my first research trip back to South Africa, I found a handful of Rowbothams in the Johannesburg telephone directory and by a stroke of luck the first person I telephoned was June Rowbotham, the daughter-in-law of Benjamin, Trix's brother. She was extremely surprised to find anyone interested in Wild and informed me that she had inherited all of Trix's papers and letters, including typed copies of Frank Wild's Memoirs and his diary of the trek to farthest south, describing the punishing attempt to reach the South Pole during Shackleton's Nimrod Expedition of 1907–09.

Gradually June Rowbotham and I built up a relationship, and on one of my frequent visits to her little house south of the city, she generously handed over all the material to me, which I in turn offered to the Scott Polar Research Institute in Cambridge.

As time went by my interest in Antarctic exploration and in particular my obsession with Wild increased. Not only had his name been besmirched by sensationalistic reporting that was repeated and often embellished, but as I picked my way through the maze I found other dark areas, shadows of intrigue and shades of wrongdoing.

Several years later, sitting ankle deep in papers, firing off stinging emails to those who repeated the inaccurate accounts about him, I knew I had to tell his story. As a biographer I would need to give up my role as Wild's minder, stand back and let the truth speak for itself.

My research uncovered Wild's determination to write his Memoirs not only for posterity but to have them published as a means to earn money. He wrote them longhand in pencil, on white, lined exercise book paper, covering events up until his time on Elephant Island, where he and 21 men faced almost certain death but were miraculously rescued. There they ended, abruptly and tantalizingly. Suddenly in 1939 he died of pneumonia before he had completed them. Fortunately, his close friend, Karl Einar Behr, who lived in Messina in the northern part of South Africa, had had his secretary type the Memoirs up with several carbon copies. In spite of Trix's efforts to fulfill her husband's wishes, they have remained unpublished until now. The story as to why they have, is a story in itself.

But 72 years after his death and more than 40 years since Trix's, their wish to publish the Memoirs has now been fulfilled.

EARLY LIFE

Wild, the eldest son and the second eldest of 13 children, was born on 10 April 1873 in Skelton, Yorkshire. He was described by his cousin Maggie Wild as a fragile baby – 'his skin hung about him like a ladies loose gown' – but it wasn't long before the attractive child with a fearless, impish nature grew in strength. Like many of his siblings, he had inherited his father's piercing china-blue eyes, a feature remarked on throughout his life. He was short in stature, less than five feet five inches tall but perfectly proportioned and exceptionally strong.

Frank's mother, Mary, the youngest of 11 children, was born in 1847. Her father, Robert Cook, a tenant farmer and Constable of the district of Lilling, was a devout Methodist and a vociferous member of the Temperance Society. Cook married Mary Hutchinson of Sheriff Hutton at the age of 40 and they lived long enough to enjoy their golden wedding anniversary. He read the Bible without the aid of spectacles and spent hours in the paddock next door to the house, lobbing a cricket ball to his bat-wielding nine-year-old grandson, Frank. The boy's passion for cricket lasted throughout his life, highlighted on one occasion by an invitation to take part in a match with the celebrated cricketer W.G. Grace.

The family, deeply religious and teetotal, had to contend with their own black sheep, Jabez, one of Mary's brothers, who finally drank himself to death, after which, due to his enormous size, he had to be lowered through the bedroom window wrapped in a bedspread. Robert Cook lived to the age of 90, but two accidents, a trampling by his pet calf and a fall against a gate, hastened his end.

It was believed by the Wild family that they were related to Captain Cook, something Frank Wild proudly claimed many times. It is only recently that this has been disputed, but it is easy to see how the story captivated several generations and absorbed many hours of letter-writing and discussion amongst the family members.

The story handed down by Frank's grandfather Robert was that his father, James, was the son

Mary Wild with Frank's brother Laurie

of the famed explorer Captain Cook. James was supposed to have drowned off the Isle of Wight but had, according to Robert, actually deserted from the navy, a crime punishable by death. Somehow the deserter made his way to Yorkshire where he married, but shortly after the birth of Robert he left both wife and child. Robert therefore claimed to be the secret grandson of Captain Cook.

Benjamin Wild

Frank's paternal side of the family came from the pottery-making area of Wakefield and Castleford in Yorkshire. His great grandfather, Benjamin, was a potter, as was his grandfather, also named Benjamin. Frank's father, yet another Benjamin, broke with family tradition and began his working career as a pupil teacher at the Wesleyan School at Sheriff Hutton, followed by two years of teachers' training. He was given the post of assistant master at the National School in Skelton in 1870 and at the age of 24 he married Mary. She was a petite, fine-boned young woman, one year younger than he was.

Within the first year of their marriage a daughter was born, who was named Sarah Ann Margaret, although known as Nancy. She was followed by the birth of Frank, and for the next 22 years it was a constant exhausting round of bearing and nursing children. In 1876 Benjamin took a better teaching post in Stickford in Lincolnshire, where three daughters were born, Cissie, (Mary Elizabeth,) Minnie Rosetta who died soon after birth and Rosetta Blanche who died at nine months old. Each death rendered Mary into wretched despondency, and she was to suffer many more bereavements.

From there the family moved to Nettleton, also in Lincolnshire, where Henry Ernest, known simply as Ernest, was born. He was the only other sibling to become a polar explorer, when at the age of 35 he joined Shackleton's Imperial Trans-Antarctic Expedition, playing a key role in depot-laying from the Ross Sea region.

The following year, now with eight children in tow, the family moved to Wheldrake in Yorkshire. Mary, in addition to running her busy household, took the position of sewing mistress at the school. Four years at Wheldrake produced three more children: Benjamin, Rupert and Laurence.

In 1884, at the age of 11, Frank, a member of the local church choir, sat the exam and was offered a place as a chorister under the Gothic spires of York Minster school. At the same time, his father was offered a headmastership at the

Left to right: Stanley Northwood, Rupert, Laurie, Frank, Christine, Harry Ernest, Percy, Stanley, Harry Bryant. Seated: Mary Elizabeth with Ernie, Benjamin, Anne with Beatie

school in Eversholt in Bedfordshire. The post was too significant to turn down, and he announced to his family they would soon be packing up and moving south. With that decision, Frank's opportunity to spend the next few years under the rigorous discipline of the choir school disappeared.

His brother Stanley recalled in a letter to his great niece: 'Nothing gave me more pleasure than lying on a rug as a child in front of the fire after church and listening to our older brother sing sea shanties accompanied by our sister Cissie, on the piano.'

The grand farewell took place at York Station, where the extended Wild family gathered to see them off. The shriek of the whistle signaled departure and with three-month old Laurence cradled in his mother's arms, two-year-old Rupert clinging to her skirt and father Benjamin gathering up the other six children, the Wild family jostled into the compartment and took their seats. The train pulled away in a pall of steam and was soon chugging through the flat snow-covered countryside. Eleven-year-old Frank would not return to his roots again until he was a fully-grown man.

On 5 January 1885 Benjamin took up his appointment as Principal Teacher in charge of some 70 children. Eversholt was a small rural village, tacked onto the side of the Duke of Bedford's rolling parklands, and the majority of its residents were employed on the estate.

The attractive red brick Georgian headmaster's house, attached to the school and a stone's throw from the church* stood out from the simple workmen's cottages.

A year after settling in Eversholt, Percy was born, a year later, Christine, and finally at the age of 44, Mary gave birth to her last child, Stanley.

The headmaster, immaculately turned out and sporting a neatly clipped moustache and beard, was a popular teacher, strict but nevertheless with a mischievous sense of humour. He recorded in the school logbook that a parent threatened to make 'mincemeat' of him 'on account of the deserved chastisement of his daughter.' Punishments were rigorously dished out, crimes such as torturing cockroaches received one stroke on each hand, as did 'irreverent behaviour,' such as pulling a girl's hair during prayers. A boy who was sent home for being dirty collected three stripes on the hand for lingering when he should have returned to school.

It was on these same tough lines that Benjamin ran his own household. If the Wild children received a punishment at school they could be sure the same punishment was meted out once they returned home. Frank's early character building had begun.

However, Benjamin encouraged all forms of entertainment and would gather scholars, teachers and the older members of his family to the school's reading room for an evening of recitations, demonstrations of hand drill for the girls and gun drill for the boys, concluding with a comedietta such as 'Love Honour and Obey,' all of which were performed with gusto. Front seats cost one shilling and those at the back thruppence. The funds were used to take the children for a day's summer excursion by train to the seaside town of Margate.

Numbers of attendance fluctuated with the seasons as the children were made to help on the land. 'Woodin' – collecting firewood after a storm – acorn collecting, hay-making and potato-picking were some of the duties that were expected of them. The biggest causes of absenteeism were the terrible epidemics of scarlet fever, mumps, measles, diphtheria and whooping cough that swept through the villages, forcing the schools to close for many weeks.

At home the boys had the freedom of a room known as the 'boys' workroom' where they kept their many pets, including jackdaws. A particular tame bird called Jack would fly into the boys' bedroom and wake them up by pulling on their hair or knocking their studs, cuff links, brushes and combs from the

*A plaque in memory of Frank Wild was unveiled in the church in 1973 by the Bishop of St Albans, the Right Rev Robert Runcie. It reads, IN LOVING MEMORY OF COMMANDER FRANK WILD R.N.V.R. C.B.E. F.R.G.S. OF THIS PARISH. FREEMAN OF THE CITY OF LONDON. ANTARCTIC EXPLORER WHO ACCOMPANIED SCOTT, SHACKLETON, AND MAWSON ON FIVE SOUTH POLAR EPEDTIONS BETWEEN 1901 AND 1922. It was unveiled by the Bishop of St Albans.

dressing table onto the floor. The undisciplined bird followed them to school and stole rubbers and pencils from the classrooms, which the Wild children were made to replace with supplies purchased with their hard-earned pennies.

The local farmers paid the Wild boys a farthing a head for each sparrow they shot with their air guns, and they grew into excellent marksmen, capable of putting a bullet through a potato thrown in the air. They were all expected to take their turn with housework duties and were rewarded with family games in the evenings. When tea was finished, one of the children was allowed to get up from the table and play a scale on the piano, while the others sang. The one to hold the highest and most tuneful note for the longest time was the winner.

Even at the age of 89, Frank's cousin, Ann Clara Bostock, was able to recall holidays spent with the family when at the age of 14 she was sent from Yorkshire to Eversholt to help out at the school. 'Frank was always climbing. I saw the belfry door ajar so I went quietly in and saw nobody either in church or vestry and heard a sound from somewhere…then I saw my boy on top of the pillar sat on the cornice with his little legs hanging down (I almost felt like having a fit as we say). So I said how are you going to get down young man, "Oh if you will draw the bell rope close to this pillar I will catch it." So I took hold of the thick rope and did my best and he caught hold of it and came down like a monkey, but to our astonishment the bell rang so we hurried out and went home.'

She remembered Frank and his brother Charles William, a year younger, caught with their pockets stuffed with apples belonging to a local farmer. The farmer took chase and the boys took off and escaped by ducking under a bridge and hiding on a ledge until it was safe to scurry home.

The irate farmer approached their father and the boys' crime was exposed. Fetching his cane, Benjamin called for his two sons. Charlie fought back the tears but Frank held out his hand and said, 'I will take it, Sir!' His father lifted the cane and brought it down missing his hand by a wisp. Frank's hand never moved. The boys explained they had found the apples on the road 'and you may have them all back!' retorted Frank.

Later that day Frank took Clara to the bridge and pointed out the ledge they had precariously hung on to, and she was horrified to find that it was no more than 12 inches wide. 'He was a little terror but to see him in the choir in his surplice, he looked a little angel who could do no wrong.'   She remained close to Frank all through his life, and he showed his fondness of her by making her a brooch fashioned from the teeth of one of his expedition dogs that had been killed in a fight with another dog. Frank's inquisitive nature was curtailed for a time when he crushed his fingers in his mother's mangle, although he did have the presence of mind to turn the handle back to release them. His sister Cissie said of him, 'as a boy he was a great reader and not a word could be got out of him till he had finished the tale or book he was reading. He liked magazines because the tales were shorter. If it was satisfactory he lay it down gently and said "a good yarn that" but if not the book would fly across the room with the one word, "piffle."'

It was hoped Frank would follow in his father's footsteps, as he certainly had the aptitude, but he showed little interest in teaching. While working as a pupil teacher in the village of Woburn, he kept the children in order by firing paper pellets at them with his catapult. His ambition was to join the merchant navy and, shockingly for his parents, he threatened to run away if they did not concede.

The family turned for advice to the vicar of Eversholt, whose two sons were sailors, with the end result that at the age of 16 Wild was given a job on the clipper *Sobraon*, the largest fully rigged composite ship of the time. Besides cargo, it carried 70 crew and 250 passengers from Plymouth to Melbourne. It was the beginning of a rigorous 11 years zigzagging across oceans on all categories of sailing ships, including 'lime juicers' on which one was expected to do 'maximum work for minimum food and wages.' It was unremitting hard work in sub-zero temperatures or paralyzing heat.

Rounding Cape Horn in winter, spray froze on the rigging and deck, covering the braces in frozen shards of ice that had to be broken off by hand. There was no escape from reefing and furling the frozen topsails, even during the most violent storms, and frostbite was common. Wild was gaining all the skills that was would be essential for his later survival.

In contrast to the cold, a passage through the Red Sea was equally calamitous. 'We had to steam in the opposite direction to our course for two hours, to cool the ship as with a following wind the heat was so terrific that five firemen had been passed up from the stoke hole unconscious, several passengers fainted and one dropped dead with heat apoplexy.'

A merchant navy man worth his salt was a hard worker, hard drinker and hard player, often bearing a badge of honour in the form of scars and tattoos. Wild, at an early age, measured up to all these traits and continued to do so vigorously throughout much of his life. He bore an eagle and snake on his right forearm and a ship and anchor on the other and while he was not a fighter, an unexplained scar was evident on the right side of scalp.

Many years later, Jimmy Dell a shipmate, recounted an eight-day stop in Simonstown, South Africa, on the *Discovery* Expedition. After a carousing night out, he and Wild came round on a 'Yankee four master' pulling out of the harbour and were nearly 'shanghied' – taken onboard for compulsory service. The skipper, on discovering they were with the Royal Navy, thought better of it and returned his human cargo to shore.

Wild progressed from 'lime juicers' and tramp steamers to Lord Brassey's

Sunbeam and then *Britannia*, where he met Edward, Prince of Wales, the future King of England. By the time he left the merchant service to join the Royal Navy he believed he had been around the world nine times.

In 1897, as Wild was coming to the end of his merchant navy career, Charles, his younger brother and a much-loved pupil teacher at Eversholt school, died of rheumatic fever. Charles was only 22 years old, and Frank was desperately sad on hearing of the death of his childhood playmate.

In August 1900, the Wild family suffered another terrible loss. Benjamin Eustace, the third youngest sibling, died of *'enteric fever' (typhoid) during the Boer War, in the small town of Kroonstad, in the Orange Free State. Initially rejected for war service because he was too short (5' 3"), he was accepted into the Army Service Corps and died within four months of arriving in South Africa from a disease that killed more soldiers than the war itself. He was only 19 years old.

Two months later Frank Wild joined the Royal Navy as an able seaman, resulting in the opportunity to apply for the British National Antarctic Expedition on *Discovery*, under the command of Robert Falcon Scott. Much to his surprise – he believed his height of 5 feet 4 1/2 inches would ruin his chances – Wild was chosen from more than 3,000 applicants.

In a fanfare of national pride topped by a visit from King Edward VII and Queen Alexandra, *Discovery* departed from Cowes, Isle of Wight, for New Zealand on 6 August 1901. Edward Wilson, the assistant surgeon and artist on board, noted 'The King gave the Victorian Order of the First Class to Captain Scott before leaving, having with great difficulty fished it out of his tail-coat pocket, which was a long way round on the wrong side of his stout figure.'

It was three years before Wild returned to Eversholt. The school closed for the day and Benjamin Wild and family left for London by train for a reception held in honour of the expedition. Stanley Wild described his homecoming.

A scout was sent by bicycle to meet Frank coming home by pony and trap from the station and getting back first to give warning of his arrival. Little coloured fairy lights were on every windowsill of our house, Chinese lanterns hung from an archway over the front gate. The door was wide open showing the dining room, lit by paraffin lamp, showing the huge dining table full of good things to eat and homemade wine to drink, with villagers wandering in and out at will. As soon as the scout arrived giving warning of the imminent approach of the pony & trap, the church bells began to ring, as the trap neared the village the band struck up with *'See the conquering hero comes!'*

* The official figures reveal that of the British Force of 556,653 men who served in the Anglo-Boer War, 57,684 contracted typhoid and 8,225 of those died, while 7,582 were killed in action. (*samilitaryhistory.org*)

As Frank got down from the trap the congregated villagers gave him three hearty cheers of welcome, while two farmers fired a double volley of salute on their shot guns.'

Throughout his life, Wild was viewed as having a character of steel, and he kept his emotions in check even during the most difficult of times. However, the softer side of his character still showed in his family life, as he cared deeply for his siblings and parents.

During his infrequent visits home, his cousin Maggie wrote: 'Frank loved to come and confess his sins to my old mother.' She recalled he would 'sit at her feet, his head against her lap staring silently into the flames of the fire as she ran her fingers through his hair, he had some then, and suddenly he broke the silence and said I remember once on the great white plain – life was at a low ebb – we were hungry cold and in pain – when a vision of mother rose before me. There and then I took a vow that if I could get back home and sit at mother's feet and feel her hand upon my head, nothing would ever again tempt me to come back to this God forsaken country; and when I got back she was dead.'

Ernest was the only sibling to follow in his footsteps – joining Shackleton's Imperial Trans-Antarctic Expedition, for which he received the Polar and Albert medals. He was described thus by Alexander Stevens, the chief scientist: 'There are some things that have great value but no glitter. Consistent...long-suffering, patient, industrious, good-humoured, unswervingly loyal, he made an enormous contribution to our well-being.' This description would describe the Wild family as a whole. At the age of 39, Ernest died in 1918 of typhoid in Malta while serving on the minesweeper HMS Biarritz.

Mary Wild died on the 23 March 1909 at the age of 62, during the final months of the Nimrod Expedition. Before she died she had told one of her daughters 'don't worry about Frank, he and all the party are well and on their way home.'

Wild's father moved to the nearby Georgian town of Ampthill, where he ran a stationers and newspaper shop in the town centre. According to Wild's cousin Charles Clark, Wild bought the business for his father for £800. Benjamin died in 1915 when his eldest son was again in the Antarctic. Both he and his wife were buried in the church graveyard in Eversholt with their son Charles.

Wild's Memoirs include four expeditions he took part in: the British National Antarctic Expedition (Discovery) 1901–04, the British Antarctic Expedition (Nimrod) 1907–09, the Australasian Antarctic Expedition (Aurora) 1911–14 and the landing on Elephant Island during the Imperial Trans-Antarctic Expedition 1914–17.

1917 – 1921 THE WAR YEARS AND NYASALAND

On his return from the *Endurance* Expedition in November 1916, Wild was met with the devastating consequences of war. So many he had known and loved had been killed. He immediately enlisted, and whilst living in London awaiting orders he took his brother Stanley on a night out.

Since the *Discovery* Expedition, Wild had become something of a celebrity. The Scots comedian Harry Lauder – a great friend – was performing at the Shaftesbury Theatre accompanied by the striking American vaudeville singer and dancer Ethel Levey to raise funds for the soldiers. Wild took Stanley, who was then 26, to dinner at the Trocadero, and then they went on to the theatre to meet up with Lauder – who was thrilled to see them and handed round generous glasses of whisky in the dressing room. Miss Levey, described by a critic as having 'the deftest precision and the most satisfying go' burst into the dressing room while Lauder was pulling on his trousers and berated him for a turn that had gone wrong in the show. Stanley – by far the more innocent of the two brothers – remarked he was 'highly interested and amused by this side light on show business!'

Stanley also recounted another London outing with his brother. 'One day during the 1914–1918 war, Frank and I were riding on top of one of London's old open top buses. Occupying the seat in front of us were a General and his ADC, a captain. The latter must have noticed Frank's Antarctic medal ribbon, for he turned round and said "Commander Wild I believe?" The General would be pleased if you would lunch with him." Frank said "I can't, I have my brother with me." The ADC replied, "The General says bring him along too." On getting off the bus Frank whispered, "you don't want to come do you?" I said "why not?" So we all went into the Strand Place Hotel and five of us sat at table together – the General, his ADC, a private clothes detective, Frank a Lieut-Cmdr RNVR, and your humble servant a mere sergeant wearing a wound stripe.'

Following Russia's declaration of war on Germany in 1914, the badly under-equipped Russians relied on Britain and France for vital war supplies. These were shipped from two main northern ports, Murmansk and Archangel, via the North Atlantic Arctic route.

In the spring of 1917, following a crash course of Russian at the Berlitz School in London, Wild was sent to Archangel as a lieutenant, RNVR, and transport officer to supervise the arrival of convoys carrying millions of tons of war supplies and munitions.

In August that year, Shackleton requested the Admiralty release Wild, with the intention that he could join him on a covert expedition to Spitsbergen, part of the Arctic archipelago of Svalbard. However, Shackleton was then ordered to join the North Russian force in charge of Arctic equipment, and Wild took over leadership of the Spitsbergen expedition.

The British government provided an armed merchant ship *Ella, to transport Wild and his men to Spitsbergen, supplying them with 60 rifles and 100,000 rounds of ammunition in case of trouble from the Germans encamped on the island. Wild was put in charge as manager of the mining company, the Northern Exploration Company. The German camp turned out to be deserted, but there was another political motive behind these activities. Ostensibly, the company was set up to mine iron ore, but in reality it was there to establish a British presence and to stake out extensive claims so as to occupy as much territory as possible.

This, it was believed, would strengthen the case in future negotiations for acquiring the archipelago for the British Empire. As it happened, Norway established control there in 1925.

In a sense, Wild was once again flying the flag for the Empire, and he took on the job with his usual diligence and zeal. However, this time he was very much his own boss, added to which he had an old chum to assist him, Dr James McIlroy, with whom he had formed a close bond on the Imperial Trans-Antarctic Expedition. Wild supervised 60 Scandinavian miners, a mining engineer, three hardy Yorkshire foremen, a storekeeper, cook and steward. Their camp at Cross Fjord was made up of army huts, which they had carried with all the provisions and equipment required for 14 months on the ship Ella. The standard army huts proved wholly inadequate against the harsh Arctic blizzards, and added to their discomfort. They also suffered from scurvy: 'our teeth were rattling in our heads,' as McIlroy wrote.

Although several tons of iron ore was mined and shipped, there not enough to make the project financially viable and the miners turned to extracting coal. A horizontal entrance was cut into the side of the mountain and the grueling work of cutting tunnels along the coal seams began. Over the next 14 months, approximately 5,000 tons of coal was sent down on a double wire known as a 'flying fox' and then hoisted onto a light railway to be transported to the shoreline.

*He was later awarded the Mercantile Marine War Medal for the voyage he led through a 'danger zone' whilst on Ella. According to medal expert Glenn Stein, Wild also qualified for it when sailing on Endurance, as the ship was classed as a mercantile vessel at the very start of the war and sailed through the South Atlantic as the Battle of Coronel took place on 1 November 1914.

Temperatures driven by ferocious winds were often as low as −50°C and as the Arctic winter took hold, so the sun vanished.

A Swedish mining camp 39 miles to the east could be reached on foot by following a frozen fjord, and 29 miles to the north, tucked behind mountains riveted with crevassed glaciers, lay a Norwegian settlement. Wild and McIlroy were unfazed by such hazardous journeys, which could be accomplished in a day's march but only by the light of a full moon. On their arrival, quantities of Swedish punch and Aquavit would await them, and the Englishmen would return the hospitality by plying the Scandinavians with navy rum.

McIlroy had a close call when on his way to the Swedish camp. He fell through a six-foot crack in the ice and only just managed to haul himself out. By the time he limped to his destination in −40°C temperatures, he had almost succumbed to hyperthermia and exhaustion.

Saturday nights were spent with a concert and a toast to 'sweethearts and wives,' a tradition that carried on throughout Wild's polar career, although on Spitsbergen the toast was not limited to just one tot.

The men set up a hunting hut stocked with food and blankets in a valley some 10 miles from the camp. From there they bagged reindeer, white and blue foxes and occasionally the much-sought-after white ptarmigan, a partridge-like bird that brought an additional delicacy to the pot.

Polar bears were an ever-present threat and fair game for the two explorers. During one encounter they were stalked for four miles by a female polar bear with cub, which Wild described as 'sheer good luck that we got her before she got us. She stood well over seven feet in height.'

On another occasion they pursued a lonely male for some 11 miles until he took to the sea and escaped. Having missed breakfast, the men returned to their hunting camp to find it had been ransacked by the bear and all that remained were packets of baking powder. They had no alternative but to continue marching the 10 miles back to base on empty stomachs in a bitterly cold −30°C.

There was plenty of time to sit around the table in the smoke-filled mess hut, the darkness of the polar winter broken only by the light of their paraffin lamps. It was believed at the time that a fortune could be made growing tobacco in Portuguese East Africa and right then a warmer climate must have seemed tempting. It was then they decided to try their luck in such a venture as soon as the Great War was won.

For now, they were caught on Spitsbergen, McIlroy attending to minor injuries and a rather more challenging case of psychosis when one of the miners suffered a nervous breakdown. The man announced he was fed up with Spitsbergen, and ran across the ice in his undergarments announcing he was 'going home.' He was brought down five miles away from the camp, and to the consternation and no doubt hilarity of the others believed his navel was becoming unscrewed. McIlroy succeeded in pacifying him by twice daily going through the motions of tightening his belly button up with a screwdriver.

'The expedition was not by any means a financial success', wrote Wild, 'but taking it all in all the experience was quite a happy one and pleasant to look back on.'

Wild had £500 in shares in the company, but unfortunately it was dissolved in 1929 and the shares proved useless. Wild was not to know then that his mining experience on Svalbard would be a vital factor in his efforts to survive in South Africa some years later.

By 1919, the Great War was over. Wild had heard 'wondrous accounts of the possibility of making rapid and colossal fortunes in Portuguese East Africa by growing tobacco.' Wild, McIlroy and fellow explorer Frank Bickerton, whom Wild had met on Mawson's 1911–14 Australasian Antarctic Expedition, pooled the little money they had and set sail for South Africa via St Vincent. Arriving in Cape Town they caught up with old friends before setting off for the coastal port of Beira. Heading up the sweltering east coast via Delagoa Bay, Beira and finally Chinde, they reached the mouth of the Zambezi River.

The men found the Portuguese authorities difficult while trying to negotiate the purchase of land, and came to the decision that their prospects would improve if they proceeded north into the British Nyasaland Protectorate, today known as Malawi.

It was an arduous journey by train from the Mozambique coast to Blantyre, the capital of Nyasaland, a wild and untouched country. Not much bigger than England, Nyasaland had little more than a thousand white settlers at the time, mostly farmers and missionaries.

Other than the disappearance of the slave trade the country had barely changed since the arrival of Dr David Livingstone 60 years earlier. His travels in Africa had fuelled the imagination of young Victorian boys and adventure in the heart of sub-tropical Africa, with all its challenges, had not lost its appeal.

The three men investigated the region and decided upon a 1,000 acres 30 miles south of Lake Nyasa, which they bought from the natives for £3/12s with an option to buy another 1,000. They did their own surveying and saw to it that they were 'not short of a 1000.' The land was teeming with wildlife: elephant, rhino, buffalo, lion and every species of buck. Labour was cheap and there was a seemingly endless supply of willing natives to hack and tame the virgin forest. Wild wrote to his cousin Maggie Wild.

'Wonderful country, splendid niggers. Both are untouched and unspoiled by contact with the white man. No missionaries within 100 miles thank the Lord. We all loved the country and the natives…'

The men built a simple, four-roomed house, kitchen and storeroom surrounded by a wide verandah, as well as accommodation for five house staff and their wives, which Wild claimed cost no more than £5 in materials. 'It was seldom we had to go more than five hundred yards from our house to get something to fill the pot…'

It was pioneering stuff and back-breaking work. Yet the men marvelled at the abundance of game, simply there for the taking. On the days they couldn't be bothered to hunt they were able to buy fowls from the natives for 3d each, 'huge' ducks for 1 shilling and four eggs for a 1d. Maize, fruit and vegetables were there for the taking. The natives, he noted, were 'wonderous clean' and bathed at least once every day.

But it was not all plain sailing. Wild found himself having to hunt down lion that frequently attacked the plantation workers, a job that put 'the wind up' him. Leopards ambushed their goats, snakes snatched the chickens, while thieving hyenas stole into their meat pantries. Rats, he complained, ran over everything and 'rather deadly beggars' – scorpions, centipedes, tarantulas and hornets – crawled everywhere. The men suffered debilitating bouts of malarial fever, and after some months Bickerton was forced to return to England. Yet with all its drawbacks, life as an African settler suited Wild.

He was convinced that he could live simply in this idyllic, verdant country on £25 a year. As they expected to make £2,000 per annum in cotton sales, he was full of optimism for the years that lay ahead, the prospects of making a fortune seeming well within his grasp. They had been there less than a year and had cleared the land and planted 250 acres of cotton when suddenly Wild was faced with a decision that would overturn all his plans for the future and reshape the rest of his life.

A young barefoot African runner, panting with exhaustion, arrived at the homestead and handed Wild a telegram; it was from Shackleton, asking the men to return and join him on another expedition. McIlroy initially hesitated, but Wild did not waver – once again it was not only 'the call of the little white voices' but the wish of 'the Boss.' He trekked back to Fort Johnston, going much of the way on foot. Forced to cross knee-deep through swamps and rivers peppered with crocodiles, he then had to pick his way through the Miombo forests teeming with game until he caught the train to Port Herald. There, he caught a boat to Chinde and thence to Beira, from where he headed to Cape Town, where finally a passenger ship returned him to Southampton. Wild was certain that he would return to Nyasaland, but at that instant his great friend and leader had sent for him and the chance to go back with him into the ice was irresistible.

Shackleton and Wild aboard Quest

QUEST EXPEDITION 1921 - 1922

Shackleton was worn down by the constant stress of financing expeditions and the Shackleton-Rowett Expedition in *Quest* was no exception. In 1920, he was determined to gather his trusted lieutenants on one more expedition to the Arctic, but this fell through when the financial backing offered by the Canadian government was withdrawn. Saving the day, John Quiller Rowett, Shackleton's schoolfellow from Dulwich College, generously offered to stump up the funds. However, finances were severely strapped from the start.

Shackleton purchased a little 'roller' the 34-meter, wooden-hulled whaler *Foca*, which his wife, Emily, renamed *Quest*. The object was to chart and map little-known islands and to take soundings and magnetic and meteorological observations in the sub-Antarctic.

On the 17 September 1921 *Quest* set sail for Rio de Janeiro and Cape Town. The ship encountered massive seas, storm after storm, so violent that Shackleton could not leave the bridge for five days. Problems with her engines meant hold-ups all along the way, delaying progress by six weeks. Anxious to reach Antarctic waters, they decided not to stop in Cape Town to collect further supplies.

Dr Macklin drew a graphic picture of conditions in a letter to his parents: 'Worsley, who is a fine seaman, preceded me up the rigging, and I cannot answer for his feelings, but my own were the reverse of happy, for by this time the wind was terrific, and the ship was jerking about in the head seas in the most awkward manner. Swinging into the rigging we crept up the cat lines, the force of wind flattening us against the stays and making it difficult to move our legs from the rung they were on to the next above. From the main rigging a loose rope ladder passes upwards to the topsail yard, and this swung jerkily in and out so that one went up slowly and carefully, clinging desperately to prevent being slung off. Once out on the yard we had the greatest difficulty in gathering in the wet stiff canvas, and more that once it was torn from our grasp. Whilst there, a particularly violent squall struck the ship, when it was all I could do to cling desperately to the yard, fervently hoping that I should not be shot like a stone from a catapult, into the boiling cauldron below, for I knew that any attempt to pick me up would be hopeless, and would, indeed, never be made. Worsley in crossing behind me to get to the end of the yard, put his mouth close to my ear and shouted something, but the wind snatched the words from his lips so that I had to signal him may times to repeat what I expected would be some sort of directions. All he said however, was "This is a blooming fine Christmas, isn't it?"'

The sponsor's wife, Mrs John Rowett, had provided the ship with a Christmas parcel containing all sort of luxuries, turkey, ham, plum puddings, muscatels and raisins and 'dainties of every description,' but due to the horrific conditions all they were given were bully beef sandwiches.

Macklin wrote: 'On Christmas day a whole gale blowing and the sea had begun to run so high that the Quest was rolling and pitching in the liveliest manner,' and nothing in the way of crockery would stay on the tables. There was a 'cold green Barney's bull of a sea running.'

On 4 January 1922, the ship sailed into Cumberland Bay and dropped anchor in the still waters of Grytviken harbour, where they were met by old friends and acquaintances at the whaling station. Shackleton went ashore with Mr Jacobsen, the manager, returning to the ship in high spirits for dinner. After the meal, he rose to his feet, saying cheerily 'good night boys, you have had a tough time, so have a sound sleep, and tomorrow we'll keep Christmas.' But they never did.

At approximately 3 a.m. Wild was woken in his cabin by Macklin and McIlroy with the shocking news that Shackleton was dead.

Macklin, who was on anchor watch between 2 and 4 a.m., recounted: 'A cold night but clear and beautiful, with every star showing. I was slowly walking up and down the deck, when I heard a whistle from the Boss's cabin. I went in, and he said, "Hullo, Mack, boy, is that you? I thought it was. I can't sleep to-night, can you get me a sleeping draught?" he explained that he was suffering from severe facial neuralgia, and had taken fifteen grains of aspirin with little effect.'

Macklin tucked a heavy Jaeger blanket around the Boss, encouraging him to take things more quietly in the future. 'You are always wanting me to give up something. What do you want me to give up now?' Those were Shackleton's last words.

Macklin recounted Wild's reaction on learning of Shackleton's death. 'Wild was most extraordinary you know. Instead of sitting up and gasping in astonishment at the act, he said 'is he dead' just like that and we said well what are you going to do. He said we can't do anything. You just go to sleep. And in the morning Wild summoned the hands. He just looked at me and asked me if I had any idea what I was going to do with the body then he said we will consider it tomorrow. We went back to bed. Extraordinary calmness.'

It was an agonising blow for Wild to lose the man he loved so dearly, but he also knew that Shackleton would expect him to demonstrate supreme self-control.

Wild said nothing to the rest of the ship until 8 a.m. the following morning, when he mustered all hands and informed them of the news. He announced that he would take command and that the expedition would continue. On that day it rained heavily and for several days more, 'fitting for our low spirits.'

Wild set a course for the Great Ice Barrier lying to the east but he was soon weighed down by increasing problems with the ship that had developed a crack in the boiler furnace and a leak in one of the water tanks. Besides a shortage of coal the pack ice was rapidly closing in and the decision to reach the Antarctic coast was little more than a false hope. Whilst the expedition's scientific exploration around the South Shetland Islands was of some significance she returned to South Georgia having been away for less than three months.

On the 6 April 1922, they entered Leith Harbour and in spite of Dell recalling of Wild's leadership that 'you wouldn't have known the Boss had gone out of it,' it was a voyage that had been fraught with difficulties.

Wild found that some of his supposedly loyal staff were not only criticizing the running of the expedition, but discussing their dissatisfaction with the sailors below. In his understated manner he wrote, 'I assembled each mess in turn and going straight to the point told them that further continuance would be met with the most drastic treatment.'

To add to the disruptions, the captain, Frank Worsley, only just escaped death when a heavily laden lifeboat that was being moved swung into him, crushing his ribs. With Shackleton gone, the tight rein on alcohol loosened and undeniably Wild and others had their share.

However, once back on South Georgia, there was more important business to take care of – the building of a memorial to the Boss. On Lady Shackleton's instructions, the great explorer's body – which had been on its way to England – was returned to South Georgia from Montevideo for burial. Wild collected together the men who had loyally served the Boss on previous expeditions – Worsley, Macklin, McIlroy, Kerr, Green and Mcleod. On a headland that overlooks Cumberland Bay, they built a cairn of stone, laboriously blasted from the surrounding hill and to which a brass plate was fixed with the words:

SIR ERNEST SHACKLETON
EXPLORER
DIED HERE JANUARY 5TH, 1922
ERECTED BY HIS COMRADES.

The cairn – upon which is fixed a wooden cross – still stands aloft, guarding entry to the bay. It is, in fact, the first thing to be seen when entering the bay's gleaming waters and the very last when leaving.

'So we said good-bye to the "Old Boss," and I who have served with him through four expeditions know that if he could have chosen his own resting-place it would have been just here,' wrote Wild.

When the restocking of the ship had been completed, the expedition departed from South Georgia and made its way to Tristan da Cunha, Gough Island and on to Cape Town, all the time suffering from another storm-ravaged journey. 'I had a spell of sea-sickness which did not help matters,' wrote Macklin, continuing, 'even

Shackleton's burial at South Georgia

Shackleton's grave

Cairn overlooking Cumberland Bay

Wild & Worsley, those hardened old shell backs felt it a bit, and it takes a lot to upset them.' Mr Jacobsen, the manager of the whaling station, had given the ship a young sow, which they named Bridget, but even she was sea-sick and had to be found a berth in the bathroom.

The meals were miserable and Green had a trying time in the galley, but somehow managed to come up with something hot at each meal, including a number of creative dishes such as penguin stew, curried penguin eggs, roast sea elephant, cottage pie of seal or whale meat, reindeer stewed or curried, roast albatross or seabirds done in a variety of ways.

Quest docked in Cape Town, causing a stir amongst the city's inhabitants. It was considered a great privilege to host the returning explorers, and invitations flooded in from all corners. Wild was the honored guest at a dinner given by the Freemasons, but nothing topped the reception held for the expedition members by the Prime Minister General Jan Smuts.

It is likely that it was Smuts – who became a close friend of Wild's, often inviting him to stay at his exquisite house Doornkloof near Johannesburg – who suggested that he return to South Africa to farm. Smuts founded the British Empire Service League (BESL) to care for the welfare of ex-service men and women and to provide them with employment, and he was behind a Soldier Settlement scheme to allot farms to war veterans as a reward for their service. Smuts no doubt thought Wild the perfect candidate.

Shortly after Quest returned to England – docking in Plymouth on 16 September 1922 – Wild re-met Vera Alexandra Altman, a dark-haired, dark-eyed woman with something of a gypsy quality. The two had previously met in Russia when Wild was stationed there in 1917. She was the fifth child of Emily and Theodore Bogosoff of Odessa, a cigarette maker and tobacco merchant. After her father died, she lived with her widowed mother and four siblings in Bristol and, like two of her sisters, became a schoolteacher.

In 1901 she married William Alfred Pettitt, a Professor of Music – it is not known why this did not last, but six years later in Bristol, she married Granville Joseph Altman, whom quite likely she met through her brother Theodore. Theodore Bogosoff worked as an assistant for Altman on his tea plantation in Brunei, British North Borneo, and later gained further employment on a rubber concession known as the Biang Estate, which also belonged to Altman.

In the meantime, Altman had been employed by the British government to work in Vladivostok, where Vera joined him. They had two sons – Valor Granville, born in 1908, and Niegel Poultney, born in 1912.

In 1917, at the start of the Russian Revolution, Vera crossed Russia, which must have been a hellish journey, and ended up in Archangel with her two children; either Altman feared for his family's safety or Vera simply took off. There she met

Wild, who was working as a transport officer at the port, and he helped the young woman and her two small boys find a passage to Britain.

Vera would not see her husband again. Altman died in September 1919 in Vladivostok. According to his will, Vera received an annual sum of £300 for life, affording her a comfortable income.

In 1920, she sailed to New York, returning to Plymouth towards the end of 1921 travelling first class. Several reasons could explain what happened next. Wild had been through a physical and emotional tempest. He had lost a devoted comrade in Shackleton and he was contemplating a future in South Africa. For her part Vera was looking for a new relationship and a father for her two sons, who were now 13 and nine years old, respectively. The fact that Wild knew and liked the boys immensely must have influenced her decision to get married. The wedding took place in the Registry Office in Reading on 24 October 1921 followed by a brief honeymoon in Bournemouth.

Wild's close friend McIlroy, who believed he knew Wild as well as he knew himself, was kept in the dark about the nuptials. 'He didn't tell me about it, he kept absolutely quiet, because he knew perfectly well that I'd do my best to stop it. So you see what the woman was … so he went off to Zululand with this woman and she started to drink, and altogether she behaved very badly and he divorced her.'

There is no evidence to suggest that because Wild was unable to come to terms with Shackleton's death, he decided to immigrate to South Africa in 1923. Britain in the 1920s had far from recovered from the Great War, and the colonies offered both prospects and adventure.

Unquestionably the loss of Shackleton was devastating, but Wild believed that that the Boss remained with him, and that was a constant comfort. 'I have his photograph signed by him hanging up at home, and once a year, on the anniversary of his death, we have a little drink together. I always feel that he knows exactly what I am doing and how I am faring. I know it sounds foolish but that is exactly how I feel about it.'

His cousin Maggie, a devotee of Wild and avid letter writer, noted: 'Only once did I see Sir Ernest Shackleton and as he talked to me of Frank his eyes shone and his voice vibrated with emotion.' She continued in another statement, 'like David and Jonathan their love was wonderful, passing the love of women.'

Shackleton wrote of Wild, '… it is hardly necessary to write about him. He is my second self. I love him, as does every decent man on the expedition. He has been a tower of strength to me. Take him absolutely into your confidence about everything, including finance. He is a man … He is a damn sight better than a good many generals we have.'

SOUTH AFRICA

Although Wild always intended to return to Nyasaland, he realised the untamed country in the heart of Africa was no place for his new wife and two young stepsons. During this period, the statesman, philosopher and military leader, Field Marshal Jan Smuts, was Prime Minister of South Africa

Under Smuts' scheme, Wild – with a partner called Spray – was allotted a 1,000 acre farm in Mkuze, northern Zululand. It was a beautiful tract of land of mostly acacia bush with the Obombo Mountains in the distance. Wild paid 15s/6d an acre for the land, which he named 'Quest,' after the ship. Wild was under no illusion that farming this virgin land would be easy. Malaria was the cause of many deaths and wild animals roamed at large.

Vera spent little time on the farm, preferring to live in the coastal town of Durban some 200 miles away with her son Nigel. While there, and on Frank's instruction, she posted a copy of the book *Shackleton's Last Voyage* to the King, with the inscription, 'Presented by humble duty by his loyal and devoted servant.'

Her son Valor, a sturdy young boy in his teens with an engaging smile and the swarthy looks of his mother, enjoyed life in the bush with his step-father.

The accepted view is that Wild's Antarctic fame was mostly ignored in South Africa, when in fact he was courted by the great and the good and none more so than by Smuts. Undoubtedly, the death of Benjamin Eustace Wild during the Boer War would have touched Smuts, who had also lost a brother to typhoid several years earlier.

On 3 October 1924, he wrote to Wild: 'I saw Vera in Durban, and if I had not found her there I might have come round to look you up in Zululand. She gave me an account of all that was happening and so I thought it unnecessary to come round that way. ....When the Xmas holidays come round we wish you to send Vera and the children to Doornkloof, and Vera should remain here while the worst heat and malaria continue in Zululand. If you could be spared from the farm you should also come for some time and feel the more bracing climate up here.' Again, he wrote to Wild on 20 Jan 1925: 'When are Vera and the boys coming up here? You know you will all be most welcome, none more so than you: and I should not like malaria to get hold of your family.

In spite of the remoteness of his daily life, Wild was invited to give lectures on his polar adventures to eager audiences. He told them, 'I should hate to settle down, and I never will until old *Anni Domini* makes it compulsory. No one can be called settled down who has to get up at 5 a.m. and look after a farm of 1000 acres. Clearing, stumping, ploughing, harrowing, fencing, etc all in different parts of the estate often entailed walking from six to ten miles in the course of the day. This farm will certainly hold me down a good deal more than I have been accustomed to but if cotton prices keep I have hopes still of seeing more of this little old world that I have already travelled over fairly extensively.'

In pre lecture notes he wistfully jotted down: 'Do I long for the sea and ice again, Good God yes. Get down to Durban get down to the point to spend a few hours or a whole day with men I understand and who understand me...find some genial chap in the Yacht Club to lend me his boat for a run in the Bay.'

He made the point that he would not be in South Africa if he didn't like it. He told of his farm in Nyasaland being only a few feet above lake level and in the Tsetse fly belt, making it impossible to keep domestic animals other than goats and he assured his audience that Zululand was 'a veritable health resort' in comparison.

Poignantly, he wrote, 'I do long for the sight again of limitless fields of snow, of still or heaving pack of the gorgeous riot of colour which only those regions know and which must be seen to be believed, to feel again the awesome silence of a Polar night, and to fight a stout ship through 400 crushing crashing monstrous bergs or barely visible growlers, with a shrieking hurricane in the rigging, blinding snow and frozen spray taking the skin off the face, the little craft rolling 50 degrees each way, scores and sometimes hundreds of tons of ice on the deck and probably the galley fire swamped and no hot food or drink for days on end. Glorious, and who knows? I may yet repeat the experience.'

Even today, one is struck by the remoteness of Mkuze and surrounding towns, but in the 1920s it was the back of beyond, linked to the bigger towns of Newcastle and Ermelo by not much more than tracks, dusty in dry weather and mud slides in the wet. Surprisingly, however, letters reached their recipients, and at the end of 1924 Wild received a registered parcel from the Office of the Governor-General in Pretoria. It contained the Gold Medal conferred on him by the American Geographical Society. The medal had been sent to the American Embassy in London, which then forwarded it to Downing Street, from whence in turn it was sent to the Earl of Athlone, the Governor residing in Pretoria. From there it continued to the Quest Estate.

It is not surprising that Vera chose not to live with Wild. Life was exceptionally difficult for white women in the African bush, except for the very few who loved hunting and the isolation it offered. Milly Selley, whose husband, Nick – a renowned engineer responsible for constructing the railway line and bridges that still stand to this day and who was later to employ Wild – said she did not see another white woman for a year. Living quarters were modest, the heat unbearable and the fear of malaria ever present. For every sleeper laid on the railway track a member of the workforce died of malaria.

Meanwhile, Percy, Frank's brother, was in South Africa from 1923 to 1928 and assisted Wild in his farming venture. In order to bolster funds, Wild accepted a contract from Nick Selley to extend the South African railway from the Swaziland border to Mtubatuba as part of the line that ran through the Quest Estate.

Frank in front of the South African Railway hut

The Selleys – with two small boys – became close friends with Frank. Percy helped both on the railway and on the farm, concluding he was 'fully entitled to the name Voortrekker.' He cleared the bush and ploughed the land with a three-furrow disc plough drawn by 18 oxen. Wild employed more than a hundred Zulus on both railway formation and on the estate. He was known by the Zulus from Mkuze to the Swaziland border 'as the little man with the bald head who is always smiling.'

Wild built a simple house of wood and corrugated iron. It was typical of the time, surrounded by a verandah and enclosed with wire netting to keep out mosquitoes and snakes. Beside it stood a 1000-gallon tank to store rainwater for domestic use, and later Wild put in a borehole and windmill. Gas and paraffin lamps were used for lighting, and wood fires burnt during the cold winter nights to warm the house. All the domestic chores were carried out by Dick, Wild's much trusted 'house boy' who hailed from Swaziland.

By 1926, less than three years after leaving England, the marriage was over and Vera took her youngest son Nigel and fled back to England. Valor remained to help Wild on the farm. On 28 December 1928 they were officially divorced. Shortly after her return to England, Vera met Reginald Markham Levinge, described as a planter and superintendent of customs, whom she married in May 1929. Vera died in England in 1954.

Cissie, Wild's sister, disparagingly described Vera as an 'adventuress' and indicated that the collapse of the marriage was 'the first disappointment that started breaking him up.' His sisters believed he would not be able to choose a suitable wife for himself, referring to his wanderlust, yet he was to prove them wrong.

Wild, in his effort to keep the farm afloat, had over a period borrowed £1,575 from Vera, which he agreed to repay back in instalments, although there is no record that he did. Wild made a will soon after his divorce, leaving everything to Vera, but she never benefitted from it. Many years later, Wild received a letter from the well-known American writer Poultney Bigelow, a

Wild (right) with trusted 'houseboy' Dick in white apron

close friend of Vera's second husband, Altman, and most likely once a close friend of hers too, because Bigelow was Niegel's godfather. 'You are lucky in being rid of that much married lady who took yr money and gave nothing in return,' Bigelow wrote.

Wild received a letter from Jan Smuts, written on 1 Jan 1931, saying the news on Vera 'was not very favourable,' and he also mentioned that the sponsor of the Quest Expedition had committed suicide. 'I was very sorry to see that poor John Rowett had gone & hanged himself – poor devil.'

Wild had been determined to make a success of the farm, but cotton farming at the time met with frequent misfortune. In October 1924, Smuts lent him £500, half of what he asked to borrow. 'I am sure you will make good and I am equally sure you will not get prematurely discouraged by the initial troubles of the settler's life,' wrote Smuts.

In the following January, again Smuts wrote to Wild: 'I see you are still in need of money....' and he sent him another £250, asking him to do things as economically as possible as he would not be able to give him any more. 'I doubt that any source will be available.'

In 1925 all hopes of a fruitful crop were devastated by 60 inches of rainfall over a 10-day period, washing away bridges and roads as well as the cotton crops. 'I watched pumpkins, dead livestock and to my horror, even dead native bodies being swept down the river,' wrote Milly Selley in her diary.

The Zululand newspaper reported 'in the remote parts of Mkuze…men of our race have watched their lands, sodden with water, gradually give up the bright promise of the early season and vanish in a sea of mud.

Two years later, the area was flooded again, on top of which insufficient transport and impassable roads hampered the delivery of cotton. The *Zululand Times* reported: 'the ten historical plagues of Egypt pale in significance before the chapter of afflictions this district has been called upon to suffer'. A settler wrote that 'most of us are ex-servicemen, and do not want to plead for charity, yet we do feel that the Government might come forward and make it possible for us to obtain loans from the Land Bank. It is the only thing that can save us now…the alternative is ruin'.

Ninety per cent of the cotton crop was entirely ruined, but the settlers believed the losses were an anomaly, and hoped for better times. The new planting season during the latter part of 1925 was filled with optimism as steady rain fell, but then it stopped abruptly, and by early 1926 the farmers were facing a prolonged drought. A pattern of flood and drought continued to repeat itself, followed by an insect infestation of Jassids (leaf hoppers) and bo weevil, beetles that desecrate cotton buds and flowers. By 1928, the majority of settlers, including Wild, were ruined.

Wild's stepson, Valor, had no option but to leave. Wild had enjoyed both the company and help offered by the strapping young lad of 19 and would have been very sad to say goodbye to him. It appears he went to work with his mother's brother, Theodore Bogosoff, who had carried on managing the Biang Estate in Brunei (British North Borneo) after the death of his father, Granville Altman. The estate had been left to Valor and Niegel by their father. Valor married Winifred Cowpe in 1964, when she was 51 and he was 56, and in 1977 he tragically committed suicide by shooting himself. Niegel Poultney, later to be known as Nigel, left for New York at the age of 17, where with the help of his godfather Bigelow Poultney he became an undergraduate at Union College in New York and later an actor.

Despite the difficulties, Wild had many good times with the Selleys. While working on the railway and living in tents, their camps were set a mile apart from each other. Spray, his partner, had a

Wild (centre) working on railway on Mkuze River

car that he left on the far bank of the Pongola river and Wild built a boat known as 'the coffin' that they used for the crossings. Milly remembered that: 'none of us had much money but what a lot of fun we had. A note would come from Frank Wild; 'We have green beans tonight, please come over!' I would send a note down to their camp 'the bread will be out of the oven, please come.'

The four would play cards late into the night, and at weekends they would cross the river in 'the coffin', jump into Spray's car and drive to the Mkuze hotel for an all-night party with a mixed bunch of settlers, engineers, storekeepers and farmers.

'We danced to the music of a portable gramophone. The most popular records were 'Lady be Good' and 'Sonny'. The men always wore dinner jackets and bow ties, while the girls wore dinner or dance frocks.....how we used to dance on those nights.....Frank living up to his (sur)name at a party but who only spoke of his Antarctic experiences on rare occasions.. *Extracts from Milly's diary, West of the Moon Ron Selley. The parties would last until the early hours and after a breakfast of bacon and eggs the revelers would leap into their cars and roar off into the sunrise.

On one occasion Milly recorded that after a day's shopping in Mkuze, followed by a hard night drinking, she and her husband Nick, accompanied by Wild and Spray, made for 'the coffin' parked on the river bank. It was a black night and none of them carried torches. Wild and Spray had packed their purchases from earlier that day in a suitcase and Wild, who had had a few too many, ignored Spray's protests and took off into the darkness carrying the suitcase. It wasn't long before he fell down a 'donga' and disappeared into a void. The remaining party panicked, thinking the worst. When Frank was found, he lay motionless, announcing he had lost the use of his legs. 'Can't get up Nick. I think I have had it,' he moaned. Selly attempted to move him, gently enquiring where it hurt most, then burst out laughing. The heavy suitcase had fallen across Wild's legs, pinning him to the ground and rendering his limbs immovable.

Wild redeemed himself a few weeks later when the small party discovered someone had left 'the coffin' on the far side of the river, which was too deep to cross on foot. Wild plunged into the water in full evening dress and swam to the bank on the other side and brought the boat across.

Milly recounted: 'Spry, Nick and I shouted at once in horror expecting Frank to be taken by one of the resident crocodiles before he made the opposite bank. He got the boat and dragged it back for us.' They enquired why he hadn't sat in it to bring it back and he answered he didn't want to get it wet. 'What an indomitable spirit he had.'

Despite all this, Wild was, in fact, afraid of swimming, having had a near-death experience when swept off a ship during his merchant navy days. He told

Nick Selley and Wild (right) with the notorious coffin

Wild's stepson Niegel (Nigel)

Wild's stepson
Valor

Tented camp near Pongola River

Nick and Milly that he was terrified of being taken by sharks or crocodiles, having witnessed horrendous attacks in the past. Nick found bangles in the stomach of a crocodile he had shot and it was common knowledge crocodiles were a threat in the Pongola River.

The general store* in Mkuze supplied the locals with everything from the basic staples of flour and sugar to hardware items – hoes, shovels and tin buckets. All purchases were recorded in leather ledgers and Wild's monthly spend, which included 'bar sales,' was 16/- or thereabouts, a modest sum when compared to his companions who spent as much as £6 per month.

With the railway contract to subsidize him, Wild earned £742 pounds in a year. However, by the time he set his farming losses against this figure, it had dwindled to less than £300. When the railway contract came to an end, he was back to living 'on fare that the poorest of the poor would have scorned.

Due to failing crops, food became scarce and meals consisted of 'mielie meal' porridge made from crushed corn, the staple diet of Africans. If one was lucky he might eat a chicken at the weekends. The farmers sold most of their possessions, and Spray had no choice but to sell his car. Undaunted, Wild devised another form of transportation to avoid the dreary walk to Mkuze village. He hitched his two remaining oxen to a Scotch cart on which he placed a comfortable armchair, a small table with a portable wind-up gramophone and some records. A young African 'umfaan' (boy) sat in the cart and was given the task of winding up the gramophone and changing the records, while another 'umfaan' led the oxen on foot. In this way, Wild and anyone who cared to join him would be conveyed into town. 'The first time I set my eyes on this equipage, I laughed so much I was overcome by hiccups,' wrote Milly in her Memoirs.

At this time Wild met Jack Scott, a 24-year-old engineer who was working on the railway with Nick Selley. Scott was later to play a pivotal part in Wild's life.

In the 1950s, the Rattray family – who over the years have owned large swathes of land in South Africa – bought the farm 'Quest' and turned it over to sisal plantations, before selling it in the late 1980s to the present owner, Charles Senekal. Michael Rattray explained 'these farmers just walked away leaving everything behind them, machinery and tools. 'Quest' always lost money!' Lions continued to be a threat even in his time, and he recalled two

---

*The store was started by the Rutherfoord family in 1918 and the Mkuze hotel a little later. Three generations of the Rutherfoords have lived and still run businesses in the area including Ghost Mountain Inn, which stands today on the site of the old hotel.

male lions escaping from the near-by game reserves and terrorizing the locals in Mkuze.

Today when visiting the area, 'Quest' still exists, although it is part of a much larger estate. It borders the small town of Mkuze, which then was no more than a settlement; the railway still runs through it, but the original house is gone. Much of it, flat and featureless, is today under sugar cane and there are plans to turn over a sector of the estate for housing. However, something shall always remain: the majestic Ghost Mountain in the distance, a magnificent sentinel that stands proud above the Umbombo mountains – a view that greeted Wild each time he stood at his front door.

Wild was next offered a temporary job 25 miles from Mkuze at the delightful little *Victorian hotel in Gollel (Golela), while the manager, Wild's friend, was away on leave. The hotel was a hub of activity, much like the Mkuze hotel, a watering hole for the farming community and a hostelry for the many travelers on their way from the coast into the hinterland.

Wild would greet everyone enthusiastically, carrying their suitcases to the building that housed comfortable bedrooms separated by a long corridor. In

*The hotel stands today on the Swaziland side of the border, in a place known as Lavumisa. It is a typical African border, with a cacophony of rumbling trucks, idling cars, people on foot and African market stalls set up to catch the constant passing trade. The little hotel had barely changed since Wild's time, but unfortunately it has recently succumbed to 'modernisation.' Some of the original features still remain, however: the corrugated tin roof, the front verandah and the typical Victorian interconnecting salons. The building behind the hotel with the bedrooms and beautifully pressed ceilings are sadly awaiting a 'makeover.' The bar, which was complete until very recently, has now gone.

Ghost Mounting standing proud above the Umbombo Mountains

the evening, dressed in black tie, the Englishman would serve behind the bar, famously known as the longest bar in South Africa. On the wall were pinned two enormous python skins, all of six feet long, which Wild had shot. The evening would gather pace, the music would be turned up and it would develop in to a raucous party, with most everyone taking to the floor.

Life was tough for the white farming communities, with much time spent in isolation, but British trends and changing social mores of the 1920s managed to find their way onto the African continent, and what was viewed by some locals as hedonistic behavior was taken up often by ex-pats with gusto. Women shortened their skirts, bobbed their hair and puffed on cigarettes. At the slightest opportunity, people would congregate at the various hostelries or private homes–sleek cars, dancing and jazz were the order of the day. The Great Depression was looming, and life would change irrevocably, but for the farming community there was still room for gaiety.

Tales of Wild's antics became legendary in the district; it was said that one evening while serving at the bar he took a bet to swim the Pongola River in his dinner jacket. The following day someone threw a stick of dynamite into the pool and three dead crocodiles surfaced. It is a far-fetched story because the Pongola is some six miles from Gollel hotel where he was working.

A Johannesburg newspaper reporter discovered Wild working in the hotel and wrote a sensational article in a national newspaper saying that he was broke, forgotten by his fellow countrymen and had been found working as a barman for £4 a month. This image of Wild as a man on skid row has been perpetuated throughout the years.

For a man who shunned publicity it was a wounding slight to which he responded quietly: 'it's a job, and I am not a loafer.' In reality the post was temporary, and he was helping out a friend.

South Africa at that time was experiencing a boom in the mining industry – gold had been discovered in 1886, and small mining outfits were mushrooming all over the Transvaal. Jobs were few and far between as the effects of the Great Depression began to bite.

After Gollel, Wild took a position as a battery manager on a small mine 80 miles west of Johannesburg, but five months later the company went bust. He moved north into Southern Rhodesia for eight months as a manager of the Usk Estate, of which little is known today. He also took the opportunity to go prospecting: 'I then went into Rhodesia and messed about prospecting and finding nothing worthwhile accepted an offer on another small mine near Klerksdorp.'

Wild was referring to Ottosdal, a small mining settlement situated on a vast flat featureless plain 150 miles west of Johannesburg, where he took a job as manager of G Stone Quarry. The village, primarily Afrikaans, consisted of no more than a general store and a few Victorian tin-roofed houses dominated by an imposing stone-built Dutch Reform church. Social life was pared down to Saturday evening 'get-togethers' and droning sermons on a Sunday morning. The isolation and unfamiliarity of this small 'dorp' (town) with blistering heat and dusty streets was sorely felt by Wild, who sifted through tons of gravel in the 'vain hope of finding diamonds.' This was certainly a low point of his time in South Africa. Ottosdal is much the same today.

Four months later, the company went into liquidation and yet again Wild was left stranded with no option but to return to Johannesburg. There, with what little money he had, he took refuge in the comfort of his club, the New Club.

The New Club was originally built in 1887 on Loveday Street in the centre of the conurbation of early Johannesburg, at a cost of a staggering £80,000. As a grand gentleman's club emulating those of Pall Mall, it was richly decorated with sumptuous paintings and imposing hunting trophies mounted on the walls. Ornate carved mantle pieces, seven in all, imported from England, dominated the

(1)

How do you like settling down after such a life of adventure

Does not the heat affect you

Don't you long for the sea & the ice again

How do you like S.A. & what do you think of cotton.

These are a few questions of the I have to answer almost every day.

Firstly, I have _not_ settled down, I should hate to settle down, & I never will until old Anna Domini makes it compulsory.

No one ~~can be called settled down~~ who has to gets up at 5 a.m. & look after a farm of 1000 acres. Clearing stumping ploughing harrowing fencing etc etc, all in different parts of the estate, often entails walking from ~~six to ten miles~~ in the course of the day.

This farm will certainly ~~hold me~~ down a good deal more than I have been accustomed to ~~but~~ if cotton prices keep up I have hopes still of seeing ~~a little~~ more of this little old world that I have already travelled over fairly extensively.

SCOTT POLAR
RESEARCH
INSTITUTE

Then, as regards the heat, People who wonder that

MS 944/5/5.

Lecture notes

high-ceilinged rooms, The sweeping staircase led from the main reception room to the panelled rooms on the floors above, and the entire building was warmed by hot-water pipes and radiators.

At this time, Wild occupied himself jotting down ideas for lectures to be given on his life as an explorer. The subjects were varied as can be seen from his notes

Wild's ambitions of profiting from this young, burgeoning country had started to fade. It is true that he had many friends throughout South Africa, including the Randlords – the entrepreneurs who were cashing in on the riches of the country and making a fortune, particularly in mining – but he was not in their league. There was once a time when he'd had the courage, physical strength and mental resilience that put him in a class of an illustrious few. Now, at the age of 57, he was living from hand to mouth with few prospects, and there was a sense of quiet resignation about him.

His club brought him a semblance of family life. He would sink into a buffed leather chair with a glass of brandy in one hand and in the other a Flag cigarette that he would have taken from his silver pocket case engraved with an image of *Discovery*. Club life was at the core of the many associations to which he belonged: the Memorable Order of the Tin Hats (MOTHS), the Navy League and the Sons of England, an offshoot of the Freemasons. These societies held regular meetings and brought together men of similar backgrounds, who, having seen war themselves, were dedicated to keeping alive the memory of those who had died during the Great War. They fiercely upheld traditions of the British Empire and were committed to maintaining 'Britishness' in Southern Africa. Wild sat on the committee of the Sons of England, and such was his admiration for the society that on 24 June 1930 he gave the bell from *Quest* to the Shackleton Lodge.

Raising funds for charity was an important aspect of these benevolent societies, and between the wars the Sons of England paid out £250,000 in charitable and benevolent works. By 1930 the MOTHS association had nearly 20,000 ex-servicemen members in South Africa alone.

On 16 December 1930, Wild's life changed very much for the better when he became engaged to Beatrice (Trix) Lydia Rhys Rowbotham, whom he purportedly met in Tanga, a port town on the east coast of Tanzania. Why either of them was there at the time is unknown.

Trix was born in Port Elizabeth of Welsh parents, a slight, dark, plain but highly intelligent woman 47 years old when they met, 10 years younger than Wild. She was self-effacing, extremely well-read and interested in 'easternised' religions and the paranormal. Considered a little eccentric, she bucked the trend by wearing trousers and rolling her own cigarettes.

2.

water, many in a single drop.

Loss of Vince. Whitfield. Smythe. Heald.

My feelings over crevasses, devils running along underneath ready to catch us. Effect on Adams & Marshall. Latter doubled his rope.

Tents wrecked, dugout 5 days, awful dread of avalanches.

Effect of winter on spirits of men & animals

Horror of loneliness much less in Arctic. Mick's lone 39 mile walk.

Shackleton's wonderful optimism against Scott's pessimism.

Boat journey, half party insane. Shackletons consideration — gloves. Shackleton's boat journey, no sleep 16 days & 7 days previously.

My difficulty in keeping up spirits of party. My own certainty of Shackleton's safety and

In March the following year, they were married and Wild wrote to Shackleton's wife Emily in 1932 saying that he had found happiness and that he had 'three valuable assets, a helpful and loving wife, good health and a sense of humour.'

Trix's father, Benjamin, had died when she was 12, leaving her mother Jeannette, née Tonkin, struggling to bring up six children. Wild was very fond of his mother-in-law, and she stayed with them whenever possible.

Trix was undaunted by the lack of money that forced them to live in rented rooms and boarding houses. They had each other, and it was a very happy union. Wild's sister Cissie wrote: 'I always feel very grateful to her for the affection she gave to my brother. He was very affectionate himself and returned it fourfold when he received it from man, woman child animal or bird.'

By late 1932, financial restraints forced Wild to give up his membership of the New Club, and he and Trix moved into a small room in Johannesburg. He sold his golf clubs to pay the rent and wrote to Emily Shackleton that, 'I was sorely tempted to part with my medals and orders but managed to scrape through so far'

Again he made notes for his lectures seen here.

At the end of 1932 Wild applied for a job with the New Consolidated Gold Fields Ltd and was put in charge of stone ore crushers on the Witwatersrand Gold Mine. 'It is not a very important position and leads nowhere, but I was glad to take anything.'

Johannesburg was in the thrall of the Depression, and people seized any job on offer. Reduction plants on the mines separating the ore from stone ran 24 hours a day, and a reduction officer could earn 17s/3d a shift.

Wild's job enabled the couple to move into their own rented house close to the mine, one they didn't particularly like in the ugly little town of Germiston but where Trix's mother was able to join them. With much scrimping and saving over three years, they managed to buy a Wolseley car, the 'County' model. It was Wild's pride and joy, and they could now plan their first touring holiday together.

In 1934 Wild and Trix received two invitations from the Mayor of Johannesburg – a luncheon at the prestigious Langham Hotel in honor of the visit of Vice Admiral 'Teddy' Evans, followed by an evening performance of the visiting Russian ballet company. Evans had served as second officer of Morning, a relief vessel of Scott's 1901–04 British National Antarctic Expedition, and he said of Wild: 'Why dammit, the man ought to be kept by the nation.' .

Someone gave Wild's brother Laurence a description of the two men meeting at the reception. Apparently Wild, standing in the background, was spotted by Evans, who went straight across to him. They were so pleased to see each other they did a little jig together.

Stanley Wild told a similar story, recounting how Wild met General Smuts at a Cape Town function and 'like two excited schoolboys they did a "highland fling" together along the whole length of the floor to the utter amazement (and some consternation) of the many dignitaries present.'

The hotel in Gollel where Wild worked behind the bar

BRIEFLY BETTER TIMES

Now that things had become more financially secure, Wild was able to take some leave, and with Trix's mother they drove north from Johannesburg to Messina on the Rhodesian border, where they left Mrs Rowbotham with her daughter Enid. Gathering up Enid's seven-year-old son Brian, they set off on a camping adventure armed with a rifle and shotgun.

They bumped along dusty roads, scattering herds of buck that took off into the acacia bush in alarm. Wild shot the occasional guinea fowl for the pot, and in the evening they would set up camp and sit around the open fire. As the embers died down they crept into a tent to sleep under the African sky ablaze with stars and listened to the eerie noises of the bush. Some nights, afraid that there might be lions or leopards about they took to sleeping in the Wolseley.

On one occasion Wild was so intent on looking at a herd of gemsbok he drove over a boulder in the road breaking a spring of his precious car which was already on its last legs. With temperatures reaching 40°C in the shade, they

Wild with nephew Brian at the Great Zimbabwe ruins

coaxed the Wolseley into the nearest town, Fort Victoria, for repairs. Wild was a stickler for making notes of temperatures. 'So long as a man has a sound heart and lungs he can stand either extreme equally well. The limits of my experience have been 127°F in the shade and 76°F degrees below zero or 108°F of frost, also in the shade, a difference of 203°F,' he declared in one of his many jottings.

One of the highlights of the trip was visiting the majestic Great Zimbabwe ruins, a mystical series of towering stone ruins and walls believed to have been built around 1300. Wild had Trix, wearing a large hat, hands in trouser pockets and looking rather crumpled, stand with her nephew by the Wolseley while he took a photograph with little Brian's Brownie Box camera. It was then Wild's turn to pose, an old man of 61, sitting on a stone with his nephew beside him.

The following year, Wild was able to take another break from the arduous job of managing the crushing machines. Taking Trix's mother with them, they headed east to Northern Zululand. The Wolseley rattled and gasped on the rutted roads as it climbed through the mountains but the discomfort was 'more than compensated by the glorious scenery.' The small party stopped in Piet Retief to visit friends and reached Gollel the following day. Here Wild caught up with some old friends before pressing on to Mkuze to stay with Captain Robinson

Trix and her nephew at the Great Zimbabwe ruins and the Wolseley

who still lived on the old farm 'Quest'. Showing Trix and her mother around the farm brought back many memories, and he boasted they were delighted with what they found.

Their destination, St Lucia on the wild Zululand coast, was finally reached the following day. They stayed in the Estuary Hotel owned by Wild's dear old friends Nick and Milly Selley, who, thrilled to see him, gave them a special rate.

The hotel, started by the Selleys in 1928, had hot and cold water in the bedrooms and 'an excellent table.' The next eight days were spent mostly lazing about, sitting on the hotel verandah, gazing into what was known as Mug's Pool, 'swarming with grunters and mullet and one only had to throw a line in the pool to pull out a fish.' They took walks along the estuary and watched hippos wallow in the shallows and they meandered along the sands to study the flocks of flamingoes and pelicans. Wild and Trix, armed with a box of sandwiches and a flask of coffee for their lunch, took a motor boat down to the mouth of the estuary where they walked across the sand dunes and swam in the Indian Ocean. On the way home they stopped to fish for grunters and to the envy of all the guests in the hotel, Trix landed a salmon.

On the return journey they spent two more nights with the Robinsons, where Wild collected some treasured belongings, which included the two volumes of *Heart of the Antarctic*, a copy of *Shackleton's Last Voyage*, a copy of *Aurora Australis* and a painting of *Discovery*.

Arriving back in the rather bleak and stiflingly hot town of Germiston at Christmas, it was a depressing thought that they would have to wait another year before taking leave again. The job – as uninspiring as it was – afforded the Wilds a reasonable standard of living, and he never lost his quiet optimism to return 'home' to England for a holiday in the next year or two, when suddenly during the sharp Transvaal winter, the unthinkable happened. Wild fell seriously ill and was taken to hospital suffering from diabetes and a weak heart. The cruel conditions and years of privations spent in the Antarctic, and undoubtedly his love for tobacco, were finally catching up with him.

He was discharged from his job at the mine, and with no safety net he became dependent on family and friends. He was left without choice and was forced to take help from a man he disliked, his brother-in-law Pat O'Brien Frost, married to Enid, Trix's sister.

The Frosts had three children – two sons, Pat junior and Brian, and a daughter named Margaret. Frost senior began by working for the Messina Transvaal Development Company, a copper mine on the northern borders of South Africa, in 1918. By 1954 he had risen to the position of General Manager, a figure of importance, in charge of 500 Europeans and 4,100 native mine workers. He was a man who liked his pound of flesh and he certainly got it from Wild.

As a getaway from the inescapable heat and dryness of the bush area of Messina, Frost bought a beautiful tract of land perched on a hill in the eastern Transvaal, near the village of Haenertsburg, 250 miles from Johannesburg.

It is one of the most spectacular areas of South Africa, with grasslands and indigenous forests. Mountainous, verdant and malaria-free, he called his land Kloof Ridge and he offered Wild the job of overseeing the building of his dream house.

Wild had barely recovered from his illness, but he took the job. Frost made it clear that he would provide them with a roof over their heads, but no income other than bare living expenses and a share of the profits from the farm that he planned to develop, warning them at the same time this was highly unlikely.

They would be dependent to a large extent on their own endeavors for a living. As to how they were to make a living in the extremely remote locality of Haenertsburg, which Wild noted was 45 miles from a railway, shop or pub, was unclear. Frost wrote in a letter to Trix 'to have Frank there to look after my interests, speaking from a purely personal point of view, it would relieve me of a lot of worry and it would enable me to proceed with the development of the place to the best of my financial ability... for the rest you must expect nothing more than a salubrious locality ...'.

The Wilds lived in a simple building known as 'the shack,' which leaked when it rained, which it did constantly, covering their worldly belongings in mould. The building was laborious work partly due to the inaccessibility of the terrain. A road had to be forged up the hill to carry building materials to the site. The house was to be built of stone that had been blasted from the surrounding mountains and brought down the slippery slopes on sledges dragged by oxen. The cold wet winters and the humid heat of the summers took their toll and after 16 months of hard labour, the arrangement was proving to be a failure.

Frank received a damning letter from Frost pointing out the shoddy work carried out by the builders. His list of complaints included 'plastering before roof was on, ceiling before roof or walls completed, burning of scaffolding poles, fires in house, the builders making a mess with foodstuffs etc on the new floors.' He added that he was disgusted with the whole business and was considering 'calling in all stock and closing down all activities on the farm, maintaining only sufficient staff to look after the house and orchard.' In his view the house was spoiled and it was Frank's lack of supervision that was to blame.

It was obvious the men had little time for each other. Frost, it was said, looked down on Trix and treated Wild with equal condescension. It was of no interest to him whatsoever that Wild had been an illustrious leader and a hero of men much greater than he. He only saw a tired man unable to carry out the demands being made on him.

That year Trix's mother died and the loss was severely felt by both of them, as had the death of Trix's brother Victor of asbestosis a year earlier.   W i l d must have had to swallow his pride and finally ask for some official help. He received a letter from 10 Downing Street informing him that through the British High Commission he was to receive £100 from the Royal Bounty Grant. As part of the Civil List this fund was set up by the government to help those in need.

A month later, just before Christmas 1938, Wild wrote to Rupert, another of his numerous brothers in England, that he would have left the present set-up 'a long time ago,' but did not have the means to do so. However, he was finally leaving to go back to Johannesburg to take a room in the house of Trix's sister. He continued: 'I am still blasting and carting stone for Frost's new house, as well as mending roads & fences, ploughing, harrowing, doctoring calves and sheep repairing wagons carts and implements, and a score of other jobs, & in the evenings writing up reports to HQ, & making up books. All for my health sake only!'

The truth was that Wild's health was failing again. Ironically, having endured temperatures in the Antarctic cold enough to shatter teeth, in Africa he suffered from the cold weather, a result of his diabetes. 'Trix', he wrote to his brother Rupert, 'shrivels up like a cockroach if the temperature falls below 60°F.' His car was in desperate need of repair, but the cost to have it mended outweighed its value.

His friend Jack Scott, whom he had known from his Zululand days, heard of his plight and sent him a letter addressed to 'Dear Commander,' and explaining that 'I managed to make a few bob on shares I hope you will accept the enclosed which may be useful.' A month earlier, Scott had married the well-known British stage and screen actress Aileen Marson.

In the same letter, Scott added that he was trying to float a mining company in London, and that soon as it was through he would have work for Wild. 'I'll get in touch with you and see if there are any jobs that you would care to accept.' It was the boost that Wild needed and demonstrated the respect Scott had for him that was so obviously lacking in Frost. Wild wrote back to Scott: 'anything you can offer will be welcome and I am looking forward to a word from you to say "come along."' A few months later, they were finally able to pack up most of their belongings and limp back to Johannesburg in the old Wolseley.

It was the beginning of 1939 and once again Frank was having to rely on the good will of family and friends; fortunately he still had many of those.

Jack Scott was true to his word. He was a hugely influential figure in South Africa and was making a fortune in mining. He lived in a splendid mansion in Johannesburg that was occupied by the Shah of Iran in 1941 after his abdication. Awarded the MBE and later decorated with a DCO, he was made an Honorary Colonel of his regiment (SAEC) at the age of 45.

He offered Wild the job of storekeeper on the Babrosco mine near Klerksdorp, for which he would be paid £23/19s a month. In early March, Wild and Trix packed up their few belongings and boarded the train at the Johannesburg Station for the four-hour journey to the small mining town a hundred miles south of Johannesburg. Wild had also been informed by 10 Downing Street that he was to be given a Civil List Pension of £170 per annum, to be paid quarterly and to be back-dated a year. Finally, he was being recognised for his services 'in the sphere of polar exploration.' The Civil List Pension announcement was made public in the newspapers on 6 May, and he told a reporter for the *Daily Mail* that 'this will not make a slightest difference to my plans,' adding that had grown attached to Klerksdorp and its 'charming people.'

They were given a simple but comfortable mine house to live in, his job made few demands on him and they were financially secure. For the first time in several years the future looked promising.

But then he received a letter from the Income Tax department in London, pointing out that the Pension was not exempt from UK Income Tax. He replied cordially but with a hint of frustration that 'the Civil List Pension of £170 is not sufficient to support my wife & myself and I have succeeded in obtaining a temporary billet which will bring me in about £24 a month. As I am suffering from diabetes and a weak heart I may have to give up work at any moment.'

Wild was hoping to retire in a year's time and, after a visit to the home country, England, they planned to move to Nyasaland, where he still owned land and they believed they could live reasonably cheaply. In May, the dreadful news reached Klerksdorp that Jack Scott's wife, Aileen Marson, had died in London whilst giving birth to twins. It cast a shadow over what was otherwise an enjoyable life in Klerksdorp. They had quickly made new friends, and with the security of £206/3s in the bank, they ordered a new Wolseley car ready to be collected from John R. Clark Motor Co. in Johannesburg on 23 August.

It was 1939 and there was much talk of war. Wild received a letter from one of his close friends in Johannesburg, the exuberant Gus Williams: 'we are all on tender hooks here. Filling up BESL (British Empire Service League) forms in case of war. I think we shall have a show down soon and you and I must be in the same mob. So make your selection and give me the once over.'

Wild wrote back to Williams to say he was planning on joining up with the RN or RNVR but that he would be visiting his friends in Johannesburg at the end of June. The 'gang' would be out in full force to welcome him, replied Williams, although one of their friends, Bill, complained about his 'war' foot and on doctor's orders had been told to lay off the whiskey and soda.

On Monday, 14 August, Wild fell ill and went to bed. 'Gradually he became worse although he never lost his high spirit,' reported a friend. By the following

Saturday, his doctor in Klerksdorp was called away from dinner to attend the now terribly ill man.

An ambulance was summoned, but it was too late. Wild had succumbed to pneumonia, and, with Trix by his bedside, he died at eight minutes past nine on 19 August 1939. Trix was inconsolable. 'If I'd only brought my dear one away from the inexperienced tactics of country doctors all would have been well….. my loss is all the greater in that he had so much more in him than most,' she wrote to her friend Mrs Dora Poultney.

Even on the day of his death, Wild had recalled an episode in the Antarctic, and it is extraordinary that both he and Shackleton – who had lived such famously dangerous lives – died quietly in their own beds.

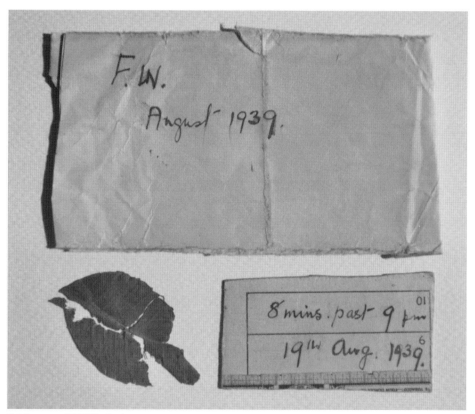

Trix's notes of Wild's death

Letters and telegrams of condolence flooded in, not only from Wild's family and friends from England but from throughout the country. With the help of her family, Trix arranged for the funeral and burial to take place at Brixton Cemetery in Johannesburg. At the eleventh hour, she was contacted by the Antarctic Society of Pretoria, suggesting that if Wild were cremated, his ashes could be sent to

Transvaal Sea Cadets marching in Wild's funeral cortège through the centre of Johannesburg

Antarctica to be buried with his beloved 'Boss' on South Georgia. The funeral was quickly moved to the Braamfontein Crematorium, about a mile away.

On 23 August, family and friends gathered in the centre of Johannesburg at the funeral directors, J.A. Hobkirks, at 243 Bree Street. They represented a mix of his private and public life. Among the chief mourners were the top commanders of the army and navy and captains of industry. Major F.H. Bradley, VC, Colonel Anderson, Lieut-Commander M. Penny and Mr E. Bateman, to mention but a few.

At 2.30 p.m., the coffin, draped in a Union Jack, was brought out by eight pall bearers and the order was given for the Transvaal Sea Cadets, 40-strong, to stand to attention. The pallbearers – who included Frost; Mr S. Raphaele, the vice-chairman of the Navy League; a retired Lieut-Commander of the Royal Navy, L.W. Walwyn; and Mr. S.S. Waters, who was the past President of the Sons of England, Shackleton Lodge – carefully placed the coffin into the hearse, which all but disappeared beneath a veritable garden of more than 40 floral tributes.

Officers leading their cadets took up their positions in front of the procession, followed by a convoy of funeral cars transporting the numerous mourners. Thus the somber cortège left the funeral parlour and slow marched through the chilly windblown streets of central Johannesburg. Traffic came to a complete standstill while bystanders stopped to stare, the men removing their hats and bowing their heads. At the Scottish Memorial in King George Street the procession came to a halt. Here, the officers and cadets boarded buses that took them to the crematorium about two miles away, and the funeral cars proceeded.

From the bridge over King George Street, onlookers gathered to watch. One old man in their midst was Mr Hudson, who was too lame to join the procession. He described Wild as 'one of the finest types of the British race.' For him it was a particularly poignant moment – his brother, Commodore Hubert Taylor Hudson, had been the navigator on the *Endurance* Expedition.

The hearse drew up at the small, stone-built chapel and in order that no one be overlooked in having the honour of carrying the great explorer, a second group of pall-bearers took their positions. They included Commander M.M. Williamson Napier, the Chairman of the Navy League; Mr Eric Burchmore, the provincial President of the Sons of England and Benjamin Rowbotham, Trix's brother.

The church was crammed to the gunnels with people, and a simple service was conducted by Reverend Pearson, which concluded with a bugler playing the 'Last Post.' On leaving the church, the mourners were able to inspect the wreaths laid on the grass. Amongst the cards bidding him farewell were his close friends General Smuts and Jack Scott, the Explorers Club of New York, Sons of England, the South African Geographical Society, Mr J.A. Robson, president of the Shackleton Lodge and the Memorable Order of Tin Hats. One card in particular, hand-written in blue ink, read:

> 'Master, I've filled my contract, wrought in Thy many lands; Not by my sins wilt Thou judge me, but by the work of my hands. Master, I've done Thy bidding, and the light is low in the west, And the long, long shift is over . . . Master, I've earned it -- Rest.

The Babrosco Mine paid £12/10s towards funeral expenses, but there is no record of a wake being held after the funeral. Trix returned to her single room in the Victoria Hotel in Johannesburg where she had been staying before the funeral; within a matter of weeks she left for Messina to stay with Enid and Frost.

War was declared on 6 September 1939, a week after Trix's husband died. She had no option but to give instructions to the funeral directors to retain her husband's ashes for safe-keeping, as there would be no possibility of them being transported to Antarctica at this time. She planned to collect them at a later date.

Two days after Wild's death, the *Daily Mirror* of London headlined a story: 'Poverty made hero into bartender,' repeating the tale that Wild had worked behind a bar for £4 a month, but adding that it was in an African township and that he had been forgotten by his fellow-countrymen, all of which he 'bore in silence.'

Heartbroken, Trix found it hard to cope now that Wild was gone, and she confided to her friend Dora Poultney that: '*I have lost my grip.*' She added, 'he was a truly noble character, and none have been more blest (sic) than I was in his companionship. Life has nothing more to offer me, but the physical insists on going on somehow. I have had messages from all over the world and I feel such a miserable sinner in that I didn't manage to save him. His new book was three parts completed and publishers waiting.'

Of some comfort to her was the assurance given by a clairvoyant friend in Sydney – 'a perfect saint' assuring her that all was well with her darling husband.

Trix received many letters from friends offering her a roof over her head, but she chose to divide her time between the room she had rented in Johannesburg, the mine house in Messina in the northern Transvaal where the Frosts lived, and their Kloof Ridge farm in the eastern Transvaal. To avoid the inconvenience of traipsing her trunks around the country she left her precious possessions for safe-keeping at Kloof Ridge.

Unfairly, the Civil List Pension ended on Wild's death and Trix faced an impecunious future. In desperation she sought the help of her husband's old allies, General Smuts, now the Prime Minister of South Africa, and Admiral Sir Edward Evans. With their recommendations, the British government agreed that she should benefit from her late husband's Civil List Pension, and in March 1940 she received a yearly pension of £105. This was barely enough for her to live on, but Trix was well skilled living a life of frugality. As a younger woman she had worked as a secretary, and her office skills would have most likely included book-keeping. She was extremely popular, and many of her friends offered her a home after Wild's death but she was proud and tried to maintain her independence. Apart from two snapshots – both of which are indistinct – no photographs of her exist.

Trix was a prodigious correspondent, carefully composing her letters and making copies before sending them out. She wrote to the newspapers requesting the return of photographs of her 'deceased' husband and she corresponded with his old Antarctic comrades Raymond Priestley and James Wordie – the latter having contacted her regarding Wild's obituary, which finally read, 'I doubt if Wild ever was the same after Shackleton's death. His great days were on the polar journey, and in the escape from the Weddell Sea ice. No one was more liked and loved, and his attraction, apart from his feats, lay partly in his simple and confiding nature, but also in his being the complete confidence-giving companion.' She also remained in constant contact with his family members in England and Australia.

In the face of grief she turned her mind and energies to her 'pet scheme' – the introduction of healthy bread to South Africa. 'Welfare,' as she put it, was a favourite topic of hers. She wrote to the Star newspaper suggesting that the government should take action and instruct the milling industry to maintain the essential vitamins in bread instead of throwing them out in the bran, which would make a 'vital difference to the health and strength of the people.' She sought the support of the Women's League, which was influential in matters of welfare. Unfortunately all her efforts came to nothing. The country was at war, and the government had more pressing issues with which to deal; besides there was a wheat shortage.

In 1943 whilst living in her room in Pritchard Street in the centre of Johannesburg, Trix was visited by the acting British Trade Commissioner, who was shocked at her 'very straightened circumstances' and secured her a cheque of £100. She was asked not to view it as charity but to treat the transaction as confidential and was told 'it is just one more testimony to the work which your late husband did as an explorer.' Soon afterwards, she was visited by Frost, who was appalled at her reduced circumstances and insisted she return with him to Messina to join her sister, which she did.

Whenever possible she seems to have spent her time with her favourite nephew, Pat Junior, who was managing his father's farm at Kloof Ridge. When her sister Enid died in 1957, Trix went back up north to Messina to act as housekeeper and companion for her brother-in-law, but more sorrow was to come her way when five years later Pat Junior died of cancer at the age of 37, having married four years earlier.

In 1965, Frost remarried, to a woman called Hester Catherina, but by then Trix had returned to Johannesburg. Her circumstances had now detoriated considerably, and the only affordable accommodation available to her was a simple room in a dreary block of flats in a somewhat dubious area of the city known as Hillbrow. Joan Provis was the only member of the Frost family to visit her.

Virtually all those whom Trix had dearly loved were now gone, and her care fell to her brother, Benjamin Rowbotham, a retired traffic policeman, and his wife Gwen. Trix ended her final days in the Queenshaven retirement home, where Gwen was employed as the matron and Benjamin the maintenance man.

She died on 10 February 1970, at the age of 86, of an embolism on the lung, brought about by having broken her leg in a fall. She outlived her husband by 31 years. She, too, was cremated at the Braamfontein Cemetery and her ashes scattered in the Garden of Remembrance, which is a large mound surrounded by a retaining brick wall in the centre of which stands an enormous Belhambra (Pokeberry) tree.

Her brother Benjamin inherited what remained of her estate, which included two letters written by General Smuts and a collection of Wild's papers, including typescripts about his experiences as an explorer on *Quest*, photographs, two telegrams sent on behalf of the King to Shackleton and Wild, a printed agreement between Shackleton and Wild engaging Wild as second-in-command of *Quest*, and the original hand-written Memoirs and 'farthest south' diary written by Wild. Benjamin also received Wild's group of medals. This memorabilia had been kept in a trunk belonging to Trix, and was sold by Sotheby's in two different sales. The medals were sold on 23 June 1971 for £850, and the Memoirs, diary and remaining papers on 3 May 1971: lots 289–293.

The trunk containing Trix's few remaining personal effects was handed over to Benjamin's daughter-in-law, June Rowbotham. These included a typed copy of the Memoirs and 'farthest south' diary, numerous letters and his silver pocket cigarette case with an etching of Discovery. It was June's foresight and interest in family history that convinced her to keep these things, although she never believed they would be of interest to others.

Familt group, Trix second from left

MEDAL AND ASHES

The Polar Medal awarded by the Sovereign symbolizes human endeavour at its finest, and embodies fortitude, bravery and self-sacrifice – all the characteristics necessary in polar exploration. No one had then or has since matched Wild's Antarctic achievements. His silver Polar Medal attached to the iconic white ribbon decorated with four clasps and his polar experience are without equal.

His Polar Medal, CBE (Commander of the Order of the British Empire) and the miniatures of the medals were part of a much larger group of medals* and there were times in South Africa when he thought he might be forced to sell his collection to make ends meet, yet he succeeded in keeping them all until he died.

The narrative of what happened to Wild's medals is a story that reflects the restlessness of his later life. They have crossed continents and passed through many hands for reasons of sentimentality and acquisitiveness, giving satisfaction to some, yet causing immeasurable dissension in others. The chief protagonist has been the Polar Medal, and with it his CBE and miniatures, because they became separated from 'the group.'

On Wild's death in 1939, his collection of medals was valued in South Africa at £82. They remained in Trix's possession until her death in 1970. In 1971 her brother Benjamin sold what he thought was the entire set through Sotheby's auction house. However, somewhere along the line, the prized Polar Medal, CBE and miniatures had been 'removed' from the collection.

His group of medals included two gold medals, one from the Royal Geographical Society of London and another the David Livingstone Centenary Medal awarded by the American Geographical Society of New York, although this medal was separated from the group between 1980 and 1988. Its whereabouts is unknown. Wild received the RGS silver medal for the 1901 *Discovery* Expedition and three medals for the Imperial Trans-Antarctic Expedition: the Royal Scottish Geographical silver medal, the Ernest Shackleton MVO FRCS, and the bronze Belgian Royal Geographical Society Medallion. Again this medallion was split from the group between 1980 and 1988 and now remains in the collection of a dealer in London. Wild received an unusual 'sports' medal for coming second in a sledge race held on the King's birthday during Scott's *Discovery* Expedition. Finally in the group were the British War Medal (unworn) and the Victory Medal (unworn). A gold medal was issued by the Chilean Illustre Municipalidad for his part in the *Endurance* Expedition, but unfortunately it was lost.

Michael Naxton, the respected medal consultant working for Sotheby's at the time, stated that:

A   Commander of the Order of the British Empire
B   National Antarctic Expedition 1902-1904 Silver Soprts Medal for coming 2nd in a toboggan race held on the King's birthday
C   Victory Medal, Mercantile Marine War Medal, British War Medal
D   Royal Scottish Geographical Society Silver medal 1907-1909
E   Dress Miniature of the Polar Medal 1904 E.V11.R., 2 clasps
F   Polar Medal
G   RGS Silver Medal for Shackleton's Antartic Expedtiton 1907-1909
H   RGS Silver Medal Scott's first Antartic Expedtiton 1902-1904
I   RGS Patron's Gold Medal 1924

'When I was contacted by Sotheby's offices in Johannesburg, by telex as I recall, to expect "the group of medals awarded to Frank Wild, the Antarctic explorer" which they had been consigned for my forthcoming auction, I was thrilled and elated at the prospect of handling something as historic as Wild's unique four-clasp Polar Medal. Imagine my excitement when the sealed package finally arrived in my office in London and the instant disappointment when, upon opening it, there was no Polar Medal inside, merely the dress miniature included amongst Wild's other awards. An urgent telephone call to Johannesburg then ascertained that the full-sized four-clasp medal had never been consigned with the rest of the items and, even worse, further enquiries with the vendors eventually revealed they had no knowledge of the Polar Medal whatsoever. My dreams of offering for sale the most celebrated polar group ever to appear at auction crumbled to dust, and I still vividly remember my bitter disappointment as clearly as if it were only yesterday.'

The medals were bought by another auction house – Spink & Son – for £850 and then sold to Peter Hlinka, an American enthusiast, the same year. Hlinka hoped to unite his newly acquired collection with the Polar Medal, but was unsuccessful and decided to sell them back to Spink in 1973, so they re-crossed the Atlantic.

By coincidence, and in truly bizarre circumstances, word was out that the unique Polar Medal was 6,000 miles away in Cape Town, South Africa. It had come to the notice of several dealers and one in particular, a woman named Natalie Jaffe. She allegedly offered to take the group of medals from Spinks to South Africa and sell them to the person holding the Polar Medal. None of these plans bore fruit, however, and the group of medals were sold by Spinks to W.H. Fevyer, the renowned medal author, collector and specialist, for £5,450. Fevyer parted with the Belgian medal and possibly the Livingstone Medal some time after that.

The value of Wild's group was steadily rising but no one foresaw the next surge in value. Fevyer sold the medals through Spink to R.C. Witte, an American patent lawyer for £11,500, but that sum was dwarfed in 2007 when Witte put them back on to the market with the British auctioneers Dix Denoon and Webb. The polar medal community was astounded when they fetched a staggering £52,000, bought by Dr Mike Wain, an English GP. It was an indication of the meteoric rise in interest of Edwardian polar memorabilia, not only in medals but books, paintings, photographs and, in fact, any object that related to the men of the Heroic Age.

Then, one spring afternoon in 2005, I was researching Wild's background at the Scott Polar Research Institute when I was handed an email from a South African man called Luigi Casaleggio, enquiring as to the whereabouts of Wild's grave. That same afternoon a member of the Shackleton family telephoned the archivist asking the same question. He was setting out on a visit to Johannesburg and wanted to know where he could find Wild's grave. According to Bob Headland, the Scott Polar Research Institute's archivist at the time, no one had enquired about Wild since Mills, Wild's biographer, visited the archives to research his book published in 1999. As if by a collective consciousness, we were all brought together on the same day on Frank Wild business.

Casaleggio and I consequently became fellow researchers. With his help, I discovered that Wild could not have been cremated at Brixton Cemetery as had been widely believed. At the time of his death, all cremations were held at the Braamfontein Cemetery, two miles away.

On my next research trip to South Africa I visited the Braamfontein Cemetery, which lies almost at the heart of Johannesburg, and there I found an entry in the large, leather-bound registry: '*Wild Frank (Commander) m 66 19.8.39 Klerksdorp TVL.*'

Wild's cremation took place on the 23 August 1939 and it noted that his ashes had been taken away by J.A. Hobkirk, the funeral directors, for safe-keeping. Then I spotted another entry – a cremation certificate had been issued on 18 July 1971 the year following Trix's death. This indicated someone needed proof that the cremation had taken place – but why?

Casaleggio now made another discovery. By trailing through hundreds of names in the Cape Town telephone directory, he finally found the whereabouts of Brian Frost, son of P. O'Brien Frost, the only living person to our knowledge who remembered Frank Wild.

I arranged to meet Frost on my next trip to South Africa. He and his second wife lived in a large 1960s-style bungalow in Constantia, a salubrious suburb of Cape Town. Now in his late 70s and frail, he could be described as somewhat taciturn, although on subsequent meetings we established a friendly relationship.

It was during that first meeting, while sitting on his verandah, that he told his wife to 'bring the medals.' She returned carrying a red box containing the CBE and Wild's miniatures, and next to them, in all its glory, lay the Polar Medal with four bars. It was a thrilling moment.

Also in his possession was a silver cigarette box purportedly given to Wild by Rudyard Kipling, along with two certificates. One was for the Back Grant, awarded by the Royal Geographic Society in April 1916 'for his distinguished and long-continued services in the exploration of the Antarctic,' and the other, an ornate certificate in colour, given to him in Montevideo in September 1916 by the Magallanes Club in Chile on his return from Elephant Island.

Frost then produced a photograph album with a photograph of himself as a plump-faced, seven-year-old boy, dressed in khaki shorts and shirt, sitting on a rock, with his little arms hugging his knees, and beside him sat an aged man

Wild with nephew Brian at Zimbabwe ruins

with wispy grey hair − it was unquestionably Wild. Behind them towered the extraordinary stone-built fortressed walls of the ancient Zimbabwe ruins. I had in my possession a letter written in 1937 from Wild to his niece, Renee (daughter of his brother Rupert in England), describing the holiday at those same ruins, so seeing the photograph brought the letter to life.

It was clear from that first meeting with Brian Frost that he was happy to share our mutual interest in his uncle (by marriage), yet it was also clear he showed uneasiness regarding the medals that were in his possession.

I asked him how he had acquired the medals, and he replied, 'I really don't know how I got hold of them but I didn't steal them. I only presume that my father gave them to me.' Did Brian Frost believe his father had a right to them? I believe he never thought to ask. Perhaps his discomfort had more to do with his relationship with his father, which had broken down many years earlier. To save his father 'from himself,' he said he had rescued what he believed were the family heirlooms before Hester, his father's second wife, could take them. As it happened he went to court and had his father certified and taken into curatorship. But the question remained: how did his father come by the medals and the other items?

Members of the Frost family at first suggested Wild sold or gave his Polar

Medal and CBE to P. O'Brien Frost either to make money or in lieu of favours. That is possible, but highly unlikely, as it would indicate that Wild sold or gave away all the other items that he treasured as well. Surely Trix would have mentioned to her brother Benjamin that Frank had sold the Polar Medal to Frost, but Benjamin insisted he knew nothing of the whereabouts of the medal when questioned by Sotheby's in 1971.

At that same meeting, Brian Frost dropped a bombshell. He believed that Wild's ashes were left in a trunk in the attic at Kloof Ridge. Frost gave me a letter from the medal dealer Natalie Jaffe, dated 19 March 1999, in which she implored him to sell the Polar Medal in order to re-unite it with the others. She lived in hope that 'we can work together in making history come right.'

An American medal collector – R.C. Witte – had bought Wild's medals on 25 November 1998 through Spink, it would be a perfect time for a dealer to try to unite Wild's Polar Medal with the group for Witte.

When I contacted Natalie Jaffe she said she was the only person who had handled all Frank Wild's awards. It was her dream, she said, to reunite them, as she believed that 'the ghost and spirit of Frank Wild roamed about restlessly, looking for peace.' This struck me as somewhat unusual, because when we arranged to meet in London on her next visit, I was surprised to find that her knowledge of Wild was somewhat scant. Nor would she disclose how she had come to handle all Wild's medals. I wrote to her again three years later asking her for the provenance of the medals and she declined to give me the information.

I suspected she wanted to meet me, believing that I had some influence in persuading Frost to sell the Polar Medal. The meeting was inconclusive, and I mistrusted her. Brian Frost was later to tell me he found her persistence disquieting, and yet she was later to play a part in the selling of the Polar Medal.

Both Frost and Jaffe alluded to the Polar Medal having been stolen many years earlier from Frost's house, but that it had somehow been returned. It was then I learnt that he had three sons and that he had broken ties with one of them.

In 2009 I received an email from Frost's wife to say that he was seriously ill and had decided to sell the Polar Medal to pay for the medical bills. I encouraged her to sell the Polar Medal privately to Dr Wain, the present owner of the group of medals. He offered the estimated price of £60,000 plus the buyer's and seller's commission. This would guarantee the collection would be reunited, something Natalie Jaffe purportedly wanted. Equally as important, Dr Wain assured me the medals would go on public display. However, Frost died on the 29 June 2009, and the medals went into auction.

Unbeknownst to me, one of Frost's sons, Richard, had brought in Jaffe as acting agent for the London auctioneers, Dix Noonan & Webb. Undoubtedly, the Frost family would have a better chance in realizing the maximum amount of money at public auction, and there were enormous commissions to be made by the auctioneer and agent. Somehow the question of uniting the medals had become irrelevant as all the players were gearing up for financial gain, that is, except for Dr Wain, who was now wildly liquidating assets to buy the Polar Medal at auction.

The Polar Medal, CBE and miniatures were set for auction on 18 September 2009, and I believed the chances of them being united were slim. However, a matter of days before the auction there was an extraordinary turn of events.

I received a message from my researcher friend Luigi Casaleggio, saying that he had received a call from Shaughn Frost, Brian Frost's absent son. He gave me Shaughn's contact details, and when I spoke to him on the telephone he informed me that he had had no contact with his father from the age of 18, and he was now in his late forties. On learning of his father's death, he had visited his estranged brother Richard and had asked about the medals. According to him, Richard shrugged the question off.

Shaughn told me he was the son who had stolen the Polar Medal from his father's safe in 1974. He took it to Don's Coins and Medals in Tulbagh Square, the same square where Jaffe had her business, named City Coins, and sold it for R10.00 (£5). Seeing the commotion it caused in the shop, and knowing he would face the wrath of his father, he asked for it back, and when he returned home he put the medal back in the safe. Don MacKenzie, the medal dealer, traced him back to school (he was wearing a school uniform), and he received a hiding from his father and was forced to study a book on Antarctica, which he did not know then was *Aurora Australis*.

It took me years to track down John, the son of Don MacKenzie of Don's Coins and Medals, which no longer traded. Don MacKenzie had died four years earlier, but the son, who was 17-years-old at the time and working for his father, remembered Shaughn bringing the Polar Medal into the shop. He recalled his father telephoning Brian Frost and informing him that he had the Polar Medal. Father and son then drove to Frost's home and returned the medal into his keeping. Whilst in the house, John MacKenzie remembers quite clearly Brian Frost showing them the copy of *Aurora Australis*. Frost promised that if he should decide to sell the Polar Medal, it would be through Don MacKenzie.

According to Don's son, they took a photograph of the medal and gave the photograph to Jaffe, a friend, colleague and business neighbour. He alleged she then placed an advertisement with the photograph in a newspaper with the words saying something to the effect of 'this is the kind of medal we deal in.' Thus, Don McKenzie's loyal collectors believed he had sold the medal to her and they showed their displeasure by taking their business elsewhere.

Natalie Jaffe had a different story. She claimed it was the well-known medal collector 'Bill' Hibbard – who had connections with Cape Town University – who returned the medal to Brian Frost on behalf of City Coins. I now had three very different versions of how the Polar Medal found its way back to Brian Frost, and each relater claimed theirs to be the truth.

In the grand scheme of things it is not hugely relevant how the medal was returned, yet there can only be one version. Don MacKenzie was taken to court for receiving stolen goods for an unrelated incident and, according to his son, his honesty in returning the Polar Medal to Frost was cited in court.

During my first telephone discussion with Shaughn Frost, he asked me if I knew the whereabouts of Wild's medals and told me his father had promised him that he would have them at the age of 21 – John MacKenzie confirmed this – but they fell out long before that. When I told him the Polar Medal with the CBE were to be auctioned in London that very week, I was met with a stunned silence.

I believed Shaughn Frost would try and stop the auction from proceeding, and he said he went as far as contacting his lawyer, but then said, 'it is time the medal came out of Frost family hands.' He offered Dr Wain £10,000 of his own money should he need it. This offer was never taken up.

By opening Pandora's box I have stirred up buried memories and bitter disagreements. Other than Shaughn, the members of the Frost family have made it quite clear they want no further dealings with me, and Jaffe has remained guarded. The auction of the Polar Medal and CBE went ahead in the Washington Mayfair hotel in the centre of London, its ornate stone frontage dating back to 1913 when Wild was preparing for the Imperial Trans-Antarctic Expedition. It was alleged that Richard Frost wanted a five-figure sum for the miniatures and the auctioneers withdrew them.

I had agreed to meet with Dr Wain, with whom I had been corresponding since 2008 on the subject of Frank Wild's medals, at the hotel. We agreed to an early meeting over coffee in order to calm our nerves before Lot 972 came up for auction. Luckily I arrived half an hour earlier than the agreed time, and I wandered into the sale room to get a feel for the atmosphere. About 60 people, some from as far as Australia, sat quietly in the room checking their catalogues, their whispers drowned by the measured tones of the auctioneer and thwack of the gavel as he progressed through the Lots.

To my horror I realized Lot 972 was probably only 15 minutes away from being auctioned and Dr Wain was nowhere to be seen. I crept out of the sale room and telephoned him on his mobile 'Where are you?' I asked, and the reply was: 'in a book shop in Piccadilly!' In a panic stricken voice, I said 'the medal is coming up for sale in a few minutes!' to which he replied, 'Get in there and bid!' With a querulous voice, I asked him what his limit was and stole back into the saleroom with my heart thumping! I whispered to Pierce Noonan of Dix Noonan & Webb the state of affairs and he said, 'Don't worry, we can do a telephone bid!' As I was giving him Dr Wain's mobile telephone number, to my amazement and with only minutes to spare, Dr Wain slipped into the chair next to me. He had jumped into a London taxi, which fortunately had not spared the horses!

The bidding started at £45,000, quickly gathered momentum in £5,000 increments and sprinted past the reserve price of £50,000 - £60,000 in seconds. The atmosphere was electric. There seemed to be at least three serious contenders in the race, then suddenly there were only two, a telephone bidder and Dr Wain. A rival bid of £100,000 was offered. '£110,000?' called the auctioneer looking at us expectantly and Dr Wain nodded. The atmosphere crackled with suspense – everyone waited for the riposte, but there was none, and the hammer came down. Dr Wain had seen off the Canterbury Museum of Christchurch, New Zealand, and the Polar Medal had finally been reunited with Wild's other medals. It had cost him £132,000 including the commission. Dix Noonan & Webb, Jaffe, Frost's wife and one of his sons had done well out of the sale. It seems the two other Frost sons have not benefited.

All the medals and in particular the uniqueness of the four-bar Polar Medal speak of camaraderie, courage and steadfastness in the face of unimaginable suffering. For those reasons Wild held on to them. No monetary value can ever reflect these characteristics, which he himself possessed in such abundance.

Yet, I was no further in discovering the fate of Frank Wild's ashes. If they were left in a trunk at Kloof Ridge, did this indicate that Trix had left a trunk at the farm containing all her prized possessions? If so, had the trunk been brought down to her in Johannesburg at a later stage?

Brian Frost had told me of Joan Provis, who had lived at Kloof Ridge when married to his brother Pat Frost, Junior. Pat Frost was Trix's much-loved nephew who had died of cancer, and Joan Provis knew her well. Joan Provis was welcoming and invited me to stay the night in her quaint house near Kloof Ridge.

When Frost retired in 1960, he left Messina and moved to Kloof Ridge, where

Provenance of Frank Wild's 'group' of medals excluding his Polar Medal, CBE and miniatures.
Sotheby's, 23 June 1971 (lot 471), hammer £850 bought by Spink & Son
Peter Hlinka (USA) bought them from Spink and sold them back some years later
The Numismatic Circular (Spink), March 1980 (lot 3091), £5,450 (Bill Fevyer)
Spink & Son, Nov. 25, 1998 (lot 1134), hammer £11,500 (Witte)
Dix Noonan Webb, Dec. 13, 2007 (lot 1), hammer £52,000 (Dr M Wain)
Collection of Dr Mike Wain (London physician)

he built himself a house on 'Shack Hill.' Trix had returned to Johannesburg.*

Joan Provis and I motored for some 20 minutes along a steep, muddy road, twisting and turning to avoid the pot holes until finally we came to the Stone House of Kloof Ridge, sturdy, strong and very handsome, just as Wild had built it.

From the verandah that surrounded it, we gazed down on the sub-tropical valleys that lie at the feet of the Magoebaskloof mountains. 'The Shack' the Wilds lived in had long since disappeared.

I returned three years later with Shaughn Frost to look at the Stone House again. He gallantly climbed a very steep ladder to peer into the attic, knowing that it was a quixotic idea that we might find the trunk that had belonged to Trix, even though Joan Provis had assured us it was taken from the house to the stables some distance away. We then clambered through the tangled pine forest floor and finally found the remains of the stables, now no more than crumpled heaps of stone and broken timbers.

It is my gut feeling that before selling the farm in 1966, P. O'Brien Frost 'took possession' of some of Trix's effects that she had entrusted to him, and they in turn ended up with his son Brian. These included the Polar Medal, CBE, miniatures, silver cigarette box and the copy of *Aurora Australis* which Brian sold in October 1995. Brian's sister, Margaret also had in her possession a first edition of Shackleton's *Heart of the Antarctic* and a box of glass lantern slides, which she generously gave to me, and I in turn handed over to the Scott Polar Research Institute.

The artifacts would have been Wild's, and subsequently Trix's, most prized possessions. Each and every object told a story, in particular the lantern slides that he used during his lectures to raise a few pounds. I believe that the remainder of Trix's possessions were sent to Johannesburg sometime before 1966 when Kloof Ridge was sold.

With regards to the ashes there is documentary evidence that Trix guarded them in the belief that they could be sent to Antarctica to be buried with Shackleton on South Georgia. However, this was impossible for her to do so until the Second World War was over. After that, she may not have had the wherewithal to arrange it, and so had held on to the ashes. She died on 2 February 1970 and was cremated on 17 February. Her ashes were scattered the following day in the Garden of Remembrance.

Beneath the details recording Frank Wild's death in the leather bound ledger at

*In 1966, four years after Pat Junior's death, the farm was bought by the international golfer Gary Player. The house, which has since changed owners twice, stands insignificant in the vast timber forest and is now rented out to tenants.

the Braamfontein Cemetery it is recorded that someone applied for a cremation certificate, number 4825 (Dated 19 July 1971, Receipt No 27751). This certificate would be needed prior to ashes being buried in a grave, scattered or interred in a niche.

Trix's brother Benjamin would have known the whereabouts of Wild's ashes. Did he wait for the sale of the medals on 23 June 1971 and then apply for the certificate less than a month later? Were Wild's ashes finally united with his beloved wife's? I believed there was no better explanation.

As I was unable to return Wild's ashes to South Georgia to be buried next to Shackleton, I had one last job to do, and that was to set the wheels in motion to have a plaque set up in the little Lutheran church where Shackleton's funeral took place and where Wild would have sat many times on the wooden pew, his head bowed in prayer.

It took two years to bring the project into fruition, but in March 2009 I sailed from Ushuaia via the Falklands to South Georgia in the *Professor Multanovskiy*. After five days at sea we docked in Cumberland Bay off the Port of Grytviken and, clutching the bronze plaque depicting Wild smoking his pipe, I was taken ashore.

Ledger at Braamfontein cemetery recording Wild's death

That afternoon I was joined by some 40 passengers and a handful of staff from the Island in a simple unveiling ceremony of the plaque that now stands on the wall in the gallery at the back of the church. Two of Shackleton's poems were read, and a historian spoke a few fine words in tribute to Wild. Before we left, we drank a tot of rum to one of the greatest men of the Heroic Age. Of that I am sure he would have approved.

One Ocean Expeditions provided the author with a passage to South Georgia. The author's husband – the sculptor James Butler, RA – modelled the plaque. With the support of the South Georgia Heritage Trust, the James Caird Society, Antarctic-circle.org, Lockbund bronze foundry and many private individuals, the bronze plaque was created.

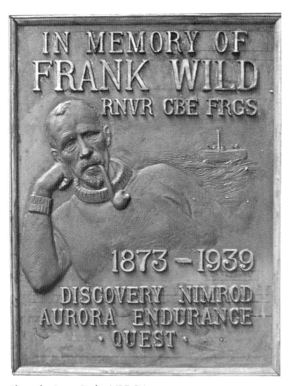

Plaque by James Butler MBE RA

AURORA AUSTRALIS

The Nimrod Expedition 1907-1909. L-R: Wild, Shackleton, Marshall and Adams

Whilst on the British Antarctic Expedition (Nimrod 1907–09), in order to keep his men busy during the long, dark winter months, Shackleton gave them the job of publishing a book. Frank Wild and Ernest Joyce were given a crash course in printing by Sir J Causton and Sons Ltd, which had donated a printing press, a lithographic press, ink, paper and type.

On reaching Ross Island, the men set about building the hut that would house them during the oncoming winter. It was divided into small areas and Wild and Joyce were allotted a cubicle six feet by seven, known as 'Rogue's Retreat.' It housed two bunks, a large sewing machine and the type cases.

Another compartment known as 'The Gables' accommodated the illustrator George Marston and the 'book-binder' Bernard Day. Hence the *Aurora Australis*, edited by Shackleton, was the first book to be written, illustrated, printed and bound in the Antarctic and all under enormously challenging circumstances.

The type-setters, Wild and Joyce, were required to burn a lamp under the type-rack as the metal letters were too cold to handle with bare hands. A candle was placed under the inking plate to stop it from freezing solid, but if left there too long, infuriatingly, the ink became too thin to make an impression.

After many weeks of frustrating mistakes, the men were able to print off two pages a day. Each book produced was unique and was recognised individually by stenciled monograms according to the contents of the packing cases that were used as covers. The spine was made from leather strips and the contents tied into the binding by threading cords through holes punched in the margins of the pages.

Marston reproduced his delicate drawings by using aluminum plates and the etching press. To his frustration, the salt in the water reacted on the plates, but he managed to overcome these difficulties and to produce very fine etchings and lithographs. Some of the expedition members contributed their accounts, observations and verse, and it is believed between 90 and 100 of the books were printed, for which the whereabouts of a third have not been accounted. These exceptionally rare books, given to friends and benefactors of the expedition and printed with many variants, today fetch exorbitant prices but very rarely come on the market.

It is known that Wild had at least five copies of *Aurora Australis* in his possession. One was given to his close friend Charles W. Cooper, along with a piece of rock taken from Mount Erebus on Ross Island. According to Cooper, the covers of this particular book were made from a butter box stenciled with the word BUTTER on one side and the other with the letters SH ANTA DITION – being part of the words British Antarctic Expedition. However this lettering differs in the Christie's catalogue.

Wild's sister bestowed a sum of money to the National Children's Home in Harpenden, Hertfordshire, which then set up a 'Wild Room' in recognition of her brother. Laurence Wild donated a copy of *Aurora Australis* to add to the Wild Room's polar memorabilia.

In 1970 a third copy of *Aurora Australis* was consigned to Sotheby's by Josephine Wild, the only child of Stanley, Wild's youngest brother. It was put up for sale for £380.00 and was unsold. After some negotiation, it was bought by a Mr Holmes, who returned it to auction in 1978, when it was purchased by Louis Starr for £1,300. The uniqueness of this particular book lies in the inside front cover with not easily decipherable lettering: CRYSTAL(lised) FRU(it) below which is BUTTER & AKED BEANS with TINNED FRUIT. Inside the front board is a typed note, signed 'Mountevans,' Wild's old Antarctic comrade, Teddy Evans.

Also included is a note from Stanley Wild, expressing regret at being unable to attend the dedication of the 'Frank Wild Room' and a message to be read out on the day.

In 1999, following Starr's death, the book came back onto the market. With the upsurge of interest in the Heroic Age and the recognition of the rarity of *Aurora Australis*, it sold for $50,000, excluding the buyer's premium, to an unknown buyer.

On 23 June 1995, a copy of *Aurora Australis* inscribed by Wild's brother Laurence to his grandson was sold by Sotheby's. It was bought by an Australian for £7,500.

The fifth 'Wild copy' of *Aurora Australis* went with Wild to South Africa and somehow was acquired by Brian Frost. In 1992, Frost must have been thinking of selling the book, because he contacted Spink & Son, who advised him that it was worth approximately £10,000. At the same time, he asked Spinks the value of the Polar Medal, which they estimated between £5,000 to £6,000.

Brian Frost eventually sold the book through Christie's on 25 October 1995 for an unusually low price of £1,600 to a buyer from the USA.

The inside front cover of this book revealed the letters GRIFFITHS, McALIS… EXPORT PROVISION M… LIVERPO[ool],' with the pencilled note BAKED BEANS, below that similarly stencilled BLAC[k]… BOTTLE. The book had been restored by the conservators of the South African Library in Cape Town for the sum of R800 (approx £50) which resulted in obscuring the original stitching holes in the inner margins. The book had its own leather-lined cloth solander box, again restored, which also contained a portion of the original spine and a length of the green twine used in the original binding.

Christie's informed Brian Frost that when cataloguing the book they discovered that Marston's sketch 'Under the shadow of Erebus' was missing, and that with the book being incomplete its original estimated value of £5,000–8,000 had depreciated to £1,500–2,000. This in itself was most unusual and ordinarily would not devalue the book. The name of the buyer is unknown.

I served five years in ships of the ——
company, the "Macquarie," "Harbinger" & Rod
& several incidents which occurred during
that time cling to my memory.

Whilst on the "Macquarie" in Sydney,
another youth & I were walking along
the beach near Miller's Point, & noticed
a number of children from eight to twelve
years of age in the water. Suddenly they
all rushed screaming out & we gathered
that one of their number had been taken
by a shark. As we stood watching we
saw the child's face appear in a blood
tinged patch of water; we rushed in &
brought the remains of the body out
but he was bitten clean in two. That
was the second person I had seen killed
by sharks. The other was always in Sydney
Harbour at Cockatoo Island; in this case
a full grown man. The shark came up
underneath him & took the whole of his
intestines. From that time I have had
an absolute horror & dread of sharks, I
never feel really comfortable when swim
even in a swimming bath.

Outward bound on the "Macquarie," w

WHY THE MEMOIRS WERE NEVER PUBLISHED

Four people have previously set out to write a biography of Frank Wild, and only one has succeeded. In the 1970s, the polar historian A.G.E. Jones embarked on extensive research on Wild for a biography, but due to ill health never completed the project. Nearly 30 years later owing much to Jones' encouragement, Leif Mills wrote and completed the first biography, *Frank Wild*, a solid and fair account of Wild's life as an explorer, but with only a brief summary of his time in South Africa.

Before that, in the 1950s, Arthur Scholes, an Australian Antarctic scientist, wrote to *The Star*, a South African newspaper, asking friends and relations of Wild's to contact him. He was intending to write 'one of the greatest stories of the Antarctic' and was keen to know why Wild had 'died in poverty stricken circumstances' and 'came to end his days so tragically in South Africa.' He was duly met with a curt reply from Frost, who stated emphatically 'that he did not die in poverty stricken circumstances, nor tragically, except insofar as the death of any great man may be considered a tragedy.' Nothing more came of Scholes' attempt.

Also in the early 1950s, Kenneth Graham Thomson, a Press Association sub-editor, did an enormous amount of research for a biography to be entitled, 'Father of the Antarctic: the Life and Times of Frank Wild.' His research was thorough, covering interviews with Wild's remaining family and meetings he had had with many of the men that had served with Wild on expeditions. However, he asked to quote from Wild's book written after the Quest Expedition – *Shackleton's Last Voyage* – the Memoirs and the diary of the farthest south journey. Years of frustration ensued throughout the 1950's as Trix prevaricated, refusing to give copyright permission or to send him the Memoirs and diary.

I owe much of my material to Thomson's research. The Scott Polar Research Institute (SPRI) contains hundreds of his letters. He kept carbon copies of those he sent and categorised the responses he received. He maintained that a biography of 'such a notable and gallant seaman and explorer as Cmdr Wild is long over due, and that his name and achievements ought to be rescued from oblivion and placed permanently on record in book form.

In one of the few letters Trix wrote Thomson in reply to the many that he besieged her with, she stated: 'the only Diary I have is written about "Shackleton's Farthest South" march, undertaken by Shackleton, Wild, Marshall and Adams, and I am sure he, FW, did not intend it to leave his possession…".

Initially, Thomson's manner was pleasant enough towards Trix, but as the months of her inaction turned into years, his frustration deepened and his letters became more unpleasant. Her brother-in-law, P. O'Brien Frost, initially handled matters on her behalf and informed Thomson that she was 'dependent on us and makes her home with us for the greater part of the year' and suggested he pay her a royalty.

Thomson responded: 'I should be very willing to come to a fair arrangement with Mrs Wild about paying over to her a percentage of any money received from sales of my book when published; but I cannot say what percentage until I have seen the manuscript, judged its length and its possible usefulness…if you are prepared to trust me, will you air-mail it right away…?'

Despite the pressure, Trix would not let the Memoirs out of her hands so easily and jeopardise her beloved husband's wish to have them published as a whole. Instead she decided to find someone to complete the last few pages of the Memoirs and publish them herself. 'I do hope your writing of the biography will be successful for you. I trust you will see my point of view that Frank's memoirs should be published just as he has written them and intended doing.'

In 1952, Thomson wrote to Laurence Wild, one of Wild's brothers, asking him to help persuade Trix 'to give me full permission to quote from any published writings of her husband's and also from any portions of diaries, letters to him, or other material whatsoever that may be in or come into my hands.' Trix ignored Laurence's letter.

KG Thomson continued to collect data, letters and first-hand accounts of Wild's life, including some from family members in Australia, but Trix remained mute.

His correspondence became a rant. He wrote to Frost that, 'I have not received the courtesy of a reply from you… the only unhelpful person who I have approached has been Mrs B. Wild, who married him after his exploring days were ended, and her brother-in-law, representing her: yourself. Do you think that is right? You are trying to compel me to "buy a pig in the poke … to promise Mrs B.W. money which has not been earned, to an amount which you have not named, in return for some Memoirs of unknown merit and value which you refuse to let me see – and the existence of which I begin to doubt. I might point out that, as Frank Wild died in 1939, you and Mrs Wild have had 13 years in which to publish these Memoirs, from which you hope to obtain money to assist Mrs Wild in her present (according to you) somewhat straightened circumstances… I am no Hitler, (but to repeat his famous phrase) my patience is exhausted."

Frost informed Thomson that he had nothing further to say on the matter and suggested that he address all correspondence directly to Mrs Wild. Unfortunately, Thomson, in his frustration, was turning some of Wild's friends and family against Trix. Increasingly bitter, he wrote four years later to James Fisher, Shackleton's biographer asking, 'Is she middle aged or old, is she stupid or shrewd, is she holding out for the higher terms or really intending to publish Wild's own Memoirs herself or is she just plain dumb or gaga and incapable of handling business correspondence? The fact that Wild has been dead for 17 years and that she has not yet published these Memoirs seems to me to indicate that they are pretty worthless…..'

The months turned into years and the situation remained at a deadlock. She would not part with the Memoirs and he would not agree to give her a percentage without seeing them. In 1956 he again wrote to Laurence Wild explaining that he would paraphrase his book. 'The book would not be so good a biography of Frank as it would be if I could quote fully from his own letters and diaries, but at least it would be a biography of him, and of course she could expect to get nothing out of it.'

Trix turned to the Scott Polar Research Institute for guidance, and the Institute offered her £60 for the Memoirs and diary and assured her they would be safe-guarded and that 'only responsible people should have access to them.' Thomson waited in the wings and offered to bolster the sum up by another £20.00.

Trix was living on no more than £105 a year, the Civil Pension given to her by the British government. Extra money would have made a considerable difference to her quality of life, which much of the time was unsettled and often dismal. Not wanting to outstay her welcome either in Messina or Kloof Ridge, she would insist she return to Johannesburg by train and spend time in her rooms in the centre of the city. She was very much alone, unwell and unsure as what to do, so she did nothing.

Then her nephew put her in touch with John Jordi, a newspaper editor who offered to complete the Memoirs and use his contacts in the publishing world. She wrote to Jordi, 'First he (Thomson) must have the M.S. (manuscript) in hand and the other copyrights before making me an offer. Also he mentioned using only parts of the Memoirs where applicable in his book. This of course, I would never agree to, nor would I send him the autobiography for his approval and for curtailment. His airmail requests keep arriving and are becoming most vitriolic. I owe the SPRI an apology for not replying to their first three letters but I was quite unable to come to any decision. I have intended all the time to deposit Franks' effects with them eventually.'

Thomson, furious with the impasse, wrote a letter that cut her deeply. 'Does not the fact that you continue to receive a pension from the British Government given you on account of your husband's services to the World (not of any merit of your own) make you feel that you owe it to the public to assist in the publication of your husbands Life?... do you dislike England, or the Wild family, or your husband's memory?...have you no memoirs written by your husband? I wonder whether you are ashamed that you married a heroic explorer who, perhaps, was no hero to you;… I wonder whether you are afraid of what a biographer might write about his last years of life, when he had already faded from public view: the years when he was too proud to write to his relations at home more than about two letters, which I have seen, in which he made it appear that he was well, happy and if not prosperous, at least comfortable – when perhaps, he was not really any of those things.'

Jordi took up a job with the Chronicle newspaper in Rhodesia and subsequently was unable to take on the task of preparing the Memoirs for publication. However, he contacted Cassell & Co., the publishers who in 1923 had published Shackleton's Last Voyage: the Story of the Quest. At the same time, Thomson approached them to publish his book and they were impressed with his research. Cassell suggested they would broker a royalty deal between Trix and Thomson. Jordi held them off while he contacted another publisher, John Murray. 'Mrs Wild has other provisional plans in mind,' he told Cassell. It was enough for Cassell to drop out of the deal altogether. To Cassell it appeared that Thomson was not going to get copyright permission, and they declined to get further involved in this hornet's nest.

Thomson wrote to Shackleton's biographer, James Fisher, that 'to see myself deprived of the fruits of many years of work by the capriciousness of that inscrutable woman is to touch the bottom in frustration and disappointment. The only bright spot in the outlook is that at least Frank Wild's achievements will go on record in a book – which would probably never have appeared if I had not aroused Mrs Wild's interest in her late husband's life by my correspondence with her.'

In 1958, Thomson discovered that Wild had left all his possessions to Vera Alexandra, his first wife, which confirmed his belief that Trix had been bluffing all along. He tried to find Vera, but failed. Had he done so, he would have discovered that Vera was not able to benefit from Wild's death. She was the sole and legal heir to Wild's estate and believed if nothing else, his most treasured possessions, his medals, were to come to her. Yet an ante-nuptial agreement signed between Trix and Wild left Vera with nothing.

Thomson's correspondence continued until 1965, ever hopeful he would succeed in publishing 'one of the greatest stories of the Antarctic,' but then all letters ceased. 'Father of the Antarctic: the Life and Times of Frank Wild.' remains at the Scott Polar Research Institute, unfinished. Trix was not ultimately successful, either. Even if she had been able to let go of the precious manuscripts that held for her the memories of her beloved husband, she did not ultimately have the robustness required to see them published.

The original hand-written Memoirs and diary were sold by Trix's brother Benjamin in 1971 to the Mitchell Library, of the State Library of New South Wales. Fortunately, the Memoirs had been typed with several carbon copies during Wild's lifetime and at least two of those copies remain in South Africa. As a result of my meetings with June Rowbotham, I have copies of the Memoirs and the farthest south diary, Trix's personal letters, some of Wild's papers and a collection of photographs.

MY QUEST

In order to get a feel of Frank Wild's world I needed to see Antarctica for myself. When I discovered it was possible to go 'south' by ship and visit South Georgia, I immediately booked a passage. Whilst there, I did the walk known 'in the footsteps of Shackleton,' admittedly only the last few miles of a well-trodden path by today's visitors. The whaling station stands silent but as I climbed the last ridge before descending into Stromness Bay, I could almost believe I heard the station's steam whistle that signaled to those men the end of their ordeal.

I entered the little wooden Lutheran church in Grytviken where Shackleton's funeral took place, and I walked to his grave some distance away. Crossing the bay, I picked my way through the belligerent fur seals that flew at my heels and climbed the tussock-covered hill of King Edward Point to the cairn and cross that his men had erected in his memory. Wild was never far from my thoughts.

When I received the initial Rowbotham material, amongst it were around 40 cards, some still with their pin marks in them, which were attached to Wild's funeral wreaths. I recognized the names of friends of my family. I even remembered as a child meeting the mining magnate Jack Scott, who gave Wild his last job. Sadly all these people are now gone, and I feel I have only just missed the boat in talking to them about him.

Throughout the years, I met only three people who had known Wild. First, in England his niece and goddaughter Anne Fright, who has since passed away. She was an ardent supporter of anyone interested in her uncle and was happy to share memories and the polar material in her possession. There was also Brian Frost, who at the age of seven holidayed with Auntie Trix and Uncle Frank and who told me he remembered Wild using a flag from the Battle of Jutland as a tablecloth. I visited Bjorn Behr, a tall, fit man, in his 80's living in Johannesburg. His Swedish father, Einaar, was an engineer at the Messina copper mine managed by P. O'Brien Frost. Behr, a small boy at the time, recalled Wild's frequent visits to their house on the mine and his father and Wild sitting in the garden at the end of a blistering hot day scooping out the brandy-soaked flesh of a paw paw (papaya) – slurping rather than sipping their 'sundowner.'

I traced step-by-step Wild's movements in South Africa, and saw for myself the glorious view of Ghost Mountain that greeted him each morning in Mkuze. The flat featureless drive I took to Ottosdal brought home the isolation he must have felt in that small town far off the beaten track. Twice I visited Kloof

Wild at Mkuze with Ghost Mountain in the background

Ridge, the house that he built for Frost, which stands robust, if not a little neglected, more than 70 years later.

It was on one of these trips that a monstrously large dog belonging to my hostess, who was central to my research and had kindly invited me into her house, bit my leg when no one was looking. Anxious not to lose her good will and more importantly not to distract her from the subject of Wild, I stemmed the blood with an airline sock and said nothing.

Cruising around the indistinguishable streets of Germiston, a reef town that was once an industrial 'dorp' but is now a much-developed urban conglomeration, I eventually found the tin-roofed Victorian bungalow occupied by Wild for four years when he worked on the mine.

It must be 20 years since I visited the Great Zimbabwe ruins on the border of South Africa and what was once Rhodesia, where the Wilds spent a carefree holiday. More recently, I have visited the wild coast of St Lucia, where Wild and

Kloof Ridge, the house that Wild built for Frost

Trix spent lazy days swimming and fishing. Whilst these countries have seen great changes, in the last decades their natural beauty spots remain much the same.

In conclusion it is evident that some writers and historians have taken their cues from anecdotal evidence rather than relying on investigative research. More often than not, this can be traced back to Dr Macklin, who had 'heard about' Wild's time in South Africa.

Frank Wild was one of the great explorers of his time; there is no question of that. Little could surpass those magnificent years when he and his fellow explorers achieved the impossible, when their lives were suspended on nothing more than a gossamer thread and the odds were stacked against them. From their survival, a brotherhood was borne that could not be replicated in civilian life. Yet, I believe that when Wild immigrated to South Africa in 1923, he was looking forward and not back.

South Africa in the 1920s was in the throes of an economic boom. The discovery of gold and diamonds and the offer of huge expanses of land for farming created a new era of imperialism and galvanized folk with a pioneering spirit. Newly married and with a ready-made family, Wild was perfect for this land of opportunity.

Africa is an untamable continent and has shattered many dreams, particularly those of the farmer. When Wild started farming, the country faced extreme weather patterns, unprecedented floods and scorched-earth droughts. He was powerless to save his farm from financial disaster, and the breakup of his marriage to Vera, followed by the loss of his stepsons, wiped him out both physically and emotionally.

I found no evidence in South Africa that he was an alcoholic, but he was certainly a heavy drinker and there were 'tipping points' demonstrated throughout his adult life.

At that time, and even when I was growing up in South Africa, cigarettes and alcohol were dirt cheap. There was an unchecked drinking culture imbedded in the 'colonial' life style adopted by the middle-class English-speaking population. The end of each day was met with a 'sundowner' and continued through the evening until it ended with a 'night cap.'

By the early 1930s, South Africa was caught in the grip of the Great Depression. About 16% of the 1.8 million members of the white population were out of work, the majority Afrikaans-speaking and known as 'poor whites.' Prospects were only slightly better for the more-educated white person. In the 16 years Wild lived there, he was in employment most of the time and, aware of the scarcity of work, remained in the same mining job for four years.

The country too was grappling with political instability. Wild's old friend

J.C. Smuts, Deputy Prime Minister between 1933 and 1939, had formed a coalition with Prime Minister J.B.M. Hertzog from which a break-away hard-line faction known as the Purified National Party emerged, the cornerstone of the Apartheid era that would continue for the next 46 years. Smuts' belief that South Africa had a place within the British Empire was not shared by the right-wing hard-liners and the British community with all its imperialistic ideologies found itself slowly but surely marginalized.

There is no doubt that at this time Wild was fed up with his time in South Africa, a country he complained as 'over boasted and over run by pests, droughts, floods, locusts, hail, army worm,

COMMANDER WILD CREMATED

ASHES MAY BE SENT TO ANTARCTIC

A suggestion has been made that the ashes of Commander Frank Wild, who accompanied five expeditions to the Antarctic—who died on the Rand and was cremated in Johannesburg to-day—should be entrusted to the next American Antarctic expedition and scattered from the air over the South Pole.

An alternative suggestion is that they should be entrusted to the captain of a whaler and taken to South Georgie to be buried near Shackleton, whom Commander Wild accompanied on his last and previous expeditions.

Representations are being made by the Sons of England and the Navy League, but these suggestions would only be carried further if it was the wish of Mrs. Wild or Commander Wild's relations in England.

Sons of England suggest that Wild's ashes be sent to South Georgia

ants, mosquitoes and politicians, the last named being the worst.'

I believe he missed England and in particular his family. He planned to return for a visit (a four-week voyage by ship), but he always demonstrated a quiet acquiescence and an ability to accept his lot with little fuss, be it on Elephant Island or Zululand.

At his death, which was sudden and unexpected, Trix was inundated with letters and telegrams of condolence, of which I have copies. It is abundantly clear from those letters that they were both popular and he tremendously admired as an explorer. His funeral was anything other than the desultory affair it has been described as. Why it has been reported that it took place at the Brixton Cemetery is understandable, since that was the original plan, but when it was suggested by the Sons of England that his ashes could be sent to South Georgia for burial, Trix switched the funeral to the Braamfontein Crematorium.

In my quest to discover more about Wild's life – and driven by the determination to find out what had happened to his remains – I returned to South Africa seven times in as many years. I never lost hope that I might discover his ashes in a discarded tin trunk at Kloof Ridge or perhaps in a niche in the Wall of Remembrance at Braamfontein, but as the years rolled by, so my faith wavered.

If truth be known, I never gave up my quest to find Wild's ashes, and many times my hopes were raised and dashed. J.A. Hobkirk, the funeral directors, had been taken over by Doves, and no records had survived. I found a cutting from *The Star*, dated 1966, with a plea from the Pretoria Antarctic Society looking for the missing ashes. In reply, a Mrs Trovis wrote suggesting that Mrs Wild had told her the ashes remained in a chapel. I had a hunch she was referring to the chapel in the Braamfontein Cemetery, and during my most recent visit to Johannesburg I returned there, and again I poured over the ledgers in the office. The African gentleman in the office – by the name of Mafemani Mkhari – escorted me to the stone-built chapel and unlocked its doors. Like all crematoriums, it was stark in its simplicity and devoid of any areas where ashes could be kept.

I then had a breakthrough as, jangling a bunch of keys, he led me to a door within the chapel, which he unlocked. We descended the stone steps into a large sepulchral vault beneath it. To my amazement I found myself staring at row upon row of marble shelves, stacked from floor to ceiling and divided into small compartments, each one numbered and containing an urn of ashes. On closer inspection, some of the recesses stood empty, and, as I carefully turned the wooden boxes in their cobwebbed tombs, I noted that several were unmarked. Mr Mkhari had left his office to take me into the vault, and as he stood beside

The Columbarium at Braamfontein cemetery

me fidgeting with his keys, I was conscious he needed to return to his post. I looked at as many boxes as I could, but soon it was necessary to ascend the stairs and step into the bright Johannesburg summer light. Yet, I left convinced that for sometime anyway, Trix had had Wild's ashes deposited in the vault for safe-keeping.

With the publication of this book imminent, I felt deep regret that perhaps I would have to finally accept that I would not find Wild's ashes and that the scattering of them on the Garden of Remembrance at Braamfontein, as had been done with Trix's, would appear to be the most plausible explanation as to what happened to them.

In one last-ditch attempt after my return to England, I contacted a friend in Johannesburg and asked him to return to the cemetery to obtain a telephone number of someone in the municipality. I was given the contact details of Mr Alan Buff, the Regional Manager (Parks and Cemeteries), and after a short telephone conversation I emailed him the relevant information regarding Wild's death.

Two years earlier – whilst researching the Braamfontein Cemetery – I had read about Mr Buff, an Englishman who had lived in South Africa for 40 years. After some quite extraordinary detective work, he had found the missing grave of Enoch Sontonga - the composer of 'Nkosi Sikelel' iAfrika' the South African national anthem – who had died in 1905. My spirits at once lifted.

On 31 January 2011, an email arrived. 'Good day, Angie.

Two sets of ash in the columbarium, Beatrice Wild and Commander Frank Wild. Regards Alan.'

I telephoned him immediately. 'What is a columbarium?' I hardly dared ask. 'The room under the chapel,' he replied casually. Buff had spent more than an hour checking records, and through a process of elimination and with the clue from the newspaper cutting mentioning 'the chapel,' he found Wild's urn on the bottom shelf on the far side of the columbarium. As it turned out, the urn next to it was not that of Trix, as her ashes had been scattered, but there was no mistaking that in niche 107, the Green wooden box with a copper plate and the words (commander) FRANK WILD 19.8.1939 AGED 66 YEARS was his.

Frank Wild wrote of Shackleton's gravesite: "*Gritviken is a romantic spot. All around are big mountains, bold in outline and snow-covered. Below lies one of the most perfect little harbours in the world, at times disturbed by the fierce winds from the hills and lashed by the gusty squalls to a mass of flying spume and spindrift. Often it lies calm and peaceful, bathed in glorious sunshine and reflecting in its deeps the high peaks around, whilst the sea-birds, "souls of old mariners," circle in sweeping flights above its surface and fill the air with the melancholy of their cries. An ideal resting-place this for the great explorer who felt, more than most men, the glamour of such surroundings*".

In 1922 after Shackleton's sudden death, his wife Emily asked that her

The green wooden box containing Wild's ashes

husband's body be returned to South Georgia for burial. Seventeen years later, with equal selflessness, Trix made the decision to have her husband cremated rather than buried in order that his ashes be returned to that 'ideal resting place' and re-united with Shackleton. Perhaps her wish will finally be granted.

Frank Wild
Memoirs

AS WRITTEN BY WILD

With the encouragement of Trix, Wild began writing his Memoirs in 1934 with the sole intention of having them published as a book. They began with his time in the merchant navy in 1889 and ended with a brief account of life on Elephant Island, towards the end of his fourth expedition, in 1916.

By all accounts, Wild had a publisher who had been introduced to him by the well-known and prolific author of the day, Valentine Williams, 'waiting' for the book. After his death, Trix sought the help of James Wordie and Raymond Priestley to help identify Wild's vast collection of photographs for the book. 'I am at a complete standstill owing to the number of slides not being entitled. Of course fully known to him.' Why nothing came of this is unknown.

Again, in the early 1950s there were opportunities for Trix to have the book published, yet, with the clash with Thomson and his malicious accusations, John Jordi's move to Rhodesia and her itinerant life style, she appeared to have lost her self-confidence. Sometime before 1964 all of Wild's slides and photographs, stored in a suitcase at Kloof Ridge, were burnt during a 'clear out.'

INTRODUCTION

Commander Frank Wild was born in Yorkshire, quite close to the birthplace of his illustrious Great Great Grandfather, Captain Cook, who was the first to sail amongst mountainous bergs and the burrows of the Antarctic. Wild commenced his travels in the bad old sailing-ship days. In 1895, he sailed on the "Britannia" with King Edward VII, then Prince of Wales, and in the same year went out to Australia with Lord Brassey on the famous "Sunbeam".

In 1901 Wild was one of those chosen by Captain Scott from 3,000 naval volunteers to form the crew of the "Discovery". Mention is made in Scott's account of that expedition of Wild's courage and resourcefulness.

Shackleton was one of Scott's party and in 1907, he commanded his own Nimrod expedition and chose Wild as one of the three to accompany him on his wonderful sledge journey to within 100 miles of the South Pole.

Wild's next venture was as Mawson's second-in-command 1911 to 1913, during which time Wild discovered and named Queen Mary's land. He was caught on a sledging trip in the snow blizzard which killed Captain Scott and his party.

In 1914, he again sailed as Shackleton's second-in-command on the ill-fated Endurance, when after seeing their ship crushed in the ice, the party spent six months on floating ice before they made a landing on Elephant Island, from where Shackleton made the most wonderful boat journey to South Georgia, leaving Wild in charge of the party on the island. Wild was publicly and privately complimented by King George for bringing his party safely through the five months privation and hardship on the island.

In 1918, Wild was in command of an expedition in the Arctic and upon his return, went to settle in Nyasaland cotton planting etc, but in 1921 he returned to accompany his old chief, Shackleton, on the "Quest". On the journey south, Shackleton died and was buried in South Georgia and the expedition carried on under Wild's command.

Wild is the proud possessor of the Polar Medal with four clasps, bars, the only one in existence.

Commander Wild has been awarded numerous medals from the British, Scottish, American and Belgian Geographical Societies, also the Stanhope and Livingstone Gold Medals. The Stanhope medal is given for the most outstanding exploration work of the year; the Livingstone medal for the most outstanding feat of exploration south of the Equator.

THE MEMOIRS

As far back as I can remember, at the age of four, I wished to be a sailor and when eight years old read a book on Arctic adventure, and ever since have had a keen desire for Polar travel. Even now, after five Antarctic expeditions and one to the Arctic, that longing is not extinguished.

There may be something in heredity. Captain James Cook was my great great grandfather and he was the first navigator to penetrate the Antarctic proper.

My first sea voyage was on the "Sobraon", perhaps the best known and most popular sailing ship of her time. She had accommodation for 200 passengers and made a regular yearly trip to Melbourne for about 50 years, and was finally sold to the New South Wales Government for a training ship. That was in 1891 and she is still afloat in Sydney Harbour.

I served five years in ships of the same Company, the "Macquarie", "Harbinger" and "Rodney" and several incidents which occurred during that time cling to my memory.

Whilst on the "Macquarie" in Sydney, another youth and I were walking along the beach near Miller's Point and noticed a number of children from eight to twelve years of age in the water. Suddenly they all rushed screaming out and we gathered that one of their number had been taken by a shark. As we stood watching, we saw the child's face appear in a blood tinged patch of water, we rushed in and brought the remains of the body out but he was bitten clean in two. That was the second person I had seen killed by sharks. The other was also in Sydney harbor at Cockatoo Island, in this case a full grown man. The shark came up underneath him and took the whole of his intestines. From that time, I have an absolute horror and dread of sharks and never feel really comfortable when swimming, even in a swimming bath.

Outward bound on the "Macquarie" when about midway between the Cape and Australia, we were running before a heavy gale with a tremendous following sea. I was on the poop coiling down the main braces when a sea came over the quarter and washed me overboard. Luckily the coils of rope went with me and I was so tangled up in them that I could not have got free had I tried. The Mate, a pocket Hercules, saw me go and hauled me aboard singled handed. Except for being winded and having a bit of skin taken off my face whilst being pulled up the ship's side, I was unhurt. We were doing about fifteen knots at the time and there was far too heavy a sea running to allow a boat to be lowered.

I got my Second Mate's Certificate and made a voyage as Third Mate on a real lime juicer – a term for a ship that was run on the cheapest lines possible, where the crew was expected to do the maximum of work on the minimum of food and wages. My salary was £3:10:0 per month and able seamen were receiving £3.

We sailed from Cardiff to Callao with a cargo of coal, from there in ballast to Calata Busno, where we loaded saltpeter, returning to Antwerp to pay off. We carried a very mixed, quarrelsome and naturally discontented crew. The Captain and three officers were British, but the others were American, German, French, Scandinavian, Finnish, Russian, Italian and Chilean. The one American stood six feet four inches in his socks and was a tremendously powerful man; he was the only man aboard who never had a fight but he always did the refereeing, standing by with a belaying pin ready to knock out any man who used a knife or committed some outrageous foul. He saved me from being seriously hurt in my one and only scrap.

On the outward voyage we had a particularly rough time rounding Cape Horn. It was in the latter part of June and July. A gale was blowing for six weeks; we were under lower topsails and reefed foresail, ice thick on the deck and all lower rigging and some frozen spray as high as the cross trees.

Every time we were ship, we had to beat the ice off the braces and then the blocks out with boiling water. In the middle of all of this the cargo shifted, giving the ship a dangerous list to starboard. For several days we were forced to remain on the starboard deck, which meant we were travelling further and further South, sighting numbers of icebergs.

One watch was under hatches all the time day and night, trimming the coal back and building a bulkhead amidships to prevent the coal gliding back. We were really working in the dark as our only lights were slush lamps which could not penetrate the dense dust of the Walsh coal. Two of my watch, a German and a Finn, had a fight with shovels resulting in a broken collar bone on one and a large portion of the other's scalp being removed. When the latter eventually healed, there was no hair and the bare part was tattooed a deep blue by the coal dust.

What a contrast was my next ship, Lord Brassey's "Sunbeam".

We were present that year, 1895, at the opening of the Kiel Canal, a most imposing ceremony carried out by His Imperial Majesty, Kaiser Wilhelm.

Later that summer, I was lent with five others to assist in sailing the "Britannia". There I had the honour and pleasure of first meeting King Edward VII, then Prince of Wales. This honour was repeated several times in later years. The Prince was most charming in his manner towards the crew. Within a few hours, he knew all our names and when years afterwards I was presented to him, amongst many others, to receive medals etc, he, sitting on his throne clad in royal robes, made me the proudest man on earth by grasping me by the hand and saying, "Oh Mr Wild and I are old friends".

After the yachting season was over, the "Sunbeam" sailed for Melbourne with Lord and Lady Brassey on board - Lord Brassey having been appointed Governor of Victoria.

We called at Madeira, St Vincent (where all hands got a severe dose of fish poisoning), St Helena, St Pauls de Loando, Capetown and thence to Melbourne.

We did extensive cruising from port to port in Australia and after spending six months in that country, I returned to England on the "Rodney". Followed were a few years of voyages to India, China, Japan, Australia, New Zealand etc.

It is well known that a Chinaman will not attempt to save another man's life, even at no risk to his own, the reason being, I believe, that the rescuer can be called upon to keep the rescued for the rest of his life.

Steaming through the Formosa Channel on a P&O boat, we had the misfortune to sink one of a fleet of Chinese fishing boats. We lowered boats and picked up several of the crew, but a number were drowned. Although other fishing boats were within a few yards of the wrecked boat, their crew made no attempt to save the drowning men.

One afternoon in Shanghai, three of us were walking along the river front and found one of our ship's quartermasters very drunk and liable to be robbed. We called a Sampan and I got into it to ease the drunken man down whilst the others lowered him; he suddenly lashed out with his feet and knocked me overboard. There is a very swift current here and few people who fall into the river are ever seen again. I knew this and although a good swimmer, was feeling far from comfortable. I came up under the sampan and it was probably half a minute before I could get clear of the flat bottom and by the time I got clear and was able to grasp hold of the gunwale, I had swallowed a lot of dirty water and was unable to speak.

My pals were anxiously watching for me to come up some distance down the river and the Chinaman in charge of the boat sat unmoved and unwinkingly staring me in the face. I was too far gone to pull myself up and it seemed a very long time before I was able to shout. When my friends did at last hear me and haul me aboard, they had considerable difficulty in preventing me from punching the Chinaman's head. I had a perfectly new suit of clothes on.

One of my Shanghai friends was a Police Official and through him, four of us received permission to attend the execution of twenty political criminals at Koosung.

The prisoners knelt in a row beside an open trench, dug by themselves I was told; the executioner went along the row and lifting the pigtail (now not worn) with his left hand, swung a heavy curved sword with his right, and off came the head, the late wearer falling into the ditch. So little concerned were the prisoners that they were actually talking to each other until speech was cut off by the sword. One of our party took photographs but, before we departed, the Officer-in-charge of the guard very politely took the camera and the owner's name and address. A few days later, the camera was delivered but with all the plates blank.

Then came the Boer War....

It will be remembered that relations between Germany and England were somewhat strained at that time and hundreds of men, of whom I was one, joined the Royal Navy from the Merchant Service expecting to have a smash at the German Navy.

In 1901, Captain Scott, who had been for a long time preparing for the British Antarctic Expedition, asked for volunteers from the Navy.

I was most keen to go, but was diffident about putting in my name as I thought Scott would choose only big hefty men. However, one of my classmates in the torpedo course on the "Vernon" persuaded me, so our names went in with some three or four thousand others. To my surprise and delight, I was one of the chosen. I was sorry my big pal was left behind, but a few years later, he tumbled into a very fine position in the West Indies, which he would have missed had he joined the "Discovery".

The voyage of the "Discovery" has been often described and little that I can write is new. Before leaving England, King Edward and Queen Alexandra visited the ship.

Whilst the King was being escorted round by Captain Scott, the Queen and one of her Ladies in Waiting were making investigations on their own. They found their way into the Biologists laboratory where the Biologist was bottling some spiders. He did not recognise his visitors and after giving them a fairly full dissertation on the domestic and other habits of the spider, he said "Now I'm going to play about with some acids, so you women had better get out or you may get your frocks spoiled". The Queen was delighted and immediately sought out the King, who also thoroughly enjoyed the joke. Later the Queen was immensely amused when one of the sailors, explaining some of the equipment, addressed her as "Miss".

The voyage of the "Discovery" was of much greater interest than that of an ordinary ship. We frequently stopped to take water temperatures and bring up samples of water from different depths and to dredge and travel at depths varying from a few hundred to 3,000 fathoms and carry out all kinds of oceanographical and other scientific work, with the details of which I do not intend to bother the reader.

We called at Madeira where all hands were given the opportunity of a run ashore where we did the usual things a sailor does there; travelled up the funicular railway, came down on sledges and failed in our attempt to get the attendants to go all out and have a race down, thus probably saving our necks. We more than tasted the delicious wine and then went aboard.

Speaking of the wine; on the "Challenger" Expedition in 1870, Sir James Buchanan bought several casks of the best wine Madeira can produce, carried them on the voyage and then bottled them down. In 1911, he gave me the last half dozen bottles to take on Sir Douglas Mawson's Australian Antarctic Expedition. On very special occasions, we drank and enjoyed this wine. On one bottle, my party engraved our names and a picture of our ship and presented it to Sir James Buchanan. On another we engraved our names and threw it into the sea. Years afterwards it caused considerable interest when it was picked up on the beach near Sydney, New South Wales.

The "Discovery's" next call of interest was Trinidad Island, off the Brazilian coast. In bygone years, this was a penal settlement, but some deleterious matter in the water caused blindness and the Island was abandoned. Rumour has it that pirates used it as a treasure deposit, and several expeditions have spent time and money trying to find treasure there, but never with any success.

At the time we landed, the only inhabitants were birds and land crabs. The birds were of great variety and quite tame having been in undisturbed possession for many years. To collect their eggs, we had to push the birds off their nests and some of them, Gannets and Robber Gulls especially, fought very fiercely.

I climbed to the top, about 1700 feet, and ate my lunch alongside a spring, under the shade of a palm. After eating, I stretched out for a nap. Lying with my eyes closed, I heard a very faint movement nearby and on opening my eyes, saw a large land crab within two feet with his claws outstretched and his protruding eyes looking into mine; I don't know which of us moved the fastest.

When we landed, a light swell was running and we had not much trouble in jumping on to the rocks, but when the time came to re-embark, a heavy swell made the proceeding very dangerous. The boats had to be anchored some distance from the rocks, the cable slacked away until the boat was as close as possible without being smashed up and then the members of the landing party jumped from the rocks into the boats as they hove madly up and down in the swell.

All hands were soaked and many sorely bruised, but the only serious accident was the loss of a valuable camera belonging to Captain Scott. Petty Officer Evans volunteered to dive for it, but apart from the danger of damage from the rough sea, there were numbers of sharks about and Scott would not allow the attempt to be made.

The scientists were delighted with the collections made by the landing party and also by the people left on board, who had carried out trawling and dredging operations and had a most successful day's fishing.

Upon arrival at Capetown, the "Discovery" was put into dry dock as a leak had been giving a lot of extra work and some of the stores were damaged.

A most enjoyable time was spent in Capetown before the voyage was resumed. An interesting day was spent on the Agulhas Bank where we caught a number of beautiful cod on hand lines.

We travelled much farther south than is usual for the ordinary ship bound for New Zealand and gave the "Discovery" her ice baptism in pack which was almost as heavy as any she battled with later on.

Many people ask, "is there any practical or commercial value in these expeditions apart from the scientific knowledge gained?"

Ships sailing to Australia and New Zealand often experience weeks of overcast and cloudy weather and have no opportunity for checking their position by the sun or stars and so are entirely dependent on the compass and knowledge of currents. There are numerous islands on or near the route followed to New Zealand – Prince Edward and Marion Islands, Crozet, Amsterdam, St Paul's, Kerguelen and Auckland Islands – and many ships have been wrecked on them.

On the "Discovery", and later on Shackleton's "Nimrod", numerous magnetic observations were taken and it was found that the charted curves of variation were in many cases wrong, sometimes more than 10°. It will readily be seen that a ship steering by compass only would be a long way off her course in a few days.

Since the results of the aforesaid observations were made known and the charts altered, not one ship has been lost on those islands.

The leak which had given trouble before Capetown was not cured by the dry docking there and upon arrival at Lyttleton (NZ), the ship was emptied of all stores and again thoroughly overhauled in dry dock.

Several most happy weeks were spent with the hospitable New Zealanders and when we sailed, we had a wildly enthusiastic send off. Our high spirits, however, received a sad check. All hands who could be spared from the actual working of the ship had taken up advantageous positions in the rigging and on the yards to return the cheers and see the last of our late hosts. One sailor was sitting on the main truck holding on to the weather vane and as he started to descend, the rod of the vane broke and he fell clear to the deck, being killed instantaneously. We put into Dunedin where he was buried with full naval honours, a gun carriage and firing party being lent by HMS "Ringarooma".

The voyage south on the "Discovery" has been fully described by Scott himself in his "Voyage of the Discovery" so I shall not dwell upon it.

I shall never forget the first experience of forcing a passage through heavy pack ice and the view of colossal icebergs at close range. There is a wonderful fascination about ice and snow and I know of nothing else that can assume such fantastic shapes and take such marvelous variety of colour.

Landings were made at Robertson's Bay, Granite Harbour and Cape Crozier. As the last named despatches were left, according to arrangement, giving directions to the relief ship which was coming down the following year, as to where to find the "Discovery". Captain Scott's intention was to sail along the Ross Barrier to the east and to try and find a wintering place.

New land, which Scott named King Edward VII Land, was discovered, but no suitable harbour, so we returned to McMurdo Sound, which is a strait between Ross Island and the mainland. On Ross Island are those magnificent landmarks Mt Erebus and Mt Terror, the former an active and the latter an extinct volcano.

During the first year of the voyage, naval routine was carried out and except when the decks were awash in heavy weather, they were washed down every morning and upper deck paint work cleaned on Saturday. Many a time when running along the Ross Barrier, the water froze almost instantly after leaving the hose and had to be shoveled off, and when washing paintwork, the cloths would freeze hard to bulwarks etc.

An excellent wintering place was found below the slopes of Mt Erebus and named "Winter Harbour", clear of ice and protected from heavy seas by a Cape to the north named "Hut Point". The ice barrier to the south, Ross Island to the east and the Mainland to the west (the latter 20 miles away) but we never had any heavy wind from that direction. The "Discovery" was securely moored about 200 yards from land and a hut built ashore in case of anything happening to the ship.

Shortly after deciding upon winter quarters, a sledging party was sent off to alter the despatches at Cape Crozier. The party was composed of 12 men and a number of dogs and, although unsuccessful in its object, the experience gained was of great value.

Many alternations were later made in our clothing and other equipment and a number of "don'ts" were added to our sledging hints. For instance, one man opened a tin of jam with his sheath knife, temperature about 30°, took some out on his knife and put it into his mouth. The knife immediately froze fast to his lips and tongue and he had to keep it there until it warmed sufficiently for him to remove it without tearing a lot of skin away. As it was, his mouth was badly blistered.

We also learned to do many things without removing our gloves, touching cold metal with bare fingers being as painful and dangerous as touching hot metal.

We found that dogs cannot be harnessed to the same load with men as the dogs' pulling pace is a trot and at a man's walking pace they are useless.

Our food supplies were wrong, many unnecessary varieties were later cast out and the method of packing entirely altered.

After a few days travelling on the barrier, we found our progress was so slow that Royds, who was in charge, decided to turn nine of the party back under Barnes's charge and he, with two others, carried on on ski and with one light sledge. Where we were sinking in soft snow from ankle to knee deep, we watched them swinging away on the surface.

Before getting back to the ship we had to cross a range of hills – roughly a thousand feet high – and just as we reached the summit, about 10am, a blizzard struck us. This was our first experience of a real Polar blizzard. The only thing to do when sledging and caught in a blizzard is to get the tents up as quickly as possible, get into sleeping bags and wait until it blows itself out. Attempting to travel invariably results in getting lost.

The majority of the Antarctic blizzards last about 48 hours but I have been held up six days (nine days on two occasions) and some of my party on Mawson's Australian Expedition were confined in their tents seventeen days.

I have known a man to be completely lost when venturing out of a tent, in less than ten feet. Ninety miles an hour of wind is common and one's face is almost immediately covered with a mask of snow, one is knocked down and all sense of direction completely lost.

I have seen recorded on an anemometer 150 miles an hour and have been picked up off my hands and knees and thrown more than twenty five yards without touching anything. If a man were made to face a wind of 100 miles an hour, he would die as quickly as when held under water, the force of the wind being so great that he would be unable to expel his breath.

To return to our first experience, not knowing the danger we carried on for some time and then, finding some of the party were getting frost bitten, Barnes gave the order to pitch tents. This was done with great difficulty in the storm and thinking it was only a sudden storm and would blow over in a few hours, we did not take our sleeping gear into the tents.

Late in the afternoon, the wind having abated so much that it was possible to see 10 to 15 yards, Barnes ordered a start. We were only about three miles from the ship and being miserably cold and hungry, we were all eager to obey.

Ordered to keep together, we followed our leader as closely as possible but very soon one man, Hare, was found to be missing. We were walking along a slope and it was thought that he had slipped and gone down. Barnes, ordering us to remain where we were every few seconds, started down the slope. The drift was not quite so thick now and we saw him for 15 yards or so, then he stepped on a patch of ice and shot out of sight. As he did not reappear, Petty Officer Evans went down and he too lost his footing and disappeared. We waited a few minutes and then Petty Officer Quartly tried it. The same fate befell him. After perhaps twenty minutes, I went down and managed to keep my footing but after descending far past where the others had disappeared and finding nothing but a continuation of the slope, I decided to return to where I had left the remaining four of the party.

Orders are orders in the Navy and we had been ordered to remain where we were. Although we were all chilled to the bone and one man badly frost bitten and staying there would have inevitably have been the death of us all in a few hours, it was a long time before I could persuade the others to move on and try to find the ship.

We were still on a slope and Vince, the frost-bitten man, required a lot of help. Suddenly, in one of his falls, we were all knocked off our feet and went sliding helplessly down. We shot down what seemed miles, but later we found to be about 1200 feet. Vince was holding on to me, but became exhausted and let go and as I checked myself in some soft snow, I saw him disappear so suddenly that I knew he had dropped. The other three had followed in the same course and I was able to stop them as they came down. When we had recovered our breath, we crawled to where Vince had disappeared and found a straight drop of 300 feet into the sea.

The climb back up that slope was a horrible nightmare – every slip brought our hearts into our mouths, and I, for one, dreamt about it for some time afterwards.

The sight of the sea had given me our position and an hour later we were aboard the "Discovery". Captain Scott relates how I guided a search party back to where we had left the tents, on my way finding Barnes, Evans and Quartly in a dazed condition, (Barnes never fully recovered from frost-bitten fingers, and Evans was lucky not to lose an ear), and how Hare returned to the ship alone after being buried under snow for 36 hours.

I do not intend to rewrite the story of the "Discovery" or to describe the numerous sledging journeys that were made and shall only touch on those I personally accompanied.

The season was now too far advanced for further sledging and the ship was made as snug as possible for the winter, a heavy awning being spread over the greater part of the deck. This, however, did not prevent driving snow during storms from heaping up under the awning and giving a lot of healthy exercise in clearing it up.

In South Africa one can see immense distances and the distance is often most deceptive. At sea, it is the same but there is no place on earth where the air is so clear and distance so deceiving as in the Polar regions. I have seen Mt Erebus 180 miles away.

South of our winter quarters were two islands, Black and White Island. One Sunday, shortly after our arrival, two men decided to walk over to White Island which looked not more than three or four miles distant. After walking three hours and the island looking no closer, they returned weary and wiser. We found later on that White Island was twenty-two miles away.

In calm weather, sound travels immense distances. I have heard a man singing five miles away and a conversation can easily be carried on between people a mile apart.

When leaders of expeditions write up their books, they usually give the impression that their parties were composed of archangels and that rows and differences never occurred. In all of my six expeditions, quarrels and squabbles have taken place and men's tempers must naturally become frayed when herded together in close quarters under the trying conditions of a Polar winter.

I was once asked to act as second to one of two men who were going to fight a duel with pistols. Fortunately, one cried off and apologised.

During the first winter on the "Discovery", one man's mind gave way. One evening during bad weather, he was missed. A search party was organized by one man going straight out from the ship with a rope; before he got out of sight in the drift, another took hold of the line and so on until some two hundred yards of rope was paid out. Then the party commenced a sweeping movement round the ship. The missing man was found a short distance ahead of the ship with a crowbar in his hand. When asked what he was doing there, he said "Well, I knew a search party would be sent out for me and I hoped _____ (here he named a man with whom he had quarreled) would find me and I was going to brain him with this bar".

During the four and a half months absence of the sun, we were not entirely confined to the ship, but much of the outside work had to be done by the aid of lanterns. Fairly long walks could be taken when the moon was up and at full moon, we even played football. The moon casts a very black shadow on the snow and frequently a man would kick at the shadow instead of the ball. Anyone who has kicked hard and missed will know what a shock it is.

To the majority of us the much talked of monotony of a Polar night was entirely absent; as there was always work to be done. Apart from keeping the ship clean, bringing in ice for water from a nearby glacier, fishing through holes made in the ice, killing and skinning occasional seals that managed to get on to the ice near us and taking regular meteorological observations etc, there was a lot of work to be done in altering our sledging equipment, which had proved unsatisfactory on our early journeys. Hundreds of food bags were made, sledge fittings altered and in fact everything so revolutionised that on subsequent journeys, it would have been hard to find room for improvement.

I was acting Assistant Meteorologist and apart from the usual instruments I had to read thermometers buried at various depths on land, a snow gauge and an ice measure. The latter gave the daily growth of the sea ice which showed a depth of 12 feet the first winter. This gadget was about a quarter of a mile from the ship, round Hut Point and near the foot of a very steep snow covered hill about 700 feet high. One day as I was about to read this instrument, I saw an object detach itself from the summit of this hill and come shooting down at a terrific rate. I first thought it was a large stone, then detecting some independent movement of the object, guessed it to be a dog, but as it shot over some rocks at the bottom and landed on the sea ice twenty yards from me, I saw it was a man. I ran towards him expecting to find him dead or seriously injured when the man got to his feet and remarked "I'd have done it alright if the d___d box lid hadn't broken". He had attempted to toboggan down kneeling on a piece of three-ply wood about three feet long, holding up the front end to make a curved bow.

This man, Buckridge, had a most interesting career. He had travelled extensively on the Australian Continent, pearling in the north, sheep shearing, gold digging etc in other parts and he came over to South Africa with the Australian troops during the Boer War. He joined the "Discovery" at Capetown.

After leaving the expedition, he stayed for some time in New Zealand and amongst other adventures there, he tried to sound one of the hot lakes, the one he chose being a particularly dangerous geyser, which erupted at irregular times without warning and very shortly after Buckridge got back to land, it blew up and killed several people on the banks.

Soon afterwards, Buckridge set off on a voyage round the world in a very small boat with one companion. A few weeks later, the companion was picked up and he stated that Buckridge had fallen from the mast and killed himself and that he had kept the body on board until compelled to commit it to the deep.

On Buckridge's first sledging journey, he fell down a crevasse and expressed disappointment when he was hauled up by his harness. He said "You can't believe how beautiful it is down there, such marvelous colouring and wonderful stalactites in ice crystals!"

Another rather alarming incident concerning Buckridge recurs to me. We used paraffin lamps without chimneys, the requisite draught being supplied by a clockwork fan. During the winter, I was one day sitting reading or writing when Buckridge brought along the clockwork part of a lamp and said to me "I can't get this thing to work, what should I do with it?" Without thought, I replied "boil it in paraffin". An hour later, the alarm "FIRE" went through the ship and the galley was found to be in flames. It was not long before the fire was put out, but quite a lot of damage was done. Apart from a perfectly good dinner being spoiled, a lot of clothes which were hanging up to dry were ruined and paintwork and timber charred and blackened. When the cause of the fire was enquired into, Buckridge confessed he had followed my advice and had boiled the clockwork in paraffin in an old meat tin. I naturally received a well deserved rub down from Captain Scott, although I never dreamt my advice would be taken seriously.

Naval routine was carried out to a great extent through the winter. Morning prayers were read on the mess deck, either by Captain Scott or a Senior Officer, the remainder of the Officers and Scientists presumably said their own prayers in their cabins.

The usual evening rounds were done and on Sunday, Captain's inspection. The Boatswain piped all hands off the mess deck and whilst the mess deck inspection was going on, all lower deck members of the crew waited in the dark on the upper deck. Then the command "Fall in" and they fell in in two ranks, the Captain formally inspecting them by the aid of a lantern held up by the Boatswain. Somewhat unnecessary in the circumstances, but as one of the sailors remarked, "Oh well, it pleases him and it don't hurt us".

Sledging journeys began as soon as possible which was early in September, which corresponds with March in the Arctic. Conditions south are, however, much more severe than north. Spring temperatures down to 70° below zero and terribly persistent and violent winds make early sledging trips things to remember.

Never before, or since, has so much exploration been done by sledging parties as was carried out under Scott, but I am writing only of those in which I took part.

By the middle of September, several sledging parties were out and I was with a party of six under Lieutenant Royds on a reconnaissance trip to the south west. A few days after leaving the ship, my fingers were severely frost bitten whilst repairing a sledge.

The weather was fine but cold, the temperature varying from 40° to 65° below zero. On the eighth day out, we had pitched our tents for the midday meal, not a cloud in the sky and not a breath of wind, so we did not bother to fasten the tent very securely. Just as the pot was boiling for tea, we heard a sudden rushing sound and down came our tent. Scrambling out, we found sun, sky, land and everything blotted out by driving snow and the wind so fierce we could hardly keep on our feet. Fortunately, the three in the other tent had been more cautious and their tent remained standing. After firmly securing it, they assisted us in re-erecting ours, but the drift was so blinding and the wind so strong, it took the six of us two hours to make the tent safe.

Our sleeping equipment consisted of three single reindeer sleeping bags and one three-man bag. When getting the gear into the tents, it was found that one of the single bags had disappeared, so the owner had to squeeze in with us in the three-man bag. This made for warmth but by this time, my fingers had blistered very badly and looked as though I were holding a double handful of black plums. Every touch was extremely painful and for many nights, I had no sleep.

Luckily it was not a long blizzard, only two days, and after one more day outward bound, our object being achieved, we commenced the return trip.

Following almost in our outward bound tracks, you can imagine our delight when we found the missing sleeping bag jammed amongst some moronic boulders. It had been blown more than six miles but was quite undamaged.

When we reached the ship a few days later, the doctor lanced my blistered fingers and the relief was so great that for the first time in my life, I fainted. He gave me some brandy and I turned in and slept eighteen hours without a move.

At this time, the sun appeared for a few hours daily but it rose so little above the horizon that its heat could barely be felt. One day, several of us were sitting resting on the sledge talking about the tropics and we all solemnly vowed that wherever fortune took us in the future, we would never grumble at the sun again.

Since then, I have travelled and tramped in many tropical places, and once when in Nyasaland, it was 125°F in the shade. I almost forgot my vow, but suddenly recollecting many paralyzing polar experiences, I looked up and said "go ahead old sport, do your best".

It was a custom to keep a sharp look out for the return of all sledging parties and when seen, to meet them as soon as possible and relieve them of their load for the last few miles.

My next experience was again under Royds, this time to Cape Crozier to alter the despatches, the first attempt when Vince was lost, having failed. This time, we succeeded in reaching the objective and had an uneventful outward journey. The day that we started our return, we were caught in a very severe blizzard and for six days were unable to move. Our tents were buried to within six inches of the top and the weight of snow pressed them in until our quarters were terribly cramped. We were a party of six; three in a tent and we in my tent had fortunately left our cooking gear close to the door. Without much trouble, we were able to get it inside and had regular meals whilst we were confined. The occupants of the other tent had replaced their gear on the sledge and for the whole of the six days had no food. When the storm subsided, we dug ourselves out and then had to release the others who were in a very weak state. This was another lesson and ever after, room was found inside the tent for food bag and cooker.

The next journey in which I took part was under Armitage, over the mountains to the west and on to the continental ice cap. Being an absolutely pioneer trip over these mountains, it was only natural that many days were lost in retracing our steps when we found ourselves confronted by impossible cliffs or country so broken up by crevasses that nothing without wings could hope to cross it.

On one occasion, we hauled our sledges one at a time up 1000 feet of steep snow slope, then thick weather kept us in our tents for two days. When the drift ceased, we found in front of us an awe inspiring sight of broken glacier and yawning crevasses. We tobogganed back down that thousand feet in a few minutes and our leader unfortunately heard some of us singing:

"Oh the mighty Duke of York
He had ten thousand men
He took them up to the top of a hill
Then took them down again".

He was a most popular man and we would not have hurt his feelings for anything, but we forgot how sound travels in that air.

We had another exhilarating slide down 2,000 feet of slope so steep that we were two days hauling the sledges up with tackle on our return.

This journey was undertaken in the middle of summer and we had mostly fine weather, the temperature little below freezing point except when we were at an altitude of 7,000 feet when it hovered around the zero mark. It was altogether an interesting and enjoyable outing. Armitage discovered a better route than the one taken by us and the following summer, profiting by this knowledge, Scott was able to save much time and penetrate much farther inland.

The most of the journey was on a glacier named by Scott the Ferrar Glacier, easy to haul sledges on but rough on the runners. One man suffered from mountain sickness and had to be placed on a sledge for 120 miles. A few, including myself, had attacks of snow blindness which is excruciatingly painful but is usually one's own fault. It is inflammation of the arteries of the eye, caused by the glare and if not attended to at once, may cause permanent blindness. The feeling is that one's eyes are full of sharp sand and the eyes become tightly shut so that to see, one has to pull the lids apart with one's fingers, tears streaming down all the time. One experience was enough for me and always afterwards, I donned goggles at the first hint of discomfort.

When descending from the plateau, Armitage had a narrow escape from death. When putting on his harness one morning, he found his hauling rope was chafed and wishing not to delay the start, instead of splicing in a new piece, he made fast each end of a thirty foot length of Alpine rope and carried the coil at his waist. During the forenoon march, he fell through the bridge of a crevasse, his chafed rope broke and down he went to the full length of the Alpine rope, about 30 feet. He was a heavy man, about 250 lbs, and had the drop been a straight one, he would most certainly have been killed; fortunately, the crevasse ran down in a slanting direction and although he was badly bruised, the rope held and we hauled him out, winded but whole.

Hauling a sledge over soft snow or uphill is the hardest work I know and if anyone asks "what do you know?", well, amongst other tough jobs, I have shoveled forty five tons of coal into baskets in one day, and that is not anything like as tiring as pulling a 200 lb load in knee-deep snow.

After even the easiest of sledging trips, it is gorgeous to get back to the base and eat decent food and sleep in a decent bed and best of all, to be able to walk about without the tug of that everlasting weight behind.

Scott has written full accounts of all the other sledging journeys, including his own. When accompanied by Shackleton and Wilson, they travelled more than 200 miles farther south than man had ever been before.

Before Scott returned to the "Discovery", the SS "Morning" was sighted. This was near the end of January and the whole of McMurdo Sound was still frozen over, so that all our mail, gifts from friends and relief stores had to be man hauled across the intervening ice. At first, this was over 20 miles, but the ice gradually broke away to the north until the "Morning" got within eight miles of our winter quarters, where she remained until it became imperative for her to return or become frozen in.

The second winter passed away in similar fashion to the first and much time was again spent in preparing for further exploring. With the return of the sun, sledging parties again set out, the main party under Scott going west up the Ferrar Glacier and penetrating a considerable distance into the interior of the continent at an altitude of 7,000 to 8,000 feet.

As summer advanced and the ice showed no sign of breaking up, all hands not on sledging journeys proceeded 10 miles to the north where a camp was set up and with 12 foot ice saws attempt to cut a passage. The experiment was a failure, the ice was six to eight feet thick and in a fortnight, we had only cut 150 yards, which, of course, was useless and the only thing to do was to wait for nature to take a hand.

The reports the "Morning" had taken home about our position caused such perturbation in England that the Admiralty took the matter of relief in hand and not only again sent the "Morning", but also a powerful whaling ship, the "Terra Nova" with orders to the effect that if the "Discovery" could not be set free, she was to be abandoned and the crew brought home.

When Scott read these orders to the party, I think every man was deeply shocked as was Scott himself. The idea of having to abandon our home was insupportable.

The scientific collections and other valuables were transported to the relief ships, which at the same time were endeavouring to ram a way through the ice. Wasted effort and funds, they might as well have tried to ram through the Rock of Gibraltar. Tons of gun cotton were used in blasting.

When at last it appeared that the time had come to leave, providence took a hand and sent down a northerly swell which in a few hours broke away all the ice and the "Discovery" left her two year bed.

Immediately after steam was up, we weighed anchor and proceeded north, when a strong southerly gale drove us on to a reef off Hut Point. There we stuck and bumped in the swell, bits of keel came floating up and things looked serious indeed, until the rising tide floated us off.

The only effect this strenuous shaking had on the "Discovery" was to stop the leak, which had given trouble the whole of the voyage, and strain the rudder. Because of this latter damage, we had to put into Robertson Bay and ship a new rudder.

Before returning to New Zealand, more exploration was carried out north and west of Robertson Bay. New land was discovered and much land that had been reported and charted previously was found to be non-existent.

On the way north, we stopped for some time at a wonderful anchorage in the Auckland Islands. The bay is named "Sarah's Bosom".

We took in fresh water from a stream there, the ship being moored to a tree, and hove so close to shore that a hose could be carried to the stream. This was the first and only time that I have seen a ship tied to a tree. Here we had a very thorough clean-up, scrubbing and painting until, to the superficial eye, all the scars received by the ship in her ice battles were hidden.

Our reception at Port Lyttleton was much too enthusiastic to be described. One of the books in the "Discovery's" library was one written by Dr Cook, describing the voyage of the "Belgica" in the Antarctic in 1898. Amongst other doubtful statements is one which states that when the man landed in Valparaiso, they could easily be picked out by their sliding, gliding motion, owing to having travelled so much on ski. Also Cook says, "The men had been so long away from civilization that when they first heard the frow-frow of a woman's skirts, they all chased her". These men had been away about 12 months. We of the "Discovery" expedition had been away two and a quarter years and the majority of us had travelled at least ten times further on ski than any of the "Belgica" party, but I am sure none of us could be recognised by our walk, nor did any of us chase skirts – not publicly.

After some wonderful weeks of hospitality and entertainment sightseeing over the country (we were given free railway passes), the "Discovery" sailed for England.

Oceanographical work was carried out and a line of soundings taken between New Zealand and Cape Horn. Our track was further south than the regular one and again we encountered a lot of ice; we also found that an island on the charts named "Dogherty Island" does not exist, as we sailed over its supposed position and found a depth of 2,000 fathoms.

Probably the most interesting part of the homeward voyage was the run through the Straits of Magellan.

Upon arrival in England, long leave was granted and we all received the Polar Medal from King Edward VII and the Royal Geographical Societies Silver Medal.

Followed two and a half years of Naval service, during which time I served on the battleship "Ocean" and from her to the Sheerness Gunnery School.

During the time on the "Ocean", we were told to tow an obsolete sloop, the "Landrail", into deep water off Waymouth and moor her there for a target for a portion of the Channel Fleet. This we carried out and lay a short distance away to watch the effect of the firing.

The firing was from five ships steaming at a distance of 8,000 yards and about fifty direct hits were registered in a very short time.

A party of fifteen was then sent from the "Ocean" to slip the moorings and with the aid of a tug, which was standing by, take the wreck into Waymouth. She sank in the Portland race. A small boat from the tug took off about half the party and the remainder had to swim. I was the last to leave and the "Landrail" then was almost gone, her stern sticking perpendicularly out of the water. As I climbed out onto the stern, I noticed the first "L" of her name (the name was in detachable brass letters) was loose and I smashed it off to use as a paper weight.

A few seconds after I dived, the ship sank and we remained about twenty minutes in the water before being picked up. The water was cold and choppy and in the confusion, no-one noticed that one of our party was in difficulties until he had disappeared. Several of us dived where he was last seen, but with no success.

Early in 1907, Shackleton asked me to accompany him on his Antarctic Expedition and being granted leave by the Admiralty, I joined up with him in New Zealand.

His ship, the "Nimrod", was very much smaller and less powerful than the "Discovery", and we had great difficulty in stowing all the essential stores aboard.

We left Lyttleton on New Year's Day, 1908, and no vessel could possibly have had a more inspiriting send off. Being a holiday, thousands of people had come to the port from Christchurch and the surrounding districts and for miles along the shore were cheering crowds. The finest full throated cheer I ever heard in my life came from the crew of HMS Powerful.

To save our coal, arrangements had been made with the Union Line for one of their ships, the "Koonya", to tow us as far as possible. Before we got clear of the land, we ran into bad weather and for a fortnight, our lot was sad indeed. We were much too deeply laden for safety and the weight of our tow, 150 fathoms of chain cable and 150 fathoms of heavy wire, prevented our bows rising as rapidly as would have been the case without it. We had on deck a large quantity of coal and also a deck-house containing ten ponies.

Portions of the bulwarks were washed away and for many days and nights together the decks were never free of rushing water, the ship rolling constantly from 40° to 50° each way.

The seas were so enormous that frequently the "Koonya" was completely out of sight. All hands suffered acutely, but the position of the ponies was much more heart-rending.

They were constantly soaked and although their stalls were padded as efficiently as possible, they all became badly chafed by the incessant rolling. Two went down and had to be destroyed.

What a relief it was to get amongst ice and into comparatively smooth water. The "Koonya" being an ordinary steel built ship, dare not risk contact with ice so when we entered the outskirts of the pack, the tow was cast off and after transshipping to us a quantity of stores, including about twenty carcasses of sheep, she bade us farewell. The "Koonya" also took back with her Colonel Buckley, an old friend of Shackleton's.

Buckley boarded the "Nimrod" at little more than a minute's notice, at Shackleton's invitation and I don't think he carried any luggage – not even a toothbrush. He has been a keen yachtsman all his life and I honestly believe that had it not been for the sufferings of the ponies, he would have enjoyed every minute of that ghastly fortnight. With the ponies, his assistance was invaluable and had he not been aboard, I feel sure we would have lost more.

Shackleton had told Scott that we would endeavour to find winter quarters east of McMurdo Sound, perhaps in the "Bay of Whales", the eastern extremity of the Ross Barrier. When we arrived there, however, a landing was impossible owing to the bay ice being in a state of disintegration and we were compelled to beat a hasty retreat from an enormous field of exceptionally heavy pack ice which was advancing upon us from the north-east and threatening to crush us against the Barrier. Shackleton was loathe to return to McMurdo Sound and talked seriously of wintering on the Barrier itself. I strenuously objected to this, having seen miles of Barrier floating away in the form of icebergs and when my arguments were backed by the discovery that in places, the edge of the Barrier was eight miles further south than we steamed along it on the "Discovery", Shackleton reluctantly consented to return to McMurdo Sound.

I have great satisfaction in recording this, as Shackleton was severely criticized and unfairly accused of taking advantage of Scott's work.

The landing of stores and equipment, building material, fuel etc on the Antarctic shores is a different matter from doing the same thing alongside a wharf with cranes and all other facilities at hand. In this case, the greater part of our equipment was put overboard on to sea ice and then sledged ashore, the difficulty being increased by the constant breaking up of the ice, caused by a slight swell from the north. The ponies were landed as soon as possible and one fell into a crack which opened up between him and the shore. He was hauled out unhurt, given a good rub down and half a bottle of brandy, well rugged and he suffered no after effects.

Whilst the unloading was going on, one party was busy building the hut for our winter quarters, Shackleton having arranged that the "Nimrod" should not remain south but return to New Zealand before there was danger of her being frozen in and come down the following summer to pick us up.

Before we had been able to choose a wintering place and finish the unloading, the short Antarctic summer was drawing to a close. There was no thought of an eight hour day, or watch on and watch off. Every man worked as long as he could keep his eyes open and stand on his feet, 24 hours without a spell was not thought extraordinary, meals being snatched when possible.

One party I was with were hauling stores over a steep cliff, by means of a derrick, without a rest for 36 hours and our food during that time consisted of Garibaldi biscuits. We called them squashed flies.

On 31st January 1908, a very sad accident occurred when hauling stores out of the ship's hold. A cask was being hoisted out and just as it was being landed on deck, the can hooks slipped off the chimes and one struck McIntosh, who was receiving the hoists as they came up. One of his eyes was completely destroyed and was removed by Dr Marshall.

McIntosh was very popular and we were all sorry he had to return, but our disappointment was nothing to his own.

The tank of landing stores was interrupted several times by heavy gales and on one occasion, the "Nimrod" was driven so far north that it took her several days to steam back. Then to our great relief when she did reappear, she looked like a Christmas card picture. The rigging was thickly covered with ice and many tons of ice on her decks. Immediately the last bag of coal was landed, the "Nimrod" set off on her return to New Zealand, much to the relief of her crew.

By this time, the hut building was sufficiently advanced to afford shelter. It was built on piles, holes being dug in the volcanic sand and rock and the supports cemented in by the simple and effective method of pouring water in. After the roof was finished, a wire hawser was passed several times over it and this wire also was secured and set up taut to timbers buried and cemented into the ground. Although the hut was built in a hollow and sheltered, there is little doubt that without the wire it would have been blown away during some of our winter hurricanes.

A full account of this expedition was written by Shackleton in his "Heart of the Antarctic".

We were fifteen in number and the hut was divided up into cubicles. The entrance was in the centre of one end, an outer and inner door separated by a small porch, where one could beat the snow off one's garments before entering the hut proper.

On one side of the porch was Shackleton's room and dark room and laboratory was on the other side. The next cubicle to Shackleton was occupied by Dr Marshall, MO and Lieutenant Adams, Meteorologist; then came Day, Engineer and in charge of the Arral Johnston motor car and Marston, artist; then Captain Armitage, in charge of ponies, and Sir Philip Brocklehurst, handyman. The remainder of that side of the hut was taken up by the pantry, with the stove next to it. On the other side of the stove dwelt the autocrat of the kitchen, Roberts, and with him Dr Mackay. Next were Murray, Biologist and Priestley, Geologist. Joyce, in charge of dogs and sledges, shared the next cubicle with me and then Mawson, Physicist and last, that very noble and courteous gentleman, Professor David VRS.

Of this company, Sir Ernest Shackleton, Sir Edgeworth David, Mackay, Murray, Armitage and Roberts are dead. Priestly is now the Vice Chancellor of the Sydney University and I am sorry to say I have lost touch with the others.

Murray and Mackay were lost on an expedition in the Arctic under Steffensen.

Professor David was particularly keen on making the ascent of Mt Erebus and as the sledging program for the following summer was already practically arranged and was a very full one, this had to be carried out before the winter darkness made it impossible.

Professor David wanted to include Joyce and myself in his party, we being the only old campaigners, excepting Shackleton, but our leader would not permit it as there was an enormous amount of settling in to be done.

Stuffed full of advice and instructions, the party, consisting of Professor David, Marshall, Adams, Mackay, Mawson and Brocklehurst made the ascent successfully and actually stood on the crater edge and saw the molten lava below them.

Mt Erebus is 13,375 feet high, the crater is about half a mile in width and the lava only some 900 feet from the top.

The party had a most stirring tale of adventure to give and were all very pleased with themselves, except Brocklehurst whose feet were badly frost bitten. He was laid up for three months and was fortunate to lose only one big toe. Their equipment and clothing were sadly battered and torn and some articles missing, but no-one damped their high spirits with reproachful comment.

The only case in my experience, of anyone contracting a cold in the Antarctic occurred when we were opening some cases of clothing to fit out the members of this party. Germs must have been the clothing as the whole party caught colds. With those of us who were working outside, it only lasted a day, but the cook was sniffing for several days until Shackleton ordered him out for a long walk.

The building of a Sanatorium for consumptives on the slopes of Mt Erebus was seriously considered in Australia and New Zealand some years ago and I am sure it would be successful, though very costly.

When Dr Wilson went south with Scott he was a very sick man with TB, but when he returned, he was absolutely cured and was so fit that later he was one of those chosen by Scott to accompany him on his last journey to the South Pole.

Many of our stores were landed on some rocks not more than thirty yards from the sea and the gale which blew the "Nimrod" away to the north, drove heavy masses of spray over the cases, these being buried under one to three feet of ice. This gave us months of hard labour and some cases never were recovered. One of the lost cases contained the results of the Challenger Expedition, and one contained bottle stout. Many volunteer search parties dug for them without success – I think I could name the case which gave the greatest incentive.

Early in the winter, Shackleton received a severe shock and the expedition a serious setback.

The eight Manchurian ponies were tethered in a valley near the hut on volcanic sand. This sand contained a certain amount of salt which was deposited upon it when heavy gales drove spray immense distances inland. The ponies somehow discovered the salt and licked up large quantities of sand to obtain it. The sand was very sharp and had a lot of feldspar crystals mixed with it. All the ponies became very ill and four died, the survivors requiring a lot of careful nursing before they fully recovered. This loss occasioned considerable alteration in Shackleton's sledging programme.

The deadly monotony of a Polar night is much overdrawn. Any well organised party have quite enough work to keep them fairly well occupied and healthy, though I admit the sight of the returning sun is a most gladsome one and has a tremendously exhilarating effect, non only on man but on ponies and dogs also.

All through the expedition, meteorological records were kept, each member of the party with the exception of the cook, taking his turn at night watchman. The nigh watchman's duties include two-hourly meteorological observations, keeping the fire going (this was of great importance as the hut was never made completely wind-proof and in windy weather, the inside temperature was well below freezing point even with a few feet on the stove), and keeping a watch on the ponies. These animals were housed in a stable built on to one side of the hut and frequently one of them would eat through his halter and leave his stall.

The dogs also slept in the stables and they invariably gave tongue when a pony broke loose, thus warning the watchman who would then have to don his outdoor clothes and with usually some unparliamentary remarks, take a lantern and go out to recapture the offender. There was never any difficulty in locating the truant, as all the dogs would follow him and run around him, barking until he was caught.

In addition to his other duties, the watchman made his night the occasion for a bath, and would wash his socks and underclothing. In the small hours, he would cook himself a more or less dainty meal and should the culinary effort prove above the average, the tempting odour would bring him visitors.

Another duty, taken in turn by all except the boss, was cook's assistant and mess-man; this job was cordially hated. The mess-man commenced his duties at 7.30am. He first lowered the table, which was hoisted up to the ceiling between meals, laid it for breakfast and called all hands. After the meal, he washed up, swept the hut, brought in ice for the cook, by which time he had to commence preparing for lunch. For this meal, the table was not lowered, the dishes being placed on a small table and each man helped himself. The evening meal was the most elaborate and the washing up would keep the mess-man going long after the rest of the party had settled down to their books, cards or work.

In fine weather, the mess-man's task was much lighter than during a blizzard when every trip outside for ice or to empty slops meant getting into full kit and much extra sweeping up had to be done on account of snow being brought in on people's clothing and boots.

A popular mess-man always received a lot of assistance in washing up and sweeping etc, but the individual who had had the misfortune to put others' backs up, was left alone.

I wrote earlier about the great distance that sound travels in the Polar regions. This was the cause of some embarrassment to me. Early in the winter, before the daylight had entirely left us, I found a cave full of beautiful stalactites and ran back to the hut for my camera. I could not find it and remembered having lent it to Professor David the day before. Going outside, I saw Joyce a few yards away harnessing some dogs. I called to him in quite an ordinary tone, "Have you seen that _____ Professor anywhere?" I was answered by the Professor himself from a distance of well over half a mile, "What do you want Wild?" he replied. I told him and later apologised for my language and he smiled and said in his super charming manner, "That is quite alright Wild; I have been called many worse things than that in my time."

When opening a case of provisions one day, I found a piece of brick and thought I would pull the Professor's leg. I truthfully told him that I had found this geological specimen near the hut and asked him if it was of any interest.

After getting a magnifying glass on it, he said, "One of the best specimens of conglomerate I have seen Wild."

During the winter, a lot of work was done in the hut, fitting sledges, altering sleeping bags and many other preparations for coming sledging journeys. Whilst we were thus occupied, Professor David entertained us by reading aloud from Dickens and other works. He was the only man I have ever enjoyed listening to.

The geologists spent a good deal of time during the dark months in digging shafts into fresh water lakes, for the purpose of examining and analysing the ice at different depths. From one lake, about one and a half miles from the hut, the ice at a depth of 20 feet was found to contain living microscopic animals, rotifers and water-bears, which commenced feeding and fighting immediately there were thawed out.

Murray experimented with them, warming them up almost to boiling point, exposing them outside to 50° below zero, then warming them up again and they still lived. The general opinion amongst the scientists was that these creatures had been frozen up for many thousands of years.

Blizzards were frequent and fierce during the winter and often the hut shook and shivered most ominously. Without the securing cable, it is certain that the hut would have been picked up and blown away like a leaf.

Provision and other cases, both empty and full, were often torn away from the stack outside and their contents scattered miles away.

A friend of Shackleton's had given him a specially fine pair of Russian boots. These were lying on the top of an opened case when one of these sudden hurricanes came on. After the storm, one of these boots was found jammed amongst the cases and the other had vanished. I found it two months later nearly two miles away.

One day, when out for a walk alone, I heard a terrific noise like thunder. Walking towards the sound, I found it came from what was known as Black Sand Beach. This was on the northern side of Ross Island. The Ross Sea was frozen over to a thickness of three to four feet — hundreds of square miles of it — and a north wind had set this mass into slow motion. The ice was being pressed on to the land and as it was checked, masses of it were forced into the air. Some of the sheets reached a height of sixty feet before they collapsed with a crash as loud as any heavy gunfire. This was going on along several miles of coastline and was a most awe-inspiring sight and sound. Unfortunately, there was not sufficient light for a photograph.

The ponies were taken out for exercise every day that weather permitted. Shackleton had decided that the Polar party would consist of — Shackleton himself, Adams, Marshall and myself and so that we and the ponies would get to know each other as much as possible, we four always exercised them.

Shackleton's pony, Quan, was the largest and strongest and the most artful. Chinaman was a quiet plodder, he was Adam's charge. Marshall looked after Grisi, which was the youngest and very nervous; if approached at all suddenly. Mine was named Socks, as he had four white stockings nearly to the knees, the rest of him being grey. He was a beautifully proportioned beast and full of spirits.

For some time we exercised them on snow, being careful to avoid all crevasses, but after a while, we found their hoofs were growing too long. None of our party had sufficient farrier's experience to pare them down, so we walked the ponies over the rocks for a few days. Nearly all the bare rock in the vicinity of the hut was lava and full of feldspar crystals. These were so sharp that one day's walk would ruin a pair of ordinary boots and in a very short time, the ponies' hooves were trimmed down. When daylight returned, we commenced training them to pull a load and they took to it very well.

During the winter, the Medical Officer told Shackleton that a pint of beer per day would be of value to the party. We were not strictly teetotal, the allowances of alcohol being one drink per man on Saturday night, when we toasted "sweethearts and wives". Besides this, we had no intoxicants except on each member's birthday.

I was in charge of stores and brought a barrel of beer into the hut – one of the three given to us by the Victoria Brewery, New Zealand. After it had stood thawing for three days, it was tapped and ran black and we thought the wrong marks had been put on the cask. Little more than half a pint was served to each man, but the effect was astonishing. The following day, the ration was very pale wishy washy stuff and we then found that in freezing all the body and alcohol had been driven to the centre of the cask and remained liquid, our first drink being concentrated beer – and very nice too.

Joyce and I more than filled in our spare time during the winter months by printing a book. Before leaving London, we had spent some time at Sir Joseph Causton's printing works and he kindly lent us a printing press and type, which we set up in our little cubicle and many an hour we spent setting up and whilst many of our companions were enjoying an afternoon nap. One hundred copies were made and long before it was finished, we cursed the day it was thought of.

I mentioned earlier that the hut was never made really weatherproof and often it was so cold that we had to burn a paraffin stove under the type rack to make the type warm enough to handle and always a candle had to be burning under the ink plate when printing to make it liquid enough to run.

The covers of the books were made by Bernard Day from three-ply wood obtained from empty provision cases and the markings were left on, so some are market "Mutton Cutlets", "Roast Turkey", "Apple Jelly" etc. The illustrations were etchings and engravings, beautifully done by Marston and nearly all the members of the party contributed an article.

Having had experience of the horrors of early spring and late summer sledging, Shackleton had made his arrangements so that no sledging journeys would commence until the beginning of November. The loss of six ponies, two on the outward voyage and four after landing, made an alteration imperative and as soon as there was sufficient daylight, preparations were made for depot laying.

A number of trips were made by small parties to Hut Point, "Scott's Discovery" quarters, and a substantial amount of food stuffs stored there.

The motor car had been tried out by Day and had proved disappointing. On very hard snow or bare ice it pulled well, but on soft snow, the wheels simply buried themselves. For a distance of six miles to the south, the ice was almost bare and on this surface, the car could pull three loaded sledges as fast as it was safe for them to travel, so that all parties had a good send off and if seen on their return were met by the car and had an easy run home.

Scott's old hut was still standing and at a short distance looked as good as new, but we found many of the boards had warped and let in the snow so that we had several hours' work with pick and shovel before we made a portion of it habitable.

I was in charge of one of these small parties when we were caught on our return journey by a blizzard. As we were on bare sea ice, it was impossible to put the tent up, but my sense of direction is above the ordinary and after three miles blind travelling, we arrived at the Glacier tongue, eight miles north of Hut Point and under the lee of the glacier, we had shelter from the storm and plenty of snow on which to pitch and secure the tent.

In low temperatures, the steam from the cooker and the moisture from the breath freezes on the inside of the tent and forms a rime. Every shake of the tent brings down a miniature snowfall. On this particular night, Priestly changed his singlet. He was not, of course, very long over it but long enough to get several of these snowfalls on his bare skin. Before he had reclothed himself, Day and I had got into the three-man sleeping bag. The rule is "last man in fastens the bag". The bag is fastened right over the occupants' heads with wooden toggles and loops, but it cannot be done with gloves on. Before Priestly had succeeded in fastening up, his fingers became frost bitten several times and his language would certainly surprise the Sydney University Students – Priestley is now Vice Chancellor there.

I know of no greater agony than that caused by frost bitten fingers. Whilst actually frozen there is, of course, no feeling, but when thawing again and the blood is forcing its way through the contracted arteries, the feeling is the same as that caused by having one's fingers heavily stamped upon, or getting them jammed in a door. I have seen strong men with tears streaming down their faces whilst undergoing this experience.

In September, a larger party set out to lay a food depot to assist the main South Pole Party. This party was lead by Shackleton, the others being Adams, Marshall, Marston, Joyce and myself. The ponies could not be risked as the low temperature would have made them unfit for the later journey and might even have proved fatal to them. We were pulling a weight of 200 lbs per man, the most of this being fodder for the ponies. All the experiences of sledging in cold weather were repeated, our lowest temperature was 68° below zero and except when a blizzard was raging, it was never higher than 40° below.

One day, whilst we were on the march, Joyce reported that one of his feet was frozen. A halt was called at once, a tent erected and several of us took turns to nurse the foot inside our clothes and next to the stomach. It was like nursing a snow-bell and none of us could stand it for more than a few minutes. Then we ran about to warm ourselves up until our turn came round again. This went on for two and a half hours before the foot was out of danger and Joyce suffered no after ill-effects.

On these very cold journeys it is impossible to sleep with one's head outside the sleeping bag and in consequence, all moisture from the breath condenses inside the bag. During the daytime, this freezes hard and after a few days, the bag seems to be all hard lumps and corners, which have to be thawed out by the heat of one's body before it is possible to sleep. I have known a one-man bag to increase in weight from 10 lbs when dry to 50 lbs in a fortnight and a three-man bag from 30 to 70 lbs in the same time.

Another difficulty is foot gear. On the march, the socks get damp. It is absolutely necessary to have dry socks on at night or frozen feet would certainly result and the only way to partially dry the day socks or at best keep them soft enough to put on in the morning, is to put them inside one's clothes next to the skin.

In the summer months, the sun is hot enough to dry things and as it then shines at night as well as day, the tents are kept quite warm and one can sleep with the face exposed and with bare feet and hands, but at -60° to -70°F, it is a constant battle to keep warm enough to sleep at all and one spends most of the night shivering and praying for the morning.

The food depot was successfully laid out with 120 miles along the route to be taken by the southern party and it was with a feeling of great relief that we commenced our return journey.

Our loads being so much lighter, we made much more rapid progress, but delays were frequent through blizzards and forced marches were imperative to enable us to get back to Hut Point before our food gave out. As it was, the last meal was eaten when we were yet twelve miles away and we were a most ravenous and weary party on our arrival.

When we left our own base at Cape Royds, two pups about three months old followed us. After repeated attempts to drive them back, we allowed them to come with us to Hut Point. Before leaving there, we shut the pups up in the hut, leaving them a plentiful supply of biscuits and there was sufficient snow to give them all the drink they required. Inside the hut, there was also a heap of small coal.

Upon our return, we were greeted by barks and yelps of welcome as soon as we were heard and as we opened the door, out burst two black pups instead of the white ones we had left. They had evidently found the coal warmer than snow to sleep on.

A very busy time followed our return to the base, making preparations for the summer sledging journeys. Apart from the misnamed "Dash to the Pole" several other parties had to be arranged.

Professor David with Dr Mawson and Dr MacKay were to attempt to locate the Magnetic Pole, a journey which entailed climbing the mountain of Victoria Land and travelling many miles on the interior plateau.

Priestley, Armitage and Brocklehurst were to lay depots for the Professor's party and Priestly was to make a geological survey of the Victoria Land coast. Several other smaller journeys were arranged for, including another ascent of Mt Erebus.

Shackleton had intended to start south late in October but several irritating delays were experienced and it was not until early November that a final departure was made.

A part of the equipment was a long rope for tethering the ponies at night. It was necessary for this to be long enough to keep the animals apart as they had a habit of biting each other's rugs and tails. When they were tethered out at Hut Point, Quan, always mischievous, ate through the rope and tore open several bags of crushed mealies. Shackleton returned to the base and was back again next day with a wire rope.

I would like to say here that the ponies were fully fed up to the time of their death and were always well treated. They were fed at the base principally on hay and clover with a little crushed mealies. On the sledging journey, they received eight pounds of crushed mealies and two pounds of maujee ration, the latter mixed with hot water into a mash.

Maujee ration was invented by a Colonel of that name and is a mixture of carrots and other vegetables, sugar and plasmon and was highly appreciated by the animals. I have eaten it with enjoyment myself.

A final start was made early in November, a supporting party accompanying us for about 30 miles. A blizzard then prevented travelling for about two days. When this blew itself out, the supporting party bade us farewell and returned to the base. That day we found ourselves in a badly crevassed area south-east of White Island; several times the ponies put their feet through the snow bridges and during the afternoon, we nearly lost Chinaman.

The ponies were pulling about 750 lbs each when the journey commenced. We were consuming nearly 50 lbs of rations per day so that at the end of three weeks, we were able to dispense with the services of one pony. Chinaman was the least fit and it was decided that he should be shot. The question then arose, 'who is to do the shooting'? Shackleton was like Scott in that they both hated the sight of blood and either of them would have gone a long time hungry if they had had to kill their own food.

I suggested each man kill his own pony as the time came, but Adams said he would rather have a tooth out. I thought Marshall, being a surgeon, would have had no qualms, but he also strongly objected, so I had to do it. I am certain it hurt me as much as it would any of them.

A portion of the flesh was carried on for food and the remainder left to be picked up on our return.

By this time, we had passed Scott's farthest south and were travelling where man had never trod before. My pony, Socks, was the fastest puller and he had a strong objection to following the others. This resulted in my having to lead and break trail. When the surface was hard this did not matter, but for many days, we were sinking ankle to knee deep in soft snow and at times, the ponies' bellies were touching and frequent halts were necessary.

I well remember a certain three days of overcast weather when nothing was visible but the snow surface in our immediate vicinity. It was like walking into a white blanket and I had a weird feeling that any minute, I should come to the edge and fall off.

When the sky again cleared and the sun shone once more, it was quite exciting to see new mountain ranges showing up, but our pleasure was somewhat spoiled as we found this new land was running more and more in an easterly direction and cutting us off from a direct march to the Pole.

Previous to this, it had been thought that this frozen ocean over which we were journeying, (an extension of the Ross Barrier and only a few hundred feet above sea level) would carry on into the heart of the continent and that the South Pole would be found at or near sea level, and to Shackleton is due the credit of pioneering the way onto that enormous King Edward VII Plateau, where the South Pole is situated 10,000 ft above sea level.

On the 3rd December, we were within a few miles of the land and no possible road was to be seen through the mountains. The surface was terribly broken up and crevassed and Socks, the one remaining pony, had many narrow escapes from death.

Leaving the pony and standing camp, we four men tramped the four miles to the foothills and climbed a 3,000 feet mountain and to every man's joy, from the summit we saw a passage leading through onto an immense glacier which apparently made a good road all the way up to the Plateau.

Shackleton named the mountain up which we climbed "Mt Hope", the entrance to the glacier "The Southern Gateway" and the glacier itself, which proved to be 170 miles long and in places 60 miles wide – the largest in the world – the "Beardmore Glacier", after one of his friends and principal supporters.

The following day, the march was resumed, Shackleton, Adams and Marshall pulling one sledge and I leading the pony with the other. I followed their track so that if they broke into a crevasse, I could avoid it, but the pony being so much heavier than a man frequently broke through bridges that safely carried the first party and Socks and I had many narrow and hair-raising escapes.

On the 5th December, we were through the "Gateway" and on the Glacier proper. That night we laid a depot at the foot of a rock that ran up vertically to a height of 5,000 feet. About here, much of the surface was bare blue ice, rippled like a lake in a light breeze, over which it was impossible for Socks, unshod, to pull. He had to be slowly led over these places and the sledge relayed.

On the 7th December, we were on a snow surface again and going well, but we still encountered many crevasses. Steel bits could not be used on the ponies as metal would burn their mouths, but they soon became accustomed to being led by a halter only.

I was only 100 yards behind the leading sledge when Socks suddenly plunged through the snow bridging a crevasse six or seven feet wide. His shoulder struck me as he fell and knocked me so far forward that I was able to grab the far side and hold on. The rein was round my right hand and gave me a nasty jerk, but the glove was loose and slipped off. As I fell, I yelled and the hauling party slipped out of their harness and ran to my help, but I had hauled myself out before they reached me. We looked down the crevasse but nothing was to be seen but a black hole. Fortunately, the harness had broken, leaving the sledge on the surface. Our sleeping bags and the greater part of our food was on it and had it been lost, we should certainly all have died. Almost my first thought was "Thank God I won't have to shoot Socks".

We were now left with 1,000 lbs weight to drag and progress was so slow owing to relay work having to be frequently resorted to, that a further reduction of food was necessary.

The first reduction was made when it became evident that the mountains would have to be crossed, thus lengthening our journey.

The day after Socks was lost, we were in such a horrible maze of crevasses that had he still been with us, he would certainly have had to be shot. When it came to camping time that night, there was great difficulty in finding an unbroken patch large enough on which to erect a tent.

Shackleton has given a full description of the journey up this glacier in the "Heart of the Antarctic". Sometimes we were able to pull both sledges and were able to do as much as sixteen miles per day, but there were many days of relay work when 5 miles was considered good work. Scarcely an hour passed in some of the bad places, without one or more falling into crevasses and we kept a keen eye on our harness to be sure there were no weak spots.

The first few falls are decidedly upsetting to the nerves and heart. To find oneself suddenly standing on nothing, then to be brought up with a painful jerk and looking down into a pitch black nothing, is distinctly disturbing and there is the additional fear that the rope may break. After a few dozen falls (I have had hundreds), the nervous shock lessens until the majority of men look upon the experience as lightly as an ordinary stumble; but a few never overcame the horror, (Adams was one of these) and it impairs their efficiency as a working unit.

The scenery was magnificent, new mountains appearing on either side and ahead, never before seen by man. Even the surface of the glacier itself was wondrously beautiful. In many places, it had the appearance of waterfalls glistening in the sun and miles and miles of it looked exactly like a storm-tossed sea.

As we had to cut steps up those waterfalls and haul the sledges up one at a time by means of a tackle and also haul them over that storm-tossed sea, the crest of every wave being an edge as sharp as a knife and taking shavings and chunks off our sledge runners – we ourselves suffering frequent and painful falls and being underfed and indescribably weary at the end of each day, our appreciation of the wonders around us was not so keen as it might have been in better circumstances.

After one strenuous day's work when we had been hauling up one of the afore-mentioned falls and had only 750 yards to show for our labour, we found ourselves close to a feed glacier coming down between some mountains named by Shackleton after his friend Buckley. After our evening meal, I asked Shackleton's permission to climb the feed glacier and from the top to see what lay ahead of us.

I found the climb not without its hazards and had to jump numbers of crevasses and make many detours to avoid those too wide to jump. I was rewarded by finding that these mountains were the last and beyond was what appeared to be an easy slope into the inland plateau. Later, this slope was found to be far from an easy one.

Anyone who has done climbing knows that coming down is the most difficult.

I did not like the idea of negotiating those crevasses again and seeing bare rock half a mile to the north, decided to descend there. It was very steep and I dislodged many tons of weathered rock, but got down safely.

On the way down, I noticed five very dark seams varying in thickness from 5 inches to 5 feet. With my ice axe, I dug out some samples and took them to camp where I found Shackleton just about to set out to look for me; the other two men were asleep.

Shackleton at once pronounced my find as coal. When we later showed the samples to Professor David, the world's greatest authority on coal, he confirmed our opinion and was wildly enthusiastic over this, the first discovery of coal on the Antarctic Continent. This was approximately 6,000 feet above sea level.

On Christmas day, we are at an altitude of 8,000 feet and still steadily rising. That evening we had our only full meal in three months. In addition to our ordinary allowance, we had some Maujee pony ration – Socks having met his end before his food was finished – and I had secreted amongst my kit some small plum puddings, given to me by Mrs James of Christchurch. To finish up, we had a tablespoonful each of Curacao, which Marshall had saved for the occasion.

Whilst we were still happily full of food, another reduction was decided upon and it was two months later when we had our next full meal.

The last 200 miles of our outward journey was on an undulating wind-swept snow surface which on sea level would have been considered good travelling. We were weakened with hunger and the long continued struggle up the Beardmore Glacier and now the altitude, over 10,000 feet, was putting a severe strain on our hearts; halts had to be called every few hundred yards.

Although mid-summer, the temperature was seldom higher than 20° below zero and for several days, we were confined to our tents by a blizzard with the temperature at 40° below zero. All the time we were on the plateau, we had to contend with a strong head wind which froze our breath into masses of ice around our mouths and our faces were so frequently frost bitten, they were covered with blackened skin and blisters.

For some days before it was finally decided to return, we knew we had no hope of reaching the Pole and getting back alive. We could have got to the Pole, but our records would have all been lost with us.

On the 9th January, Shackleton decided that any further advance would be suicidal.

Queen Alexandra had given Shackleton a Union Jack which she asked him to plant at his farthest south point. I was the custodian of the flag, a heavy silk one, and for many nights on that bitter plateau, I slept with it wrapped around me.

At 9am on the 9th January 1909, this flag was hoisted 97 miles from the South Pole.

I am perfectly certain that had Shackleton only himself to consider, he would have gone on and planted the flag at the Pole itself.

Shackleton and I were packing sledges ready for a start when he suddenly stuck his one and only biscuit into my pocket. My expostulations were in vain; he said "your need is greater than mine" and threatened if I did not keep it, to bury it in the snow. All the money that was ever minted would not have bought that biscuit and the remembrance of that sacrifice will never leave me.

On our outward journey, we had built a mound of snow, six to eight feet high, at each halt – midday and night – noted course and distance between each, hoping they would be of assistance on our return. They proved most successful and we missed only one. (It was not practicable to do this mound building on the glacier.) this saved the necessity of taking observations and when we were obliged, through weakness, to throw away everything not essential to the preservation of our lives, the theodolite and sextant were sacrificed. We carried on only sufficient clothing, food and the geological specimens. The weight we were then pulling was roughly 60 lbs per man, but in our weakened condition, it felt heavier than the 250 lbs we had once been able to haul.

We were incredibly hungry, all our thoughts, dreams and conversation seemed to be of food. One night, I dreamt I was dining with the King of Sweden, why he I don't know, as I never met him; I had a most delicious steak in front of me and how I longed to get at it. Etiquette forbade me to commence before the King and I woke up.

Providentially, the winds were all from the south, giving us considerable assistance, otherwise we had surely died. Before arrival at each of our depots, our food was entirely finished. Two hours after reaching one depot, a blizzard struck us and held us up for two days; we missed death by just that two hours.

Where Chinaman had been killed, his blood ran down into the snow and this mixture of frozen blood and snow was dug up and made a beautiful soup.

At this time, Shackleton was snow blind and as we came to crevasses, I had to tell him where to jump to clear them. He had many falls but never grumbled.

Well for us that we were assisted by the wind, (the tent floor cloth made a good sail) as we had reckoned on returning much faster than when outward bound and had laid food depots accordingly, but we had not made allowance for loss of strength and all the way back, it was just touch and go whether we should reach the next depot in time or not.

The perpendicular rock near the foot of the glacier, at the foot of which we had left a depot, was visible more than 60 miles away. When 20 miles distant, our last morsel of food had been consumed and we were pitiably weak. Several times I fell into crevasses, as did everyone, and whilst hanging in the harness, I prayed that the rope would break so that I should have a nice long rest.

However, we stumbled and struggled on. Adams fell unconscious and it was a long time before we brought him round, but at last we pitched camp about a mile from the depot and whilst Shackleton and I were securing the tents, getting hot water ready etc, Marshall walked to the depot and brought back a sufficiency of food for the night.

Words cannot express our feelings when we said 'goodbye' to that awful glacier and got once more on to snow, free of those frightful crevasses.

Here another calamity befell us. The last pony to be killed, Grisi, was in a state of exhaustion when his end came and his flesh, almost our only food for some days, was in consequence poisonous and gave us all violent diarrhea. For 24 hours, we were too weak to strike camp and I believe we all thought the end had come. I remember that night Shackleton asked me to sing "Lead Kindly Light", but one verse was all I could do.

There were several reasons for our failure, if such an achievement could be so called.

The first was the mistake in using ponies instead of dogs. Then came the loss of four ponies through eating sand. The next was the choice of the party, neither Adams nor Marshall were good pullers and if their places had been taken by Joyce and Marston, the British Flag would have flown at the south Pole and Scott and his gallant companions would not have perished.

All through this journey, Shackleton strained every muscle and nerve to the limit, as he always did during the 20 years I knew him, when strenuous action was called for.

I am convinced this was the reason for his breakdown when with Scott and Wilson, and I firmly believe that if he had exercised half the consideration for himself as he did for others, he would be alive today.

I have served with Scott, Shackleton and Mawson and have met Nansen, Amundsen, Peary, Cook and other explorers, and in my considered opinion for all the best points of leadership, coolness in the face of danger, resource under difficulties, quickness in decision, never failing optimism and the faculty of instilling the same into others, remarkable genius for organisation, consideration for those under him and obliteration of self, the palm must be given to Shackleton, a hero and a gentleman in every truth.

It was a great relief to turn our backs to that biting southerly wind and with it to help us, our progress was much more rapid.

Just before arriving at the badly broken ice of the Beardmore Glacier, we marched 26 miles, 26 miles and 29½ miles on three successive days.

Apart from the flesh of the pony, we had nothing for several days except one biscuit which was served out in the morning. I had been the first to go down with this sickness and the first to recover.

One morning…..

Shackleton had arranged that a food supply should be laid out for us on certain bearings south of Black Island. Several days before reaching this spot, we came across sledge tracks and studying the spoor, we could see that dogs had been pulling and from the length of the men's steps, going rapidly. Later on we learnt that these tracks were made by the depot party after laying the depot, they went further south to look for us and had they gone on one more day, would have met us. We were, however, so much overdue that they had no thought of finding us alive.

At one place where this party had halted for lunch, we found three small pieces of chocolate the size of a bean and a piece of dog biscuit the same size. We drew lots for them and Shackleton drew the biscuit, which had much the least value.

This depot party had made a thoroughly good job. They built a solid mound at least 12 feet high and placed the food on the top with a flag on a staff another 12 feet.

To me was given the honour of first sighting it and after taking a bearing of it, we sat down and demolished all our remaining food, four biscuits each. As I have mentioned earlier, distances are very deceptive in that clear air, and it took us four and a half hours to reach the depot – nine miles instead of the three we had reckoned on.

Besides the ordinary sledging rations, these good people had deposited a variety of delicacies, rich fruit cake, plum pudding, crystallized fruits, cooked chops in a basin, nuts and other things, altogether more than sufficient for three weeks. Shackleton and I had previous experience of overeating after starvation and warned the others, but we all disgustingly gorged ourselves and lay gasping for breath in our sleeping bags for hours before we could sleep.

In spite of this lesson, the following day Marshall, the doctor, ate quantities of the rich fruit cake and this brought on a serious attack of diarrhea. He was much too weak to pull and we three were not strong enough to drag him along on the sledge.

Shackleton had left orders that the ship should not wait for us after the 28th February. If we were not back by that date, we were to be considered dead and waiting later meant a great risk of the "Nimrod" being frozen up for another year. We struggled on for three days to the south-east corner of White Island and then Shackleton decided to leave Marshall, with Adams to look after him, and he and I were to make a dash for Hut Point where we expected to find a party looking out for us and, if the ice was cut, the "Nimrod" also waiting.

Only sufficient food was packed for one meal, (this was all wrong – three meals at least should have been taken, but the packing of the food was left to

Adams), sleeping bags, tent and cooker and we set off on our 33 mile tramp at a very good pace. After we had covered a mile, Shackleton stopped and grasping my hand said "Frank old man, it's the old dog for the hard road every time". He and I were then 35 years of age and the two we had left behind were under 30.

In all my experience, I have found the man of 30 to 40 years a better stayer than the younger man. In a short strenuous spurt as in a football or boxing match, the young man wins, but when it comes to days, weeks, and months of solid toil and hardships, the older man invariably beats the youngster.

Instructions had been left that a party should keep a constant lookout from Observation Hill, close to Hut Point, and we kept our sail set, even when there was no wind, so that we might more easily be seen. By the time we had done 20 miles, we were exceedingly hungry and began to look anxiously ahead for a relief party. When about eight miles away, we saw five men almost ahead of us, coming towards us. With joy, we altered our course and our bitter disappointment may be imagined when we found that they were penguins.

Our progress by this time had become a ghastly struggle and when within three miles of Hut Point we found ourselves cut off by open water, it seemed really the last straw. To get round the open water, it was necessary to make a detour to the east and climb over the mountains near where Vince was lost on Scott's Expedition and as it was impossible to drag the sledge, it was left with our sleeping bags, tent etc on the barrier ice.

Weary, footsore and famished, those hills seemed to be miles high instead of the actual 1,000 feet and when finally we came into sight of the hut and saw no signs of life, we were past speech.

On the boarded up window of the hut was a note from Professor David to say that the "Nimrod" would be lying at Glacier Tongue, eight miles north, until the 26th February and would then sail. This date was already past.

To give way to despair was not possible for Shackleton. It was now nearly midnight and dark and we set about making a distress signal.

Amongst the wreck of the magnetic hut were some tins of carbide and with this and the hut timbers, we quickly made a huge flare. This was kept going until we were too exhausted to do more. Luckily, a primus with paraffin still in it was found in the hut, also some tea and biscuits.

After a meal, sleep was necessary but with no sleeping bags and a temperature 30° below zero, this was difficult. The hut contained a dark room for photography, about five feet square, and we sat in there with the primus between our knees until the atmosphere became too vitiated to live in. The primus was then extinguished until the air freshened and we were almost paralysed with cold, then relit and so on until daylight, when stiff and unrefreshed we staggered out to make a smoke signal.

McMurdo Sound was clear of ice, but frost smoke, caused by the air being much colder than the water, hid the Glacier Tongue and all the land to the north. Before the fire got going properly, the masts of the "Nimrod" suddenly appeared through the haze. No happier sight ever met the eyes of man and an hour later, we were being greeted by our comrades, the most optimistic of whom had given us up as dead. We then learnt that McIntosh had the night before become obsessed by a feeling that we were returning and at midnight, climbed to the masthead and from there saw our flare.

Presuming upon Shackleton's death, many of his instructions had been disregarded, including the installing of a lookout on Observation Hill, which would have saved us many hours of mental and physical agony. However, Shackleton forgave those responsible and never made mention of it, so I will let it go at that.

Shackleton's first instructions to Captain Evans were to prepare a sledge and equipment and choose three of the fittest men on board to go back with him and bring in Marshall and Adams. Shackleton asked me if I would go and I said "yes, if you stay aboard as there is no need for two of us". He replied, "I must go". In three hours, the party set off and as I stood on the bridge watching them away, Captain Evans remarked, "Shackleton is a good goer, eh?" I replied somewhat forcibly in the affirmative; he said then, "Ah well, he has a party there that will see him out". I said, "wait until they get back".

The party Evans had chosen was Mawson, McKay and an athletic stoker who Evans considered would wear them all down and remain fresh.

48 hours later, all hands were astonished to see the party, including Adams and Marshall, waving for a boat from Hut Point. In a few minutes, they were aboard. McKay fell into the Wardroom crying out to the ship's doctor, "Into thy hands oh Doc, I delivery my body and my spirit". He and Mawson went to bed for two days, the all round athletic stoker went to bed for five days, while Shackleton went on the bridge and conned the ship out of the Bay. What I said to Captain Evans may not be recorded.

Worn down to a degree almost unbelievable, by a march of 1,740 miles, pulling a sledge 1,400 of those miles on the scantiest of rations for three months, Shackleton finished up by doing 99 miles in three days. The story of that last march has never before been told.

This rescue party left the ship at 3pm and marched until 10pm. The tent was then erected and the three fresh men got into their sleeping bags. Shackleton cooked a meal and fed them. At midnight, he gave the order to march and at 8am, a halt was made for a meal, which was again prepared by Shackleton. At 8pm, they arrived at Marshall and Adams' camp. Two hours only was spent there, the 'boss' again doing the cooking.

Marshall was still unable to pull, but walked nearly all the way. On the return, two halts were made for food which Shackleton cooked but no time taken off for sleeping. Is there any wonder I have such a great admiration for this wonderful leader?

Until the party which was left at Cape Royds and stores and dogs were taken aboard, there was little time to relate our different experiences. During this operation, a nasty sea was running and one boat was smashed up against the ice foot. There were several men and dogs in the boat and the last man was hauled up the ice wall, just as it was finally crushed and sank.

Later we learnt how Professor David, Mawson and McKay had actually reached the Magnetic Pole, a very fine performance, entailing a march of 1,200 miles, several hundred miles of this being at an altitude of 7,000 to 8,000 feet. Professor David was then 51 years of age.

I have previously spoken of the Professor's exceeding courtesy and the following is an illustration. The party was camped on a glacier near the sea; McKay had gone down to the sea ice to hunt for seals or penguins; Mawson was in the tent and inside his sleeping bag, using this as a dark room for changing plates in his camera, and the Professor was fossicking about the moronic deposits on the glacier. Presently, the Professor's voice was heard calling, "Mawson", who replied gruffly, "hallo". "Are you very busy Mawson?"; "Yes, I'm in the sleeping bag changing plates". A long pause, then, still very politely, "If you are not too busy Mawson, I wish you would come out and give me a hand, the fact of the matter is I am down a crevasse and I can't hold on much longer". Needless to say, Mawson dashed out and rescued the Professor who was hanging over a hole hundreds of feet deep and the bridge to which he was climbing was so rotten and crumbly that he dare not struggle.

Another party, Armitage, Priestly and Brocklehurst, doing geological work on the Victoria Land Coast and laying a food depot for Professor David's party, camped one night on what they believed to be land ice, and were horrified to find in the morning that they were out at sea and drifting rapidly north. For many hours, they drifted helplessly along, with killer whales continuously bumping underneath in the hope of breaking the ice and making a meal of them. Some freakish twist of current or wind then took them back inshore and one side of their little floating island just touched the land ice.

They had barely time to rush their sledge across when the floe moved off again, and they watched it until it was out of sight, getting further and further from the land all the time.

Another party had a narrow escape from being blown to eternity by a blizzard on the upper slopes of Mt Erebus, details of which may be found in Shackleton's "Heart of the Antarctic".

On the South Pole journey, it was a custom to change tent mates every week. One tent only was pitched for the midday halt and two at night. We all fed together, but slept two in each tent.

On the return journey, while sharing a tent with Shackleton, he asked me if I would join him on another attempt at the Pole. One of my diary entries reads like this – "this trip has completely cured me of any desire for further Polar exploration, nothing will ever tempt me to face that awful glacier and terrible plateau again". However, so great was my regard for the 'boss', that without any hesitation, I replied, "yes"! We then went on to discuss details. Shackleton was sure that he could raise sufficient funds in Australia and under his organisation; it would have been possible to return that same year, 1909.

One of the first items of news given us when we boarded the "Nimrod" was that Scott was preparing for another Antarctic Expedition and as soon as we were alone, Shackleton said, "that knocks us out Frank, we must give Scott his chance first". Such were his high principles.

I have never known or heard of anyone putting on weight so rapidly as we four did when we returned to full and plenty. We were all in excellent health. (Marshall was quite recovered), only fined down through lack of food and practically all we ate made good. In the first three days, I put on 14 lbs and in 21 days, I gained 37 lbs weight. The others, all bigger men, gained much more than I did. I was pleased to lose most of this again as I found it difficult to fasten my boots.

The return voyage to New Zealand was almost without incident. Before going on to Lyttleton, we put in at Stuart Island where Shackleton landed to cable home his report, he having a contract with the Daily Mail that they should be the first to receive news.

Our reception and the hospitality of the people in Lyttleton and Christchurch was too wonderful for description and we all spent several happy weeks amongst old and new friends.

My own pleasure was spoilt by the receipt of a cable to say that my mother had died a few days before our return. Two days before her death, she said to my sister, "Don't worry about Frank; he and all the party are well and on their way home".

Five of us, Priestley, Marston, Joyce, Day and myself, returned to England on the "Paparoa".

One of the young lady passengers captured Priestley's heart and before the termination of the voyage, they became engaged and later she became Mrs Priestley. There was a rival for the lady's hand on board and Priestley was a bit handicapped through being on the Sports Committee. Numbers of times a Steward came to me and told me that Mr Priestley wished to speak to me. I would find him sitting beside his lady love and he would say, "Look here old man, I have to attend a Committee Meeting - keep my seat until I come back". I found it no hardship.

Upon our return to England, we were feted and feasted and made very much of. We were all presented to King Edward to receive medals, Shackleton, Joyce and I receiving clasps as we were already in possession of the Polar Medal.

The King spoke to me at great length so that I almost forgot to back away from his presence. One unfortunate did turn round and was ignominiously turned back by one of the magnificent "Gentlemen in waiting".

I was granted six months leave by the Admiralty and during that time, lectured all through Great Britain and Ireland. I was then offered a lucrative post in Canada and retired from the Navy.

Early in 1910, I met Dr Mawson again and he asked me to go with him as second-in-command on an expedition he was organising. I promised to do so and when shortly afterwards I met Captain Scott at Newcastle-On-Tyne, I had to refuse his invitation to join him on his last Antarctic Expedition.

During the winter of 1910 and 1911, I made another extensive lecturing tour of the British Islands and Holland and although it was quite successful financially, it became monotonous telling the same old tale over and over again.

In April that year, three of my brothers accompanied me on a yachting trip. Our yacht was one of the "Nimrod's" boats, an open whale boat 18'5" in length. We sailed from Liverpool with the intention of going up the west coast as far as Oban. Bad weather kept us riding at anchor for two days in the mouth of the Mersey and we were all terribly seasick. I think I was the worst of all. The wind moderated and we got well away into the Irish Sea when a sudden north-west gale drove us into Millom. A crowd of excited people watched us run over the bar before a terrific sea and they were as greatly surprised as I when we arrived safely in the harbour after twice touching bottom on the bar.

The weather held us up for four days and we decided then to run north as the wind was more favourable and we were not particular where we went. Bad luck was still with us and on the second day out, we were caught in the heaviest gale that had been known in the Irish Sea for 12 years. For three days and nights, we lay to a sea anchor, our boat tossed about like a cork and we were all drenched with sleet and spray. My three land lubber brothers stuck it out like heroes and somehow managed to make fairly regular hot meals. The worst hardship was lack of sleep, the bitter cold and violent motion made that impossible and the sight of a small coasting steamer approaching us was very welcome.

With some difficulty, we were taken aboard and our boat into tow and 12 hours later found us in Ramsay. In our dilapidated state, we felt a hotel out of the question and were directed to a quiet boarding house. We had all decided we had done enough yachting for a while but had to stay three days in Ramsay, as there was no passenger boat to Liverpool earlier.

I knew there would be some report of our adventures in the Ramsay paper and in case it got into the London news, I sent a wire home. When we boarded the boat for Liverpool at Douglas, a steward approached me and asked, "Excuse me, are you not Mr Wild?" I answered, "Yes". "Then" he said, "These three gentlemen will be your brothers?" I said "Yes, but how do you know?" He then produced a "Daily Mirror" with my photograph and a long garbled account of our trip, with a huge heading "Four brothers rescued from the sea". It appeared that our conversation had been overheard in the Ramsay boarding house by a reporter.

I went back to Ramsay in June with Marston (artist on the "Nimrod"). I had left the boat in care of a boat builder and Marston and I half docked her, fitted a false keel and an awning to cover all the open part. We then sailed up the west of Scotland, generally putting into a small fishing port for the night. That summer was one of the finest for 30 years and we had a wonderful holiday, meeting everywhere true hospitality and kindness. The only rain we had was two days in Loch Ness. We went through the Caledonian Canal with its 27 lochs and spent King George V Coronation Day at Inverness.

It had been my intention to sail the boat to London, but in Newcastle-On-Tyne, I received a wire from Mawson asking me to join him as quickly as possible as he was almost ready to sail, so the boat was put aboard a London steamer and a few days later, saw it hoisted to the davits of the "Aurora".

When the "Aurora" left England, only two of the proposed landing party were aboard, Lieutenant Ninnis and Dr Mertz, in charge of dogs. The latter was a Swiss doctor of law and was an expert on ski, at one time holding the record amateur jump of 140 feet. When he joined the expedition, he knew very little English but picked it up rapidly. He heard the word "bloody" frequently used on board and naturally concluded it was a proper superlative. When the "Aurora" was coaling in Cardiff, he went ashore with Gray, the second officer. (Percy Gray was later an officer on the SATS "Botha".) Gray introduced Mertz to some lady friends and Mertz swept off his hat with a beautiful continental flourish and said, "How do, bloody fine day isn't it?" Gray has fortunately a keen sense of humour and his burst of laughter eased the situation.

As the "Aurora" was approaching Capetown, Mertz, who by then had more than a working knowledge of English, approached Gillies, the Chief Engineer, and asked, "Oh Gillies, is it perhaps possible you can tell me what time will the pilot come on board?" Gillies, a great leg puller said, "I don't know, you had better ask the Captain but for goodness sake, don't say "the pilot", that is only a vulgar sailor's term, the proper name is "Harlot"."

Captain John King Davis was one of the best navigators afloat and I have not met his equal at ice navigation, but his sense of humour was not highly developed and at sea, he kept up an almost unapproachable dignity. He came on deck just as Gillies spoke and Mertz went up to him, saluted, and said, "Oh Captain, is it perhaps possible you can tell me what time ze harlot come on board?" The Skipper gave him one withering glance and with a "What the hell are you talking about?" swung away on to the bridge. Poor Mertz scratched his head in puzzlement and then, seeing Gillies grinning from the engine room skylight, he tumbled to the joke, chased and caught Gillies and gave him a good rubbing down with a piece of dirty oily waste.

Dr Mawson was, at that time, attached to the Adelaide University and made that city his headquarters for the organisation of the Australian Antarctic Expedition, the full account of which will be found in Mawson's "Home of the Blizzard". The actual port of departure was Hobart, where the "Aurora" received a final overhaul and took on board all stores etc.

I did not sail from England with the "Aurora" but went to Adelaide on the P&O "Macedonia", taking out with me a number of chronometers and scientific instruments. This ship also carried an aeroplane which Mawson intended to be the first to fly over the Antarctic Continent. I was met at Adelaide by Watkins, pilot for the aeroplane and Bickerton, mechanic, and as soon as possible, the plane was landed and conveyed to the Cheltenham racecourse, about 12 miles from the city and there assembled.

Like almost all British Explorers, Mawson had found great difficulty in raising the necessary funds for his expedition (the American Government and people are much more liberal in these matters), and he had planned to use the aeroplane to assist in this. For this purpose, a huge marquee was erected on the racecourse, thousands of invitations sent out and a sufficiency of refreshments of every kind provided for the guests. The Governor of South Australia promised to attend with his family and to open the proceedings by taking the first of a series of short flights which would be given during the day at a charge of £5 a trip.

Previous to the great day, the aeroplane was thoroughly tuned up and several trial flights made until the pilot was satisfied that everything was in perfect order. At 6am on the gala day, a final test was decided upon and I went up with Watkins. The passenger seat was in front. The plane took off all right and had climbed to 500 feet when, in making a turn, it suddenly side slipped. We were almost down before Watkins got the plane straightened out and the sensation was far from pleasant. We climbed again to about 150 feet when the plane put its nose down and dived. We were then over the centre of the racecourse and as the earth rushed at us, all my past life did not panorama before me. I felt no fear, just had time to think, "Frank, old boy, your days of exploration are done," when we struck and the plane fell over on its back on top of us. A heavy weight was on my chest and I could hardly breathe, but was fully conscious. One leg was touching a hot cylinder and I was drenched with oil and petrol, and in horrible dread that the machine would burst into flames.

It seemed I had been lying a very long time when I heard Watkins grunt and then gasp out, "Poor old bus, she's jiggered up." Although breathing was difficult this made me laugh, then Watkins said, "Hallo Wild, you're alive?" I said, "Yes, but I can't get out, how are you?" He replied, "I'm all right but can't move." It felt to me at least an hour later (it was really only three minutes) that I heard Pickerton's voice and felt the weight on my chest ease up. Then the whole plane was lifted and with little assistance, I scrambled out. Watkins was again unconscious, but I was able to walk to the jockey's hospital. An ambulance very soon arrived and we were taken away to a nursing home, but whilst waiting I had to do a lot of telephoning to cancel everything that had been arranged for the day.

I spent 10 days in hospital, no bones broken but sorely bruised. Watkins's sternum was crushed in and he also had internal injuries and was invalided home. The plane was a wreck and never flew again but the engine and boxy were repaired and it did a little work in the Antarctic as an aero tractor.

Shortly after leaving hospital, I proceeded to Hobart where the "Aurora" was now lying ready to embark equipment and stores. I have frequently offended Sydney people by expressing the opinion that their harbour is not so beautiful as that of Hobart. I know of no finer view than that which meets the eye as one steams into the harbour and approaches the wharf. The town nestles on the slopes of Mt Wellington and when the latter is capped with snow, the effect is one to remain in the memory forever.

Many good friends were made in Hobart and in spite of the strenuous work of preparation; we found time to see quite a lot of the country. I had a car placed at my disposal by Mr Jones of XL fame and had several delightful excursions to various beauty spots.

Mawson's programme was an extensive one and houses, stores, fuel etc had to be carried for three parties. The first to be landed was a party of six with all material for a wireless station on Macquarie Island; the main party of 18, under Mawson, and a party of eight, under my command. It was found to be impossible to stow everything on the "Aurora" and a small steamer, the "SS Torca" was chartered to take part of it as far as Macquarie Island.

With the exception of Ninnis, Mertz, Bickerton and myself, the landing parties were Australians. They were nearly all from the Universities and, with few exceptions, young men from 21 to 27 years of age, full of life and enthusiasm.

Macquarie Island lies about 900 miles SSE of Hobart and belongs to New

Zealand. Stormy weather can be expected in those seas ten months out of the twelve and the "Aurora" had a rough passage. She carried a very heavy deck load of timber for the houses and petrol for the air tractor and amongst other top hamper was a large motor boat and the huge case containing the aeroplane.

Scarcely were we clear of the harbour on December 2nd when a heavy south west gale sprang up and Captain Davis gave the order to heave to. To a 20,000 ton liner, the mountainous sea that was running would not have been considered dangerous, but to us on the little "Aurora" of 500 tons, very much over-laden, it was a really anxious time. Many tons of water were constantly coming aboard and the deck cargo had to be frequently relashed at great risk to life and limb. The petrol was our greatest worry as there was always the dread that a sea might stove in some of the tins, when a fire would have been almost certain.

During the gale, the bilge pumps became choked and the hand pumps on deck had to be manned by the scientific staff, who all received many cold baths. Somehow, the sea water found its way into one of our fresh water tanks and in consequence, we were on short rations for a week or so. On the third day of the gale, the starboard side of the bridge was washed away, several people narrowly escaping serious injury. The motor launch was stove in and a great deal of damage was done to the deck cargo. After six days of this buffeting, the weather moderated sufficiently to allow a course to be set for Macquarie Island, which was sighted on December 11th. All the new chums and some of the old hands were seasick and relieved to reach Macquarie Island.

There are no good harbours and during the time we stayed there, the ship had to steam from one side to the other several times as the wind changed.

The island is a great breeding place for penguins and many other sea birds. Every beach has its rookery and I have found penguins nesting high up in the hills near the coast. One rookery was on a small level patch of ground nearly a thousand feet above sea level. There would be at least 100,000 birds; Victoria penguins. A small stream ran through the rookery down to the sea and the birds used the water course as their road. It was most interesting to watch the wonderful traffic control. There were many thousands going up and down all the time and every bird kept to the right. Occasionally, one would stumble and get on his wrong side, when he would receive a few pecks and buffets until he scrambled back. I walked up with them and was taken no notice of, but when out of curiosity I tried going against the traffic, I was instantly attacked and glad to get back to the correct side.

King penguins bred there in their millions and at one time, they were killed by the hundreds of thousands for their fat, which makes a valuable oil. The work was done in a frightfully cruel manner. Hugh boilers were erected and broad ramps built from the ground to the top of the boilers, and the birds were driven up these ramps and boiled alive. I did not see this in practice, but did see the boilers and ramps and enormous piles of bones. I know that Capt Scott protested against it to the New Zealand Government and it was stopped.

In addition to the millions upon millions of King, Victoria, Royal, Jackass, Rock Hopper, Gentoo and Ringed penguins, there are numerous Albatross, Giant petrols, Skua gulls, Gannets and other sea birds, also seals, sea lions, sea leopards and sea elephants. Collecting blubber from the sea elephants has been carried on for many years and when we landed from the "Aurora", we found a party of men there who were marooned owing to their ship having been driven ashore and totally wrecked.

We took several salted sea elephants tongues from them and Mawson arranged passages for them on the steamer which brought stores for us from Hobart. This ship "SS Torca" also took the barrels of oil these men had collected. All this slaughter has been stopped and Macquarie Island is now a sanctuary for birds and beasts.

I have read many tales about the ferocity of the sea elephant and what a dangerous calling their hunters have. All bosh! A fully grown bull is often over twenty feet in length and will weigh more than four tons and when approaches closely to one of these monsters, he will rear up and roar and certainly looks somewhat alarming, but they never attack. The only time they put up a fight is against other bulls in the mating season. I have seen men get on their backs and all they do is to scramble as fast as possible to the sea.

The island is covered with tussock grass and Kerguelen cabbage. Sheep and cattle have been tried there but the climate is too wet.

Having no really sheltered harbour, the landing of stores was difficult and often risky. One heavy case of machinery fell into 12 feet of water. After trying in vain for two hours to fish it up, Madigan stripped and, after a few attempts, succeeded in getting a chain sling round it; a very fine performance as the temperature of the water was 35°F. The masts for the wireless were the heaviest weights but gave the least trouble as they were floated ashore. The site chosen for the wireless station was near the north end of the island and on a hill 410 feet high, with several acres of level ground on the top, but precipitous sides. A flying fox was rigged, consisting of two wire ropes made fast to buried timbers on the top of the hill and set up tents with tackles to a convenient rock at the bottom. The material was hauled up on one wire and the weight of the hoist lessened by sacks of earth going down on the other. The heavier hoists were too much for one wire and had to be slung on both and man-hauled to the top.

I was in charge of this job and as bad weather often made it difficult to go backwards and forwards to the ship, a camp was made ashore which saved a lot of time and the change from ship life and routine was greatly appreciated by my party. There were a number of land gulls amongst the tussock grass and we found we could entice them almost within hand reach by tapping two stones together, the noise this produced being a fair imitation of their own call.

The boatswain and a number of sailors were landed to erect the wireless masts on "Wireless Hill" and this and the landing of stores being completed on December 23rd, we said goodbye to the five men of the island party and made for Caroline Cove at the south west point of Macquarie, to take in a supply of fresh water. No accurate survey of this island had been made up to that time and many outlying rocks not on the chart made navigation a risky business. On an earlier call at Caroline Cove, the "Aurora" struck a submerged rock which caused her to keel over at an alarming angle, but fortunately did no damage. On that occasion, the second officer, Gray, made himself temporarily unpopular with our austere Captain by calling out in joke, "Save the women and children, save the women and children!"

Caroline Cove is beautifully sheltered, but being only about eighty yards wide, there is not room for a ship to swing at her anchor, so we had to run a kedge out astern. Watering ship was a long and tedious job, two large barrels were taken ashore, filled by buckets from a stream nearly 100 yards away, towed back to the ship and then the performance repeated until 11pm.

During the night, a northerly breeze sprang up, causing the ship to drag the stern anchor and swing on to the rocks to the danger of the propeller and rudder. The only thing to do was to weigh and get out; slipping the kedge as there was not time to haul it aboard. The watering was not completed but it was decided to carry on with what we had and a course was set for the next objective, which was to land a party of 18 men, Mawson in command, to explore the unknown sector of the Antarctic Continent, west of Cape Adair.

This was Christmas day and beautiful weather which continued with us until we had entered the pack ice. The usual equipment for oceanographical work was carried and a series of soundings was made, dredging operations carried out etc, all of which is of great interest to science, but becomes tedious to the performers, particularly in high latitudes and low temperatures when the instruments and wire are coated with ice and more than painful to handle. The first ice was sighted on December 29th and that evening, we entered the pack and commenced another strenuous fight. The killer whales and rorquals were seen in large numbers, the former is the most formidable mammal in the Antarctic waters and accounts for large numbers of seals and penguins. The killer is from 25 to 30 feet in length and has a large mouth with formidable teeth and I have seen one take a seal of at least 500 lbs in weight in one mouthful. They are generally able to catch a sufficiency of food in the water but frequently they can be seen to poke up their heads and look over the floe ice and if they see penguins, seals or men, they dive under and come up underneath with a terrific bump. So powerful are they that they have been known to break ice more than two feet thick, actually measured by myself. The sea leopard is the only other dangerous beast and he contents himself with fish and penguins.

The water we had taken aboard at Caroline Cove had become a bit muddy in the tanks and we took the opportunity, when held up by heavy pack ice, to replenish the supply. A party of men, armed with picks, jumped on to the ice and breaking off sizable chunks, threw them aboard. When the sea first freezes, the ice contains too much salt to be of any use, but after a few months, all the salt precipitates and the ice becomes perfectly fresh.

On January 6th, land was sighted and we steamed along the coast for some miles, trying to find a landing place, the depth of the water varied alarmingly and progress was necessarily slow. Soundings taken every few minutes showed from 10 to 200 fathoms and there were many exposed rocks and grounded icebergs. One of these bergs looked exactly like a battered battleship.

This land was first seen by d'Urville in 1840 and named Adelie Land. We could see no possible landing place and continued our course to the west and about 50 miles further on, I sighted a rocky exposure in a bay about 15 miles away. Steaming in, this turned out to be an archipelago of tiny islands afterwards named Mackellar Islets. A boat was lowered and Mawson and I went ashore to explore. As we advanced towards the mainland, we saw a small bay which turned out to be a beautifully sheltered boat harbour. To the south of a rocky area which was about a mile and a half by half a mile, the inland ice rose in a fairly regular slope, giving promise of a good road inland and Mawson decided to make his base here at what he named Cape Denison Commonwealth Bay.

Although it was 8pm when we returned to the "Aurora", a start was at once made to land stores. The motor launch was lowered and it and the whale boat loaded and taken ashore, whilst Davis sought for an anchorage under the ice of the land. The weather had been fine all day but as the boats approached the harbour, a strong breeze off the land sprang up with fine snow drift and several of the party were frost bitten. The boat was landed as quickly as possible but before we reached the ship again, a strong gale was blowing.

Captain Davis was having considerable difficulty in finding a suitable anchorage, the depth of water varying from six to forty fathoms in half a cables length. Finally, the anchor was dropped about 500 yards from the face of the cliff that formed the coast line, just west of the landing place.

The boats had been hanging astern and as they were being brought forward for hoisting, the motor boat broke adrift and was carried rapidly out to sea. Luckily, Bickerton had remained in the boat with two others and just as it appeared the launch was about to be dashed to pieces on one of the small islets, he managed to get the spray soaked engine started and brought her safely alongside. For two days, it was impossible to land, then with the return of fine weather, the material was rushed ashore as rapidly as could be.

The motor boat would take two whale boats in tow and frequently a raft composed of hut timbers and wireless masts. I rigged a derrick ashore to facilitate the handling of the heavy lifts and if the weather had been kind, three days would have seen everything ashore. Frequent gales interfered however and the last load was not landed until January 19th, and our farewells over, the "Aurora" steamed away to the west to find, if possible, another landing place for my party, Mawson's instructions being that this must not be less than 400 miles from the main base.

For a few hours only we were able to keep within five miles of the land and then the ship was forced to the north by impenetrable pack for three days, when we were able to make south again.

We sailed over the charted position of Cote Claric and Cape Carr and soon afterwards sighted new land but were unable to get within 12 miles. Several days of southerly gales drove us again to the north, and driving snow rendered everything invisible. Collisions with icebergs were frequently averted with only a few yards to spare. When the weather cleared again, our observations placed us on Sabrina Land so that also was wiped off the charts.

Battling on to the west, we passed within a few miles of Totten High Land, also charted by Wilkes, but saw nothing of it. I have never seen so many icebergs in sight at the same time as we encountered on this trip. From the "Aurora's" masthead one morning, I counted 127 and many others must have been hidden by high ones in the foreground. One thing about these icebergs we appreciated thoroughly was the shelter they offered in bad weather. A ship can ride out a gale under the lee of a large berg as comfortably as though in harbour. The largest iceberg I have ever seen was 40 miles long and 15 miles wide with an average height of 200 feet, which would mean 1600 feet under water.

On the 14th February we found ourselves in a fairly open sea bounded on the east by a huge ice shelf and on the south by new land. Unfortunately, 25 miles of solid unbroken floe, anything from 10 to 40 feet thick, prevented us reaching the land. By this time, the coal supply on the "Aurora" was getting very low and it was necessary to make a landing somewhere or return to Hobart with the "Aurora". The latter could not be thought of and I asked Captain Davis to take the ship as near the ice shelf as possible, so that I might make an examination of it, with a view to making our base upon it. The edge of the shelf was a wall of 60 to 100 feet in height and later was found to extend 180 miles to the north and at least 200 miles to the east. It was Shackleton's birthday when we landed on it and at Davis's suggestion was named the Shackleton Ice Shelf. With ice axes and alpine rope we had not much difficulty in climbing the cliff. I took Hoadley and Harrisson with me. I found that for 200 yards, the ice was considerably crevassed and pressed up and showed every sign of movement but beyond that was quite sound enough to satisfy me. The whole sheet was undoubtedly moving, but I was confident that only a few yards broke away yearly and the work of landing stores was at once commenced. This was done in the same way as at Macquarie Island. A flying fox over shear legs on top of the cliff and set up taut to an anchor on the floe. We of the landing party worked on top and the ship's company broke the stuff out and sledged it along to the foot of the cliff. In this manner, about 40 tons of material and stores was hoisted in four days.

Before the ship left us, I spoke to each one of my party separately, giving them the chance to return on the "Aurora", but each said in almost the same words, "If it is good enough for you, it is for me". I did this because Captain Davis had expressed anxiety about the safety of the position and it had also been a subject for discussion amongst the crew. Later, some of the ship's company gave their opinions to the Australian press and at least one paper stated that "Wild's party is camped on moving ice and there is little probability that they will ever be seen again". It certainly was most unfortunate that just as the ship was leaving, many tons of ice broke away from the shelf, sending up a huge wave which not only caused the "Aurora" to roll heavily, but also broke up a lot of the floe ice where we had been landing stores.

At 7am on February 21st 1912, my party waved and cheered as the "Aurora" left us on the sea ice. Mawson had more or less left the choice of my party to me and later on, I had the satisfaction of congratulating myself on having made no mistake.

The party was made up as follows:-

G Dovers, cartographer, 21 years of age
C T Harrisson, biologist, 43 years of age
C A Hoadley, geologist, 24 years of age
S E Jones, medical officer, 24 years of age
A L Kennedy, magnetician, 22 years of age
M H Moyes, meteorologist, 25 years of age
A D Watson, geologist, 24 years of age
and F Wild, leader, 38 years of age.

Our first care was to haul up all the stores and gear to the top of the cliff, pitch tents for temporary accommodation and then commence hut building. It was also only prudent to move the stores further back from the badly broken edge of the ice shelf.

Harrisson, Hoadley, Kennedy and Jones were told off as house builders and Dovers, Moyes, Watson and I sledged along supplies. The site for the hut was about 500 yards from the store heap, but owing to crevasses and pressure ridges, the distance covered on each trip was nearer 800 yards. We had nine dogs but they were untrained and in poor condition after the voyage. The weather was kind to us and the house was habitable with stores set up in a week and at last we could have a decently cooked meal in comfort. The building operations were only stopped one day by a moderate blizzard and the temperature hovered between 25°F and -12°F.

Whilst working on the roof, Harrisson saw what appeared to be land to the east and later this proved to be an island, entirely ice covered, a little over 30 miles distant, 20 miles in length and 15 miles wide. It was named Masson Island.

Sunday, March 3rd, was a beautiful calm day and as we were now safely housed, I made a holiday of it. Instead of 6am, we turned out at 8.30am and after breakfast Divine Service was held. After lunch, we unpacked our ski and all went for a run east, towards Masson Island. The surface was excellent for sledging but I found a number of crevasses up to 85 feet in width, all well bridged and safe for man on ski, but dangerous for an unroped man on foot. This fine day was followed by a two day blizzard and outdoor work was impossible, but there was a sufficiency of indoor work to keep us fully occupied, as preparations for a sledging trip to be made before the winter set in were in progress. Several hundred small food bags were needed and the sewing machine intended for my base had been landed by mistake at the Main Base so it all had to be done by hand, slow and tedious work to unaccustomed fingers.

This blizzard blew itself out on the 5th day and we found 12 feet snow drifts collected all round the hut and a shaft had to be dug and a ladder made for exit and entrance and then all stores rescued. This was barely done when another fierce blizzard struck us and lasted, with only one short lull, until the 12th. During this lull, we fed the dogs and Jones, Dovers and Hoadley brought in a load of ice from a pressure ridge a short distance from the hut and had great difficulty in finding their way back as the wind freshened again.

This bad weather had its compensations, the temperature always rose during a blow and instead of being well below zero remained somewhere about 30°F. The snow piled up around the hut so that only the peak of the roof was visible and even with gusts of over 100 mph, there was not more than a very slight tremor to be felt. During our confinement, the interior of the hut was put in order much earlier than it would otherwise have been and although the delay in our sledging was disappointing, we realised we were more comfortable than we would have been camped on the glacier.

The 13th was calm and, after an early breakfast, all hands turned to erecting two masts for our wireless receiving instrument. Whilst this work was going on, we felt the glacier give a slight quake and then we saw many thousands of tons of ice calve off into the sea. An enormous wave was set up which smashed all the floe for miles and also carried away all snow ramps leaving perpendicular cliffs 100 feet high. This left us with no chance of getting seals or penguins for fresh meat for ourselves or the dogs, a rather serious matter.

The sledges were packed and all ready for a start at 1pm. The load weighed just over 200 pounds per man. Watson and Kennedy were to remain behind to keep observations going at the hut. It was my intention to travel inland to lay a depot or depots to assist the next summer sledging.

The mainland was visible 17 miles to the south running almost due east and most rising rapidly to about 3,000 feet and then more gradually to the great inland plateau of the Antarctic Continent. No bare land was visible and the lower slopes appeared to be badly broken up by icefalls but also showed a number of possible roads between.

The most accessible spot appeared to be south-east and a course was laid accordingly, over a good surface almost free of crevasses, Jones falling to the waist in the only one seen that day. All hands being a bit soft, I halted for the night at 5pm having done seven and a half miles. As it became dark soon after 6pm, the marching hours were from 7am to 5pm to enable us to get breakfast and dinner in daylight. When we commenced our second day's march, the temperature was -8°F but pulling over what we called a pie-crust surface soon warmed us up. This pie-crust was a hard frozen surface not quite strong enough to bear a man's weight and let us through from six to eight inches into soft snow underneath and is very tiring.

As we approached the land, the surface of the glacier became undulating, similar to a long swell at sea, the distance between the crests being about three-quarters of a mile and a drop between of 30 feet. Many more crevasses were encountered and we all had falls, Hoadley dropping with his head below the surface into one five feet wide. Narrow crevasses from two to eight feet in width are much more dangerous than those 30 to 100 feet, as the snow bridges over the latter are usually much more substantial.

As we neared the land, the crevasses increased in width so the harness was lengthened to prevent more than two men being on the bridge at the same time. We crossed one at least 60 feet wide with a badly broken bridge and a black bottomless pit showing through all the holes. This one looked so dangerous that we went over one by one on an alpine rope and hauled the sledges over after crossing ourselves. It was impossible to tell exactly when we actually got on the land but camping soon after we crossed the crevasse mentioned, we found we had risen 200 feet. On either hand were to be seen splendid ice falls but the road ahead seemed clear. This was March 15th.

A gale and heavy drift confined us to camp all the next day and until 11.30am on the 18th. The tents and sledges were buried in snow giving us two hours hard work digging them out before we could get going again. The surface was now névé and heavy sastrugi and the slope becoming steeper, we were compelled to relay. We camped that night at an altitude of 1,400 feet. The next three days was difficult travelling over waves or ridges of sastrugi from three to four feet in height and the sledges had many capsizes. On one of these days, Hoadley, who was taking meteorological observations every two hours during the day, found his book had fallen off the sledge.

To save his fingers at the 8am readings, he slipped the book under the strap which secured the instrument box, instead of unstrapping and putting it into the box itself. The book might have been only a few yards away or it might have been miles, as we had travelled at least three miles in the two hours. As we were making a track very easy to follow and there was no sign of wind, I sent Hoadley back to find it and we carried on with the sledges until the noon half for lunch. This meal usually took only half to three-quarters of an hour but this time, we sat waiting until after 1pm and still nothing to be seen of Hoadley. There were no crevasses on the route but he might have slipped and hurt himself and I was just on the point of taking a party to look for him when he appeared over a ridge a few hundred yards away. He had found the book two miles back so had walked an extra four miles. That had not worried him, but the utter loneliness of that three hours had quite unnerved him. Needless to say, his book went into the box after subsequent observations.

On the 21st, we were 2,300 feet above sea level and as we camped that evening, a heavy blizzard struck us. The drift was blinding and masks of snow over our faces made the erection of the tents a painful and slow process. This lasted seven days and later on we found that it corresponded in time to the blizzard in which Captain Scott and his party perished at a distance of 1700 miles from our position.

Owing to changes in the direction of the wind, large quantities of snow came through the tent ventilators and the warmth of our bodies thawed this and made our sleeping bags very wet. When it is understood that for no purpose whatever is it possible to leave the tent during a blizzard and that a section of the floor snow must be used for drinking and cooking, it may be partially realised how irksome these storms are.

At noon on the 28th, the wind eased off and we at once dug ourselves out. Nothing could be seen except the very tops of the tents which meant that there was a deposit of nearly six feet of snow. This was so soft that we sank thigh deep at every step and sometimes to the waist.

We were all weakened through our long confinement and it was nearly 5pm before we had rescued the sledges and all gear. The temperature was 20oF and Dovers got a frost bitten nose. This was his first experience of frost bite and he was terribly afraid he would be disfigured and possibly lose the affection of a certain girl in New South Wales.

Although a fresh wind blew all night, the surface was as soft as ever the following morning and as it was impossible to drag the whole load, the only thing to do was to leave the food depot on the nearest ridge and return to the base. It took us well over an hour to drag one sledge half a mile up a rise of 100 feet with a load of only 80 pounds a man. As we got on the ridge, Moyes found he had a frost bitten foot and as there was too much wind to attend to it in the open; he had to return to camp. Sufficient paraffin and food to last three men for six weeks and a minimum thermometer was left at this depot.

We commenced the return journey next day and we and the sledges were sinking so deeply into the snow that 40 yards was as much as we could do without a rest and only 900 yards was covered before lunch and this was downhill. When we made our evening camp, after one of the hardest days I have ever experienced, the sledgemeter showed one mile and a quarter. We were pulling in pairs, Hoadley and I leading, sinking thigh to waist deep, and at one time tried going on our hands and keens, but found our faces went under. After one of our 40 yard struggles, I thought I might be halting too frequently and asked Hoadley if he thought so. He replied, "My God sir, if you go another yard I'll die!"

A two-day blizzard held us up again and slightly hardened the surface and on April 2nd, we did five miles, six hundred and ten yards. As we left the hills behind the surface improved and on the 4th we had done seventeen and a half miles by camping time and as there was only six miles more to go and the party all fresh, I decided to carry on by moonlight.

After supper, we marched on for two and a half hours by which time we had had enough and I was beginning to think we had passed the hut. The next day was Good Friday but far from good for us. A heave gale sprang up and it was impossible to move. During the forenoon, Hoadley and I had to go out to secure our tent, the snow having partly blown off the skirt allowing the tent to flap considerable and a lot of drift was coming in. The other tent was only five yards away but we could not see it. At noon, Hoadley went out again to attend to the tent and became absolutely lost within six feet of it. I heard him yelling and guessed what was the matter at once, and Dovers and I yelled our best in reply, and Hoadley groped his way in with a mask of snow over his face. He told us that the wind, which was a good 80 miles an hour, knocked him down immediately he got outside and when he got to his feet again, he could see nothing and had no idea where the tent was.

The weight of snow had bulged in the weather side of the tent to such an extent that we did not light the primus and had frozen pemmican for our evening meal. About 11am the following day, the wind suddenly died away to half a gale and we turned out and had a good hot meal. We then looked out to see how the others were getting on and saw their tent had collapsed. Getting into our burberrys, we rushed out and then saw one man in his sleeping bag outside. It was Harrisson and to our relief, he said he was all right. We carried him into our tent when he climbed out all well, but very hungry. We then rescued Jones and Moyes who were under the fallen tent. They told us the tent had fallen down the day before at 10 o'clock, which was when Hoadley and I were out securing our own.

After the three hungry unfortunates had eaten a meal, they declared themselves fit to travel and shortly after the march commenced, Dovers saw the wireless masts and a little later, we were safely in the hut much to the surprise of Kennedy and Watson, who did not expect that we would be travelling in such bad weather.

The sledgemeter showed that the last camp was only two miles, one hundred yards from the hut and had we been able to see anything, we could easily have got in on the night of the 4th. The total distance covered on this trip was 125 miles and the highest altitude reached was 2,600 feet. Of the 25 days we were away, travelling was only possible on 12 days. No one was any worse for the hardships except for a few blistered fingers from frost bite. All the party had worked splendidly and were always cheerful, although conditions had been exceptionally trying. I was also most pleased with the amount of work done by Kennedy and Watson during our absence. In addition to the observations they had trained five dogs and all stores were transported from the landing place to the hut - this in spite of the weather which had been as bad at the base as with us. We were amused to find one end of our long table full of dirty crockery and two stay-at-homes having decided it was more trouble to wash up after each meal than to have one big wash up a week.

The next day, Easter Sunday - April 7th, we were perforce resting as a particularly heavy blizzard was raging. I dared not allow anyone to go out to feed the dogs on that day or the next, but these animals can go for a week without food, and for drink they have the snow.

Winter routine was now established. Harrisson was put in charge of lamps and paraffin, Hoadley in charge of foodstuffs, Jones and Kennedy looked after the acetylene plant, the former showing himself to be a very useful plumber and between them, the hut was well lighted. Moyes was out all hours with the meteorological work. Watson looked after the dogs and Dovers relieved other members of their duties when they were cooks. Each man, except myself, took a week in turn as cook, and night watch was kept by each one in turn. Work commenced at 10am during the winter and finished at 1pm, unless anything special had to be done. Divine Services were held every Sunday at which Moyes and I officiated in turn.

Drift snow had accumulated to a depth of 12 feet all round the hut, and a tunnel was driven from the door a distance of 40 feet and a trap door built over the tunnel and raised well above the outer surface to prevent it being drifted over. A ladder to this door was our communication with the outer world. The tunnel was continued on an incline until it came out and the entrance left open so that sledge loads of ice or stores could be run in, but each blizzard closed this up, giving two men a day's work to clear it again. On each side of this tunnel, roomy caves were dug out to accommodate stores and ice and by the end of April, all stores were housed.

Bamboos had been stuck in to mark the positions of the different piles of stores, but the drift snow was in some cases, over the top of the bamboos and shafts had to be dug 10 to 12 feet deep until they were located. We were two days searching for the carbide.

With everything housed, we were self-contained and could afford to laugh at our frequent blizzards. Our house then received the title of "The Grottoes".

Late in April, Kennedy, Harrisson and Jones built an igloo to be used as a magnetic observatory and on the afternoon of the 30th, all hands were invited by the magnetician to a tea party to celebrate the opening. He had tastefully decorated the place with flags and after the reception and formal inspection of the instruments, tea was served. The outside temperature was -33°F and as it was not much higher inside, our visit was not prolonged. Previous to this, Kennedy had been carrying out his observations in the open, much to the detriment of his fingers, temper and language.

On the 1st day of May, Harrisson, Hoadley and Watson went away south towards the land at the head of the bay taking four dogs and the load being only 342 pounds, the dogs pulled it easily. These four were all the dogs left at that time; Nansen and Crippen had died, Sweep had disappeared, two bitches - Tiger and Tich, had refused to do any work so had to be shot, as food for the dogs was scarce; this left Sandow, the leader, Amundsen, Switzerland and Zip. I took the rest of the party for a day's run to the north hoping to find some place on the glacier low enough to enable us to get down to the sea ice. We found several places not more than 40 to 50 feet high but no snow ramps on which to descend. A flat sheet of unbroken frozen sea stretched away to the north for at least 30 miles and no penguins or seals were in sight.

The next three days a moderate blizzard kept us indoors. Saturday was clean ship day, when the hut and darkroom were scrubbed, the verandah tunnel and caves tidied and the windows cleaned. The window cleaning was taken in turns and was thoroughly detested. The windows were in the roof and each week collected ice from an inch to two inches thick. To chip and scrape this off, one had to sit on the rafters with the fragments of ice falling on to one's face.

On Sunday, Harrisson, Hoadley and Watson returned. Although less than 20 miles away, they had missed the strong winds blowing at the base. They had discovered some old icebergs containing geological specimens and which were good subjects for Harrisson's sketches, but they had seen no bare rock. Watson had a badly cut nose through a fall on rough ice.

Apart from daily routine, we were now kept occupied for several days overhauling tents, poles and sleeping bags. The bags had all shrunk through getting wet and drying again and required enlarging.

May 15th was a beautiful day and with Dovers, Watson, Hoadley and Harrisson, I went two miles south to Icy Cape to try to find a road down to the sea ice and was fortunate at last. By climbing down a partially filled up crevasse, which opened up into a magnificent cave at sea level, we walked straight out to the level sea ice. There was not a seal or even a blow hole to be found.

Another howling blizzard, with wind up to 100 miles an hour, kept us indoors from May 22nd to 24th May. It was impossible to take observations at the meteorological screen or to feed the dogs. Moyes and I went out on a rope attached to the trap door on the 24th and succeeded in finding the dogs and gave them biscuits.

We spliced the main brace that night in commemoration of Empire Day. The most bigoted teetotaler could not call us intemperate. On each Saturday night, one drink per man was served out when we drank to "sweethearts and wives". The only other occasions when any intoxicants were issued were on each member's birthday, King's birthday, Midwinter's Day and on the return of a sledging party.

This blizzard caused a lot of damage. The dogs' shelter was entirely carried away, a short mast which was used as a holdfast for sledges was snapped off and the sledges buried, and worst of all, Kennedy's igloo had lost its roof and the delicate instruments inside were all buried in snow. The dogs had not suffered though under a deep snow blanket. As usual, the temperature had risen during the blizzard from -37°F to 50°F.

Fine weather continued until June 2nd. During this time, we were occupied in digging a road from the glacier down to the sea ice in the forenoons and hunting for seals or amusing ourselves in the afternoons. Kennedy and Harrisson rebuilt the magnetic igloo. At this time, daylight lasted from 9am to 3pm and we had magnificent sunrise and sunset effects and too frequently, the sun was surrounded by a marvelously brilliant halo and mock suns. I say "too frequently" because a blizzard invariably followed these displays and if one appeared when we were on a sledge trip, we took extra precautions in securing the tents.

Blizzards never meant idleness; there was always sufficient indoor work to keep us in employment. On this day, June 2nd, Watson and I were making a ladder of rope with wooden rungs to assist us in getting down and up the cliff and also to be used by Watson and Hoadley who were about to dig a shaft in the glacier to examine the ice structure. Jones was making a harpoon for seals, Hoadley opening cases and stowing food on the verandah, Dovers cleaning tools, Moyes repairing a thermograph, Harrisson cooking and Kennedy sleeping after a night watch.

From June 4th to 22nd was a remarkably fine spell. An igloo was built as a shelter for the geological shaft, and every day parties went out seal hunting. One day, Dovers and Watson found a Weddell Seal, two and a half miles to the west on the sea ice. They killed it but did not cut it up as it had sores on the skin. Jones went over with them and pronounced the sores to be wounds received from some other animal, so 50 pounds of meat was brought in and was a very pleasant change after tinned meat.

The frequent snow storms had by this time built up huge drifts under the ice of the cliffs up to 50 feet in height and almost to the top of the glacier and we had great fun in skiing down those ramps. Falls were frequent, but before long, the whole party became quite expert. The only serious accident happened to Kennedy who twisted his knee and was laid up for a week.

I was frequently called during the night by the watchman to have a look at "Aurora" displays, only to find them very ordinary, but on the night of June 18th, Kennedy, who was taking magnetic observations, called me to see the most magnificent display I have ever seen, either in the Arctic or the Antarctic. A double curtain of yellow light 30° wide came up from the eastern horizon to the zenith where it spread out into a Prince of Wales feathers and became brilliantly coloured, waves of light shimmering along it so rapidly that they travelled the whole length in two seconds. Although the temperature was about -30o, we all stayed out to watch until danger of frost bite drove us back to bed. Kennedy's instruments showed a great magnetic disturbance during this display.

Hoadley and Watson set up a line of bamboos a quarter of a mile apart and three miles long, on the 20th, and from then onwards took measurements for snowfalls every fortnight. Final results showed that the surface of the glacier retained an average accumulation of 13 inches per year out of an estimated snowfall of 30 feet, the remainder being blown away.

On Midwinter's Day, the temperature ranged from 35°F to 25°F and we had daylight from 10am until 3pm. A general holiday was proclaimed through "Queen Mary Land" which was the name I gave to this new land.

There was a special dinner in honour of the occasion, followed by speeches, toasts and a gramophone concert.

Now commenced serious preparations for spring sledging which I hoped to start about the middle of August. Jones made a valuable addition to our rations. After a number of experiments with glaxo, he succeeded in making a biscuit consisting of a mixture of butter and glaxo compressed by means of a steel die and a heavy hammer. One of these three ounce biscuits was equal in food value to four and a half ounces of plasmon biscuits and pleasant to the palate.

The first two days of July were quiet and we were able to get out for work and exercise. On July 2nd, the sun, which at this time was barely clear of the horizon at noon, had on either side and above a red mock sun connected by a rainbow tinted halo. This display was, as usual, followed by a blizzard and on the 5th and 6th, a terrific hurricane was raging. Had we not known that nothing short of an earthquake could move the hut, we should have been very uneasy.

In addition to the work of sledging preparations, we had other and lighter means of passing away the time, such as chess, card and dominoes and a competition was started for each member to write a short article connected with the expedition, humorous or otherwise. These were read by the authors after dinner one night and gave considerable amusement. A nine hole golf course was laid out, but every blizzard blotted it out and made it necessary to lay it out afresh.

Sandow, the leader of the dogs and Zip disappeared about the middle of the month. After two days, Zip returned but we never saw Sandow again. All along the cliff edge were snow cornices, some weighing hundreds of tons. These were constantly breaking away with a thunderous sound that could be heard for miles. On July 31st, Watson and Harrisson had a narrow escape. They went down to the floe ice over one of these hanging cornices which almost reached a sloping ramp below. A few seconds only after they got clear, the cornice collapsed, the huge mass of hard snow crashing down and cracking up the sea ice, which was four feet thick for more than a 100 yards. Doubtless, Sandow had been caught by one of these falls.

July had been an inclement month with only three really fine days and the early half of August was little better. On Sunday the 11th, Dovers and I went out in the wind to feed the dogs and to clear the chimney and on our return, found the hut in confusion. Jones had been charging the acetylene generators when one of them caught fire. There was grave danger of an explosion as the gas tank was floating in kerosene. Throwing water over it would have made matters worse, so blankets were used to smother the flames. As this failed to extinguish them, the whole plant was pulled down and carried into the tunnel where the fire was put out. The damage amounted to two blankets burnt and dirtied; Jones's face singed and scorched and Kennedy had one finger jambed. It was a fortunate escape from disastrous calamity.

A large iceberg frozen in the floe 11 miles north had been of interest for some time as it had capsized and exposed its base. On the 14th, Harrisson, Dovers, Hoadley and Watson took food and equipment and went off to examine it. They found the berg on its side and an interesting collection of stones and pebbles was made from what had been the bottom. During the absence of this party, Jones sighted seven Emperor Penguins two miles to the west. Taking a sledge, we at once made after them. When a mile off, they saw us and came to meet us with their usual stately bows. It hurt us to kill them but we were sorely in need of fresh meat. The four we secured averaged 70 pounds in weight and were a heavy pull up the glacier.

Everything was now ready for sledging, the object of the first journey being to lay out a food depot to the east, to assist the long summer journey to be made in that direction. The party would consist of six men and three dogs, Hoadley and Kennedy to remain at the base, the former to complete the geological shaft and the latter to carry on magnetic work. There was also plenty to keep them occupied in preparing stores for later sledge journeys.

Bad weather delayed the start until Thursday, 22nd. After an early breakfast, we packed up and left the hut at 7am. For four days we were blessed with fine clear weather, a good travelling surface and temperature from -30°F to -35°F. On the second day, we sighted two small nunataks eight miles to the south, the first bare land for more than seven months. Our course was almost due east parallel to the coast and to the north was Masson Island. As we went on, another smaller ice covered island opened up, Henderson Island, then a three-day blizzard held us up. As usual, the temperature rose with the wind and Jones, Moyes and I, having a three-man bag, were very warm but thoroughly tired of lying down so long. The 31st was again fine and bright and, passing Henderson Island, we saw a bay 17 miles wide running back in the mainland. This was named the "Bay of Winds", as we encountered a blow every time we crossed it.

In the centre of the Bay was a nunatak which from its shape was named the "Alligator", and ahead, apparently 15 miles distant, another nunatak, the "Hippo", and four definite outcrops could be seen on the mainland. This bucked us up as we had begun to think all the land was ice-covered.

We found the Hippo to be 22 miles away and the surface being heavy sastrugi. We were a day and a half before coming up to it. It was surrounded by huge ridges of pressure ice which prevented us getting the sledges near it. We climbed to the top, 420 feet, and found it to be 400 yards long and 200 yards wide and composed of grains and schists. Dovers took a round of angles, Watson collected geological specimens and Harrisson sketched until has fingers were frost bitten.

Moss and lichens were found and a dead young snow petrel showed that the birds bred there.

At each end of the nunatak were wide gaping crevasses, to the south the glacier shelf appeared to be very little broken, but to the north it was terribly torn up. 20 miles east was another bare rocky island. That night the temperature was -47°F.

We had felt a few gusts of wind during the night, but were surprised to find when we got away from the shelter of the rock, that a strong gale was blowing. The surface was very hard, slippery névé and neither men nor dogs could keep their feet and the sledges were blown sideways. We were 84 miles west of the base. I had hoped to do 100 miles, but our sleeping bags were getting very wet and none of the party getting sufficient sleep, so I decided to leave the depot here and make up by starting the summer journey earlier.

One sledge was left with six weeks allowance of food for three men. The sledge was placed on and in a hole three feet deep and a mound six feet high built around it and a bamboo and flag lashed on the top.

On September 4th, we were homeward bound, heading first to the mainland to examine some rock outcrops and that night, the tents were pitched in a most beautiful spot. A wall of solid rock rose sheer for more than 400 feet crowned by an ice cap of 200 feet and magnificent ice falls came down on either side. The site of the camp was in what appeared to be a sheltered hollow a quarter of a mile from the "Avalanche Rocks". One tent was up and the others in process of erection when the wind suddenly veered from the west to east and a strong gust flattened out both tents. Later, while preparing for bed, a tremendous avalanche came down, the noise was awful and seemed so close we all turned to the door and started out. The cliff was completely hidden in a cloud of snow and we stood ready to run, Dovers thoughtfully grabbing a food bag. None of the blocks came within a hundred yards and as it was now blowing hard, all hands elected to remain where we were. Several more avalanches came down in the night but none so heavy or alarming as the first one.

A strong breeze was blowing in the morning but not too bad for travelling, so I called the party. Moyes and I lashed up the sleeping bag, passed it out and strapped it on the sledge; Jones starting the cooker. Suddenly a terrific squall struck our tent, splitting it from top to bottom and Moyes and I were knocked down. When we got to our feet again, we went to help the other men whose tent was still standing. The squalls were now frequent and fiercer and the only thing to do was to pull the poles away and allow the tent to collapse. Looking round for a lee, we found the only shelter to be on the sunken bridge of a crevasse 300 yards to windward, but the wind was so strong that it was impossible to convey the gear there. All hands were repeatedly knocked over and blown along the surface 30 to 40 yards, even with an ice ax stuck hard in the snow. The only thing was to dig ourselves in.

We dug a hole three feet deep, twelve feet long and six feet wide. The snow was so hard this occupied three hours. We would have gone deeper, but came to solid ice at three feet. Everything movable was stowed in the hole, the sledges and tent poles placed across the top, the good tent laid over all and weighted down with snow and ice blocks. It was a slow and difficult task as many of the gusts must have been well over 100 miles an hour. One of them lifted Harrisson clean over my head and dropped him 20 feet away. At noon, we had everything snug, made a meal and climbed into our sleeping bags. We remained in this hole five days, the wind at hurricane force the whole time and horrible avalanches crushing down at frequent intervals, every one giving me pains in the stomach; I could not get over the dread of being flattened out like a squashed beetle. Had we been able to sit upright, we would have been much more comfortable. After a while, the heat of our bodies and the cooking raised the temperature of the dug-out above freezing point and the sleeping bags and our clothes became very wet; in fact we were lying in water, so we took the most of our meals cold and sucked ice for drinks.

We took it in turns to look out for a change in the weather and on the morning of the 10th, the lookout reported a clear sky and bright sun, and though the wind was still strong and gusty, we immediately got out and packed up. Our wet clothes at once stiffened, the temperature being -25°F. For several miles we travelled on bare rippled ice and the strong following wind caused the sledges to turn sideways and frequently capsize and the runners were badly torn. Later, the surface changed to snow and that night, we camped with twenty miles, one hundred yards to our credit.

We all had lacerated and bleeding legs, caused through our frozen clothes bending in sharp angles and chafing the back of our knees at every step. That night, another blizzard sprang up and, contrary to custom, the temperature remained low at -30°F and we had a bad time in our wet bags. For two days we travelled by compass, the sky being overcast and drift snow hiding the land.

On the 14th, an extra early start was made, we were all anxious to reach the hut that night, distant about 31 miles. We had very little sleep and plenty of shivering for the last four nights.

Unfortunately we marched on a magnetic bearing from Masson Island of 149° instead of 139°. Instead of reaching home at 5pm as expected, we travelled on until 8pm, the last two hours in the dark amongst a lot of pressure ridge and crevasses none of us could recognise and at one time found ourselves within a few yards of the cliff edge of the glacier, so were compelled to camp. The low temperature of -35°F gave us a chilly time in our wet bags. Next morning we arrived at the base and found the last camp had been four and a half miles to the north. Before having a meal we all weighed ourselves and found the average loss to be eight pounds. In the evening, Moyes and I weighed again; he had gained seven and I five and three quarter pounds.

Hoadley and Kennedy had experienced similar weather at the base to that meted out to us.

Plans were now made for the summer sledging. There was to be a Western Coast Party under the leadership of Jones and an Eastern Coast Party led by myself. The earlier idea of an inland journey was abandoned in favour of the greater importance of the coastal work.

Before commencing the main journeys, it was decided to lay out a depot to the west to assist Jones and to bring in the food left on the mountains in March. Ten days of continuous wind and drift delayed the departure of Jones's party until September 25th. His party included Harrisson, Hoadley, Dovers and Moyes and the three dogs. Watson, Kennedy and I assisted the others down to the sea ice and saw them off with a good start.

Watson was slightly lame at this time and we did not get started until the 29th and then found a soft surface and very heavy pulling. The first day we did nine miles, but during the next six days, the snow became deeper and only 19 miles were covered. Crevasses were nearly all invisible and falls were frequent. A head wind and drift made the climb more laborious and finally, at 2,000 feet, Kennedy severely strained his Achilles tendon and I decided to return to "The Grottoes". At 2pm on October 8th, the mast was sighted and soon afterwards, we climbed down into the hut finding it cold, dark and empty. The sun had been very powerful that day and both Watson and Kennedy had a touch of snow blindness.

A blizzard raged for thirteen days after our return, so that Kennedy's injury had really saved our lives. We travelled light depending on the food at the depot for our return journey and had we gone on, the blizzard would have caught us before we got there with practically an empty food bag. Our sympathies went out to the Western Party lying in wet bags waiting for a break in the driving wall of snow. On October 23rd, they had been away for four weeks for which time they took provisions and I had no doubt they would be on short rations.

On the 24th, I went to the masthead with the field glasses but saw nothing of them. That day we weighed our provisions and prepared to go in search of them. I intended to go on the outward track for a week and left instructions to Jones to hoist a flag at the masthead and burn flares at 10pm each night, if he should return whilst I was away.

More wind and drift prevented us starting until the 26th. A sledge was packed with 14 days' provisions for eight men and we started off on the search expedition at 10am. We camped at 5.30pm after a march of nine miles. Before turning in for the night, I had a last look round and was delighted to see Jones and party about a mile away. It was now getting dark and we were within 200 yards before they saw us. They were anxious to get to the hut as they only had one serviceable tent. Kennedy and I offered to change with any of them (Watson had started the cooker as soon as the party was sighted) but they were all too eager for blankets and good beds, and decided to slog on, arriving at the base at midnight.

Jones reported that they had been stopped on their march on the sea ice, after doing 45 miles, by a badly broken glacier on the far side of which there was open sea. The only thing to do was to find a way on to the mainland, and in order to accomplish this, had come a long way back eastwards towards the base. They had bad weather and very rough travelling and when finally they succeeded in making an ascent, were stopped by a blizzard which lasted 17 days. One tent collapsed and the occupants, Jones, Dovers and Hoadley, had to dig a hole in the snow and lower the torn tent into it. This was 1000 feet above sea level and only 28 miles from the hut.

When the blizzard at last held up, they at once made their way to the sea ice and headed for home and when they met us had done 19 miles. They were all stiff and sore the next day and no wonder, a march of 28 miles, after 17 days in wet sleeping bags, is a very strenuous day's work.

Final arrangements were now made for the summer journey. Jones, Dovers and Hoadley, the Western Party, were to attempt to link up Queen Mary Land with Kaiser Wilhelm II Land, at Gaussberg, Kennedy and Watson to accompany me to the east. I had arranged that Harrisson and Moyes were to remain at the hut to do biological work and to carry on the meteorological observations. Later, Harrisson begged me to allow him to accompany me with the dogs as far as the Hippo depot. As on the return he would have to travel nearly 100 miles alone, I did not like the idea, but he demonstrated that he could erect a tent by himself so I agreed that he should come.

Each party was taking provisions for 14 weeks and I had a further supply for four weeks for Harrisson and the dogs, making a total load of 970 pounds.

We started on the Eastern journey on October 30th and arrived at the Hippo Nunatak on November 6th. Here we received a nasty shock. The sledge which we had left and buried two feet deep in hard snow and with a mound of snow six feet high built around it and stays attached to two heavy food bags, had completely disappeared, both stays being broken. This was serious as the total load to be carried amounted to well over 1,000 pounds, much too great a weight for one sledge. The only thing to do was to take Harrisson on, so that we could use his sledge, although that would leave Moyes alone under the belief that Harrisson had perished.

An extensive search was made for the missing sledge the next day, prospecting with a spade in possible snow drifts and crevasse lids and then we walked out fan-wise for several miles in the direction of the prevailing wind, with no result. I decided then to take Harrisson on. I was extremely sorry for Moyes, but I knew he was a level headed man and it could not be helped.

Hippo Nunatak was left behind the next day and the search into the unknown resumed. November 12th was an interesting day, although travelling was difficult over rippled ice, with many pressure hummocks and crevasses. The coast line was two miles on our right and was most beautiful with blue cascades and icefalls and numbers of outcrops of dark rocks. 15 miles ahead was an island 20 miles long, later named David Island.

On 14th, a depot was laid and Kennedy took a round of angles to make sure of its position. On the next two days, our course lay amongst pressure ridges and crevasses so numerous that the dogs could not be used and the sledges had to be lightened and several journeys made backwards and forwards over the most dangerous areas. One large lid fell in just as the sledge cleared it, leaving a hole 12 feet wide and hundreds of feet deep.

Our direct course east was now stopped by a glacier (Denman Glacier) 12 miles wide, rolling down in magnificent cascades from a height of at least 3,000 feet, breaking up the ice-shelf on which we were travelling to such an extent that nothing without wings could cross it. Our object was to map in the coastline as much as possible and I had to decide whether to go north or south. From our position, the north looked as though it smoothed out about 10 miles away, while to get round the head of the glacier appeared to be at least a 30 mile climb inland, so north we went.

There was half a mile of exceptionally bad travelling that afternoon and Kennedy said he felt like a fly walking on wire netting. The camp was pitched amongst pressure ridges with crevasses within a few yards on every side. On that night, as in many others in this disturbed area, sounds of movement were often heard. Sharp reports and dull booms and moans and groans went on all the time.

November 18th was bright and fine and we covered more than five miles to the north before lunch; then I went with Watson to mark out a road through some difficult broken country and came suddenly to the most wonderful sight I have ever seen. The Denman Glacier moves much more rapidly than the Shackleton Shelf and in tearing through the latter, breaks it up and also shatters its own sides. At the actual point of contact is an enormous cavern over 1,000 feet wide and 400 feet deep with crevasses at the bottom which appear to have no bottom. The sides splintered and gashed with caves of avery blue, from the palest blue to black and the whole thing glittering in the sun. Enormous blocks of solid ice forced high up into the air beyond. The whole was the wildest, maddest and yet the grandest thing imaginable.

The next two days we had falling snow and bad light, nothing could be seen but a white blanket above, below and around, so, with sudden death waiting for us in the bottomless crevasses in every direction, we remained in camp. This was followed by a blizzard which kept us confined two more days. We had all been suffering from sore lips through sun and wind and these four days gave them a chance to heal. Through the combined direct glare of the sun and reflected glare from the snow, one became far more sunburnt in the Polar Regions than in the tropics.

When the weather cleared, we climbed to the top of David Island, 900 feet, and from there we could see that for 12 miles to the north the road to the east was impossible, but beyond it appeared to become smoother and we decided to cross in that direction.

On the 24th, we marched over pressure ridges and crevasses and camped near an especially bad patch. Watson had the worst fall that day, dropping vertically 10 feet before his harness stopped him. I am now going to give a few extracts from my diary:-

"Monday - November 25th - a beautiful day so far as the weather and scenery are concerned, but a very hard one. We have been amongst "pressure" with a capital "p" all day, hauling up and lowering the sledges with an alpine rope and twisting and turning in all directions, with waves and hills, monuments, statues and fairy palaces in all directions, from a few feet to over 300 feet in height. It is impossible to see more than a few hundred yards ahead at any time, so we go on for a bit, then climb a peak or mound, choose a route then struggle on for another short stage."

"Tuesday - November 26th - another very hard day's work. The first half mile took three hours to cover; in several places we had to cut roads with ice axes and shovels, and also to build a bridge across a water lead. I never saw or dreamt of anything so gloriously beautiful as some of the stuff we came through this morning.

After lunch, the country changed entirely. In place of the confused jumble and crush we have had, we got into névé slopes; huge billows half a mile to a mile from crest to crest meshed with crevasses. We all had falls into these during the day, Harrisson dropping 15 feet. I received rather a nasty squeeze through falling into a hole while going downhill, the sledge running on to me before I could get clear. So far as we can see, the same kind of country continues and one cannot help thinking about having to return through this infernal mess. The day's distance was only 1,050 yards."

"Wednesday, November 27th - when I wrote last night about coming back,

I little thought it would be so soon. We turn back tomorrow for the simple reason we cannot go on any farther. In the morning for nearly a mile along a valley running south-east, the travelling was almost good, then our troubles commenced again.

Several times we had to resort to hand hauling through acres of pitfalls. The bridges of those that were covered were generally very rotten, except the very wide ones. Just before lunch, we had a very stiff uphill pull and then a drop into a large basin, three quarters of a mile in diameter. The afternoon was spent in a vain search for a road. On every side are huge waves split in all directions by crevasses up to 200 feet in width. The general trend of the main crevasses is north and south. I have therefore decided to go back and, if possible, follow the road we came by, then proceed south on to the inland ice-cap and find out the source of the chaos. If we are able to get round it and proceed east, so much the better; at any rate we shall be doing something and getting somewhere. We could push on further east from here, but it would be by lowering the gear piecemeal into chasms 50 feet to 100 feet deep, and hauling it up on the other side; each crevasse taking at least two hours to negotiate. For such slow progress, I don't feel justified in risking the lives of the party."

Snow fell for four days and it was useless to stir in our precarious position. The dogs' food had run out and we fed them on our own as I was anxious to keep them alive until we were out of the pressure. When at last we commenced the return, we found 18 inches of soft snow obliterated our former tracks and the bridged crevasses were entirely hidden and we had frequent falls through weak lids.

At 9am, Harrisson, Watson and I roped up to mark a course over a particularly bad place. We had only gone 200 yards when I got a very heavy jerk on the rope and looking round found Watson had disappeared. He weighed 200 pounds in his clothes and the crevasse into which he had fallen was 15 feet wide. He had broken through on the far side and the rope cutting through the bridge stopped in the middle so that he could not reach the sides to help himself in any way. Kennedy brought another rope and threw it down to him and we were then able to haul him up, but it was 20 minutes before he was out. He came up smiling and no worse, except for a bruised shin and the loss of a glove.

At 2.30pm, we were all dead beat and camped with less than a mile on the meter. The course was a series of Zs and Ss and hairpin turns, the longest straight stretch 150 yards, knee deep in soft snow and the sledge sinking to the cross bars.

The next day was a repetition, a terribly hard two and a half miles, with many painful falls into crevasses. One snow bridge, 10 feet wide, fell in as the meter was going over it. On the 5th December, we had to remain in camp, falling snow and drift making it impossible to travel."

From the diary again:-

"Friday, December 6th - still bad light and a little snowfall but we were off at 10am. I was leading and fell into at least a dozen crevasses. At 1.50pm, we arrived at the open land we had crossed on the outward journey and found the same place. There had been much movement and we had to make a bridge, cutting away projections and filling up the water channels with snow and ice; then Harrisson crossed with the aid of two bamboo poles, and hauled me over on a sledge. Harrisson and I on one side and Kennedy and Watson on the other then hauled the sledges backwards and forwards, lightly loaded one way and empty the other, until all were across. The glacier at this place was undoubtedly afloat. We camped tonight in the same place as on the evening of November 25th, so with luck we ought to be out of this mess tomorrow.

Switzerland had to be killed, as I cannot afford any more biscuit. Amundsen ate his flesh without hesitation but Zip refused it."

Two days later, we were again close to David Island. As we were camping a skua gull flew down and I snared him with a line, using dog flesh for bait. We had stewed skua for dinner. While I was cooking, the others climbed up the rocks and brought back eight snow petrels and five eggs. After supper, we secured 60 eggs and 58 birds. It seemed a fearful crime to kill these beautiful pure white creatures, but it meant 14 days life for the dogs and longer marches for us. The snow petrels' eggs are almost as large as hens' eggs. Many of them were partly hatched, but although they did not look so nice, they tasted as good as the fresh ones. I was very glad to get this fresh food, as owing to difficulty in obtaining seals and penguins, we had lived on tinned meats most of the year and there was always danger of scurvy.

The light was too bad to make a start until the evening of December 11th when we dodged through four and a half miles of tumbled ice and camped on the mainland for a midnight meal. There were advantages in travelling at night; the surface was firmer, our eyes were relieved from the intense glare and our blistered lips and faces healed up.

On the 14th December, while still on the lower slopes of the mainland, we came to two nunataks jutting out of the ice. At the first, "Possession Nunataks", we made a depot of spare gear and sufficient food to take us back to the Hippo. Our course was set on a sharp peak inland which was hidden as we ascended by the contour of the intervening ridges and it was not until we had reached an altitude of 3,000 feet that we saw it again. At this time, we were again pulling in daylight. The surface then became abominably soft, and hauling became a steady, dogged strain. On the 18th, we only did a little over four miles and on the 19th, the sledge was burying itself to the crossbars and pushing a mound of powdery snow in front of it. The peak now close ahead was named "Mount Barr Smith". It was fronted by a steep rise, which we decided to climb next day, but had to put it off for 24 hours as a blizzard came up.

The next day we set off to scale the mountain. 15 miles to the south was another and higher mountain, later called Mount Strathcona and the course of the Denman Glacier was between these two mountains, the immense weight of the inland ice squeezing it down through a steep valley.

Our tramp to the mountain from our camp was through eighteen inches to two feet of soft snow. A struggle to walk through, we knew from experience what it was like for sledging. There was only sufficient food for another week and the surface was so heavy that in that time, without allowance for blizzards, it would have been impossible to travel as far as we could see from the summit. Also, by turning back at that point, we stood a chance of saving the two remaining dogs who had worked so well they really deserved to live, so I decided to return.

The altitude of Mount Barr Smith was 4,320 feet. The latitude was 67° 10.4' and the distance from the hut in a bee line, 120 miles.

The return journey commenced on December 23rd, the snow was very sticky and frequent halts were made to scrape the sledge runners.

Christmas dinner was celebrated at the depot at the Possession Nunataks. After dinner, the Union Jack and Australian Ensign were hoisted and I formally took possession of the land in the name of the Expedition, for the Empire.

These rocks were garnetiferous gneiss and many of the garnets were as large as pigeons' eggs but all badly fractured. The surface becoming again very soft, night travelling was again resumed.

At 6am on the 28th, we camped under the lee of David Island. 56 snow petrels were caught and these with the eggs, which all contained chicks, were fed to the dogs.

Next day, we arrived at Hippo and found the depoted food in good condition; we continued on to the Avalanche rocks, camping about a mile away. While we were erecting our tents, several avalanches came down and after supper, Watson, Kennedy and I walked towards the rocks to try and get a photo of one falling, but they refused to oblige us.

We found the site of the hole, where we had spent five wretched days on the depot journey, and saw that one or more avalanches had thrown blocks of ice, weighing at least 20 tons each, 200 yards past and over the hole. They had thus travelled 600 yards from the cliff.

On January 2nd, we explored the Alligator Nunatak. It was a half mile long, 400 feet high and composed of gneiss like most of the rock we had seen. On the 4th, we made our best day's run for the trip - 22 miles, and the next day, assisted by a strong following wind, we carried on until 9pm hoping to reach the hut, but the wind increased to a heavy gale and we were forced to camp with 35 miles on the meter. After an hour's march next morning, we saw the wireless mast and soon afterwards the hut. Just before reaching home, we struck up a song and in a few seconds, Moyes came running out.

When he saw there were four of us, he stood on his head for joy and was so overcome with emotion; it was some time before he could talk to us.

As we expected, Moyes had never thought of Harrisson coming on with us and had quite given him up for dead. When the time had elapsed for which Harrisson had food, Moyes packed a sledge and went out for six days, then, realizing the hopelessness of searching for anyone in the white waste of nothingness, he returned. He looked well after nine weeks of loneliness, but said it was the worst time he had ever had in his life.

My orders were to be ready to embark on the "Aurora" on January 30th and preparations were commenced at once. Geological and biological collections were packed and the cases, as well as boxes containing personal gear, were sledged to the glacier edge.

Harrisson made a winch which was mounted on a small sledge for sounding and fishing; through a crack in the sea ice a quarter of a mile from the cliff, he found bottom at 260 fathoms, and also succeeded in trapping fish, a squid and other specimens from the bottom.

On the 21st, we sighted Jones's party coming in from the south and all went out to meet them, very soon shaking them by the hand and listening to their story.

They left the Grottoes on November 7th, heading for the depot left in the spring, which, owing to strong winds and a difficult surface, was not reached until 5.30pm on the 10th. The food picked up at the depot and the extra sledge brought their load up to 1,200 pounds which, of course, meant relay work.

The lower slopes were much too badly broken up to travel over and they were forced far inland and this, frequent gales and snowstorms made their progress painfully slow.

A few extracts from Jones's diary follow:-

"November 17th - the night's camp was situated approximately at the eastern edge of the Helen Glacier. The portion of the ice cap which contributes to the glacier below is marked off from the general icy surface on either side by a series of falls and cascades. These appeared impassable near sea level, but we hoped to find a smooth passage at an altitude of 1,000 feet."

"November 18th - a start was made at 7am. The surface consisted of ice and névé and was badly broken by pressure mounds, 10 feet to 20 feet high and by numerous crevasses old and recent, many with sunken or fallen bridges. While crossing a narrow crevasse, about 40 feet of the bridge collapsed lengthwise under the leading man, letting him fall to the full extent of his harness rope. Hoadley and myself had passed over the same spot unsuspecting and unroped, a few minutes previously while looking for a safe track................ by evening had one four miles.

The next day was gloriously bright with a breeze just strong enough to make hauling pleasant; erecting a sail we made an attempt to haul both sledges but found them too heavy. At 4pm, we arrived at what at first appeared to be an impasse.

At this point, three great crevassed ridges united to form the ice falls on the western side of the glacier. The point of confluence was the only place that appeared to offer any hope of a passage and as we did not want to retrace our steps, we decided to attempt it. The whole surface was a network of huge crevasses, some open, the majority from 50 feet to 100 feet or more in width. After many devious turns................ it was found that by travelling along a narrow, knife edge ridge of ice and névé, with an open crevasse on each side, a good surface could be reached within a mile.

The ridge had a gradient of one in ten and unfortunately also sloped down towards one of the open crevasses.

During the next four days, a heavy blizzard raged. There was a tremendous snowfall and after the second day, the snow was piled four feet high around the tent and by its pressure greatly reducing the space inside. By midday on the 23rd, the weather had improved sufficiently to allow us to move. The sledges and tent were excavated, the new level of the snow's surface being four to five feet higher than that on which the camp had been made four days earlier. While crossing the ridge of ice, one man hauled the sledges while the other two prevented them sliding sideways downhill into the open crevasse."

Over the type of surface described, these three men hauled their sledges to Gaussberg, a distance of 215 miles from base, but with relay work they covered over 300 miles.

At one time, on the outward journey, they got down to sea level, where they found an enormous rookery of Emperor penguins covering several acres of floe ice. Jones said the sound of their cries reminded him of a sports ground during a well contested game. Here, they also found Adelie penguins, Silver grey, Wilson and Antarctic petrels and Skua gulls, the eggs giving them a most welcome change of diet. The nesting place of the Antarctic petrel had not previously been found. Numbers of islands and rock outcrops were discovered and examined and on Christmas Day, they were on, and examining, Gaussberg, discovered by Drygalski in 1908. Gaussberg is an extinct volcano about 1,200 feet high and stands right on the margin of the continent, the northern slopes descending into the sea.

The return journey was commenced on December 26th and the party arrived at the hut on the afternoon of January 21st. The full story of this journey is in Mawson's "Home of the Blizzard" and was an achievement of which Jones, Dovers and Hoadley have a right to be proud.

It gave me great pleasure to hear of the success of this party and between us, we had charted about 400 miles of new land.

We were now looking forward to the return of the "Aurora", but in view of the possibility of her not being able to reach us, large numbers of seals were killed and two holes dug in the glacier near the hut, the blubber for fuel in one and the flesh in the other. The nearest crack in the sea ice where seals came up was two and a half miles away, a long and tedious pull with a heavy sledge.

In January, the weather was mostly fine and we often worked at our sledging and butchering in singlets and sometimes with the upper parts of our bodies bare. The highest shade temperature recorded was 37°F and several times 33°F.

February was a bad month and there was not one fine day until the 20th and by this time, we were all beginning to think seriously of being left here another year. At two places, I had erected direction boards close to the cliff edge, one at two miles and the other five miles north of the hut, and also fitted a lamp and reflector at the mast head which was lighted every night and would be visible at least eight miles.

On Saturday, February 22nd, an eighty mile blizzard kept us inside and we carried out the usual scrubbing and cleaning up. On Sunday, the wind dropped to a light breeze and looking out with the glasses after breakfast, I saw the sea ice had broken out to within a mile and a half of the hut. Harrisson's sounding sledge was within a few yards of the open water and Jones and I went out to bring it in. We had gone less than half a mile when we saw what at first appeared to be a penguin standing on some heavy pack-ice in the distance, but which we soon made out to be the mast head of the "Aurora".

It was evident that she would not be alongside for some time so Jones went back to tell the others to bring down a load of gear, and I went on to meet the ship. Before the "Aurora" reached the fast ice, all the party were down with two sledge loads, having covered the mile and a half in record time.

As the ship came alongside, we gave three hearty cheers for Captain Davis and were surprised at the subdued nature of the return cheers from the ship and an atmosphere of gloom over the whole ship's company and then we received the sad account of the death of Ninnis and Mertz. There was little time to exchange news before leaving as Captain Davis was naturally extremely anxious to start on the homeward journey. There was a hazardous voyage of 2,000 miles to be made and only a small amount of coal remained in the bunkers. It took but a few hours to rush our gear down, take in a supply of ice and then head away for home.

Before going on with the story, I would to pay a tribute to the good fellowship, industry, enthusiasm and loyalty of my comrades. During the whole of the expedition, under the most trying conditions, all duties were most cheerfully performed.

At the earliest opportunity, Captain Davis and I "swapped yarns". After leaving us on the Shackleton Ice Shelf the previous year, Davis had a few anxious days before clearing the ice and then a fairly good run to Hobart and from there to Sydney, where the "Aurora" was refitted. There was no loafing in pleasant harbours, however. Two extensive cruises were made in the seas south of New Zealand and Tasmania and all kinds of oceanographical work carried out and calls made at Macquarie and Auckland Islands, returning to Hobart about the middle of December, where preparations were made for the relief of Mawson's and my parties.

The "Aurora" left Hobart on December 24th and again ran into very heavy weather immediately after leaving harbour. Although heavily laden, Davis got her through with very little damage and after the usual bumping and grinding through pack ice, arrived and dropped anchor at the main base on January 13th.

Davis was handed a letter from Mawson to the effect that he had planned for all sledging parties to be back not later than January 15th and in the event of himself not returning, Davis was to take charge.

By the 18th, all parties had returned, except Mawson, Ninnis and Mertz. Davis decided to wait until the 30th if necessary; later than that would seriously endanger the relief of my party. In the meantime, it was arranged that if Mawson did not return, a party should remain to search and stores were landed for this party for another year. Madigan was to be in charge with Bage, McLean, Hodgeman, Bickerton and Jeffreys.

Bad weather ruled the whole of the time, making boat work difficult and dangerous. On two occasions, the cable parted and the engines were being driven at extra full speed for a whole week at one time to keep the "Aurora" near the land. The ship was coated thickly with ice up to the mast heads and at least 100 tons was covering the decks. Davis was on the bridge the whole of this time.

The morning of the 31st arrived and Captain Davis decided to pick up those of the shore party who were returning home and make for the western base. However, the wind came away again and communication with the shore was impossible until February 8th. Davis said he had never experienced such severe squalls before and he was expecting the masts and funnel to go overboard any minute.

At 11.30am on the 8th, the party was taken on board and the "Aurora" headed away west and at 8.30pm, a wireless message was received to say that Mawson had arrived at the base.

Davis at once altered course and returned to Commonwealth Bay, but was met by another heavy gale which rendered it impossible to lower a boat.

On an earlier page, I mentioned that Davis had not been at all satisfied about the safety of my position on what was undoubtedly moving ice, and the season was now so far advanced that not only was there a doubt of being able to reach us, but the ice conditions in that 1,500 miles were so appalling that there was the grave danger of losing the ship. Knowing that the main base party was well supplied for another year, Davis decided to delay no longer and headed away west on the evening of January 9th.

Mawson's book contains a full account of the dangers and difficulties and many narrow escapes the "Aurora" encountered before her arrival at my base. Captain Davis looked an old man, and had been on his feet on the bridge for so long that he had to bandage his legs to strengthen them.

It was some time before full details of the sad end of Ninnis and Mertz were received and of Mawson's marvellous lone return journey to the hut, not, in fact, until we arrived in Hobart. Previous to this we had all been shocked to hear of the tragedy and of Captain Scott and his party.

The account of that sledging journey on which Mawson lost his two companions, as written by him, is the most wonderful and amazing story of polar travel, of suffering, endurance and perseverance ever known.

At a point 2,400 feet above sea level, 315 miles from the base, Ninnis with a team of dogs and a sledge, went to eternity down a crevasse.

The lost sledge carried nearly all the men's food, all the dogs' food, the tent and greater part of the general equipment. All that was left was 10 days' men food, a sledge, cooker and tent cover, and six dogs in poor condition. No depots had been left as the intention was to return on another route. I cannot attempt to give a full account of the appalling sufferings to which these men were subjected, but will give a few short extracts from Mawson's own story.

George, one of the dogs, was killed to provide food for the other dogs and to eke out their own supply, but it was very stringy and lacked nourishment. Then followed day after day of hard work and hunger, dog after dog being sacrificed as they became too weak to travel and on Christmas Day only one, Ginger, was still alive. At this time, the total weight of food consumed per day was 14 ounces, consisting mainly of dog meat, an ounce or two of chocolate or raisins, three or four ounces of pemmican and biscuit mixed, and very dilute cocoa to drink. The usual sledging ration is over two pounds of concentrated rich food.

On December 26th, Ginger could walk no longer and was dispatched. Mawson writes, "As we worked on a system which aimed at using up the bony parts of the carcass first, it happened that Ginger's skull figured as the dish for the next meal. As there was no instrument capable of dividing it, the skull was boiled whole and a line drawn round it marking it into right and left halves. These were drawn for, after which, passing the skull from one to the other, we took turns in eating our respective shares. The brain was certainly the most appreciated and nutritious section; Mertz, I remember well, remarking specially upon it. Before retiring to the sleeping bag, I spent another four hours cracking and boiling down bones with the object of extracting the nutriment for future use and at the same time, ridding the load of a lot of useless waste in the form of inert bone."

Follows three days of plodding along over varying surfaces and then Mawson discovered that Mertz was failing rapidly and talking things over, they decided to leave the dog meat alone for a time and go solely upon the ordinary food, of which they had some days supply still in hand. Mawson says, "I will always remember the wonderful taste the food had in those days. Acute hunger enhances the taste and smell of food beyond all ordinary conception. The flavour of food under such conditions is a miracle altogether unsuspected by the millions of mortals who eat their fill."

The struggle continued in wind and drift both men weakening rapidly and on January 3rd, Mertz developed dysentery and for the first time, his fingers were badly frost bitten. He had always been so resistant to cold he could not believe it until he bit a considerable piece off one of them.

On the 4th and 5th, a blizzard kept them in their wet sleeping bags, under the miserable make-shift tent. On the 6th, there was a following wind and the grade was downhill, but the surface was slippery and falls were frequent, which told severely upon Mertz who at last, was persuaded by Mawson to ride on the sledge. After two and a half miles, he became so chilled that they had to camp. From Mawson's account again:-

"Starvation, combined with superficial frost bite, alternating with the damp conditions in the sleeping bags, had by this time resulted in a wholesale peeling of the skin all over our bodies; in its place only a very poor unnourished substitute appeared which readily rubbed raw in many places. As a result of this, the chafing of the march had already developed large raw patches in just those places where they were most troublesome. As we never took off our clothes, the peelings of hair and skin from our bodies worked down into our underclothing and socks and regular clearances were made from the latter….. The night of the 6th was long and wearisome as I tossed about sleeplessly….. I was aching to get on, but there could be no question of abandoning my companion whose condition now set the pace."

The next day was moderately fine but Mertz was too weak to be moved and was unable to assimilate the food which Mawson prepared for him, and shortly after midnight, he went to sleep.

The hut was still 100 miles away, a stiff proposition over very broken and crevassed country and the task of pitching and breaking camp alone in high winds was most difficult. Mawson piled a mound of snow over the body of Mertz and erected a rough cross.

The 9th and 10th were blizzard days and Mawson was not able to move until the 11th. He says, "From the start, my feet felt curiously lumpy and sore. They had become so painful after a mile of walking that I decided to examine them on the spot, sitting on the lee of the sledge in brilliant sunshine. I had not had my socks off for some days for, while lying in camp, it had not seemed necessary. On taking off the third and inner pair of socks, the sight of my feet gave me quite a shock, for the thickened skin of the soles had separated in each case as a complete layer, and abundant watery fluid had escaped, saturating the sock. The new skin beneath was very much abraded and raw. Several of my toes had commenced to blacken and fester near the tips and the nails were puffed and loose….. I smeared the new skin with lanoline, of which there was fortunately a good store, and then with the aid of bandages, bound the old skin casts back in place for these were comfortable and soft in contact with the abraded surface. Over the bandages were slipped six pairs of thick woolen socks, fur boots and finally crampon overshoes, the latter having large stiff soles, spread the weight nicely and saved my feet from the jagged ice encountered shortly afterwards."

So this nightmare of a march went on. Hours each day, Mawson spent doctoring his feet and other raw patches, festering fingernails and inflamed frost bitten nose. On several days, blizzards made marching impossible and on the 17th, he had a miraculous escape from death in a crevasse.

How Mawson managed to struggle out and his subsequent superhuman exertions and incredible sufferings make such a breath taking story as had never been or since been written.

On January 29th, another miracle happened. Mawson says, "I was travelling along on an even down grade and was wondering how long the two pounds of food, which remained, would last, when something dark loomed up through the haze of the drift a short distance away to the right. All sorts of possibilities raced through my mind as I headed the sledge for it. The unexpected had happened - in thick weather, I had run fairly into a cairn of snow blocks erected by McLean, Hodgeman and Hurley, who had been out searching for my party. On the top of the mound outlined in black hunting was a bag of food, left on the chance it might be picked up by us ……. On reading the enclosed note carefully, I found that I had just missed the party by six hours.

On February 1st, Mawson reached what was named "Aladdin's Cave", a comfortable dugout on the mountain side, five and a half miles from the hut, and there he was kept prisoner a whole week by a fierce blizzard. On February 8th, the weather cleared and he was able to descend the slope, being met by the party before his arrival at the hut. Mawson says, "My heart was deeply touched by the devotion of these men who thus faced a second year of the rigours and extreme discomfort of the Adelie Land blizzard. For myself, that wonderful occasion was robbed of complete joy by the absence of my two gallant companions, and as we descended to the hut, there were moist eyes amongst the little party as they learnt of the fate of Ninnis and Mertz."

How Captain Davis received the news of Mawson's return and failed in his attempt to pick up the party has already been told.

Whilst exchanging our experiences on the voyage to Hobart, it almost appeared that we of the western base had had a year's picnic as far as the weather was concerned, compared with that experienced at the main base. For a whole year, their average wind velocity was 50 miles an hour; compare this with Europe's average of 10.1. Their highest monthly average was 63, highest daily 98, highest hourly 116, and a puffometer showed gusts of 200 miles an hour.

Although we could not compete with them in this respect, we held the record for the longest blizzard - 17 days - the one which caught Jones and his depot laying party.

On my eastern sledging journey, I managed to bring back two dogs alive. This could not have been done had we not fortunately found nesting snow petrels on David Island. For the last 100 miles of the journey, the dogs were allowed to run free. When we returned to the base, these two dogs, Amundsen and Zip, were woefully thin and weak, all their ribs showing and backbones sticking up like sharp wedges. At the base, there was an abundance of food for them and they gorged day and night, putting on weight at a surprising rate. When we arrived at Hobart, they were as fat as butter.

I gave Amundsen to a friend in Hobart. There happened to be a heat wave on at the time we arrived and the dogs suffered terribly. My friend, MacDonald, packed ice all around Amundsen's kennel, but the combination of atmospheric heat and his own fat was too much and he died of heat apoplexy. Zip was taken on to Sydney and given to a lady who kept him for several years. Zip has long been gathered to his fathers but his children, down to many generations, are still living in and around Sydney.

Soon after my arrival in Sydney, I met Bernard Day, who was in charge of the motor tractors on Captain Scott's expedition and he gave me many details and particulars. Amongst other things, he told me that an insufficient supply of paraffin had been left at the depots, upon which Scott had to rely on his return from the South Pole. This shortage is mentioned in Scott's diary and no doubt was one of the causes of their breakdown.

I spent a very happy holiday in Sydney, making many new friends and renewing acquaintance with old ones, amongst the latter was Professor David. The Professor arranged for us to give a lecture to the Royal Society, to which the elite of Sydney were invited. I was the guest of the parents of Hannam, the expedition's wireless expert, and two days before the lecture, the whole family and I went down with ptomaine poisoning. On the day of the lecture, I was so ill that I would certainly have remained in bed had it not been for letting Professor David down. I was still deeply tanned from the effects of the Antarctic sun, and nearly all the people to whom I was introduced remarked, "My word, you do look well; the Antarctic has not done you any harm." Anyone familiar with Ptomaine knows the frightful sudden spasms of intense pain in the stomach. Whilst giving my address, I had several of these seizures and had to hang on to the desk on the platform and for some seconds, was unable to speak. As I was talking without notes, I have no doubt the audience thought I was at a loss for words. The thing that hurt me the most was having to say, "No thank you" to all the delicious refreshments which were provided after the lecture.

It was with great regret that I said "goodbye" to my comrades and all Australian friends and embarked on the "SS Macedonia", the same ship on which I had made the outward journey, to join the expedition, and was more than pleased to be warmly greeted by many of the same ship's company.

In the foregoing pages, I have said nothing of the trials and tribulations of Mawson and his party during their second year in the "Home of the Blizzard" nor of the work done by the several sledging parties at the main base. Neither have I mentioned anything of the strenuous times experienced by Ainsworth and his party during their two years on Macquarie Island. Full accounts of all this may be found in Mawson's own book.

The voyage to England on the "Macedonia" was very ordinary, the only thing I can remember worth recording was passing through miles upon miles of dead locusts in the Red Sea; they were so thick that although there was a fresh breeze, the sea was as smooth as though covered by a heavy oil.

Returning from India many years ago on the ill-fated "Egypt", I had a remarkable experience in the Suez Canal. The tables were all laid for dinner and being in the canal, they were specially laid with all the best glass and other tableware and floral decorations. Just as the bugler was sounding "The Roast Beef of Old England", the ship suddenly gave a tremendous roll to port and everything shot off the tables with a terrific crash. I believe hundreds of pounds of damage was done, several passengers and members of the ship's company received bruises and one fireman was killed. It appeared that bad steering or a wrong order by the pilot had resulted in the ship running on the bank of the canal. It was several hours before she was hauled off.

For some time after my arrival home, I was kept busy writing the story of my experiences on Queen Mary Land to be included in Mawson's "Home of the Blizzard".

When I named the new land discovered by me and my party "Queen Mary Land", I was ignorant of the fact that I ought first to have obtained permission from their Majesties to do so. In 1914, I received a message asking me to go to the Royal Geographical Society's headquarters. Arriving there, I was met by three gentlemen, two knights and a commoner, who informed me that I had committed a very grave breach of etiquette in neglecting this most important formality. Sometime later, I had the honour of an audience with His Most Gracious Majesty, King George V. Amongst other questions King George asked was, "Where were you when Scott died?" I replied, "On Queen Mary Land Sir, and I believe I owe you and Her Majesty an apology for so naming it without your permission." The King said, "Oh, did you think that necessary?" I replied, "I did not, Sir, but I was told it was a gross breach of etiquette not to do so." The King asked sharply, "Who told you so?" I gave the names and His Majesty said, "You may tell them from me that I was pleased and the Queen was pleased and they know nothing whatever about it." Needless to say, I lost no time in conveying the King's message to the three gentlemen concerned.

During the winter of 1913 - 1914, I made another extensive lecturing tour. The bugbear of all lecturers is the prosy long-winded Chairman. Usually, the more ignorant the man is, the longer he speaks, often making ridiculous false statements that have to be contradicted by the lecturer. When lecturing to a Literary Society in Paisley, I was asked would I mind doing without a chairman, and I said I would be delighted. I was then told that it had been the custom for the members of the Committee to take it in turns to act as Chairman. Sir Robert Ball was giving a lecture on the Moon and the man whose turn it was to be Chairman swotted up the Moon, and spoke for three-quarters of an hour, then asked Sir Robert Ball to carry on. Sir Robert rose and said, "Mr Chairman, Ladies and Gentlemen, I came here tonight with the intention of giving a lecture on the Moon, but as your Chairman has already given the lecture, nothing remains for me to say but goodnight," and walked off the platform.

I have given many hundreds of lectures and have only once been late. This was at a place about 20 miles from Edinburgh and I motored there with friends from Edinburgh. We lost our way and arrived at the lecture hall over an hour late. To my surprise, the audience was still there and after apologizing for my late appearance, I remarked upon this extraordinary patience and was told, "You don't seem to realise you are in Scotland, these people have paid for their tickets and they want their value."

About the same time that I returned to England after Mawson's Expedition, Sir Ernest Shackleton commenced preparations for another Antarctic Expedition and asked me to accompany him as his Second In Command. His main object was to cross the Antarctic Continent, starting from the Weddell Sea, crossing the Pole and continuing on to the Ross Sea. His intention was to land a party of 14 men in the Weddell Sea area, six to make the trans-continental journey, three to go westward, three eastward and two to remain at the base. Two ships were necessary to carry out Shackleton's programme. The "Endurance", a new ship built in Norway specially constructed for Polar work, was to carry the Weddell Sea party, and the "Aurora", bought from Dr Mawson, was to proceed to McMurdo Sound, under the command of Aeneas Macintosh (who it will be remembered lost an eye on Shackleton's "Nimrod" Expedition), and a party to be landed there to run out food depots as far as the Beardmore Glacier, so that the trans-continental party would be safe as regards food for the last 400 miles. All details of this Expedition will be found in Shackleton's book "South".

Although Shackleton commenced his preparations in the middle of 1913, there was no public announcement until January 1914. Immediately applications to join the expedition came pouring in and amounted in all to nearly 5,000. For a long time, I had the task of replying to these. The majority was from totally unsuitable people and I had cards printed "Sir Ernest Shackleton regrets, etc" If any letter appealed to me, I showed it to Shackleton and if he also thought well of it, an appointment was made. 14 of these applications were from women, and one was a joint one from two young women and was so well written that I made an appointment instead of sending the usual card. Unfortunately, Shackleton came to my desk that afternoon and whilst talking, was idly turning over the letters and, noting this particular one, asked, "Friends of yours?" I have never been able to tell a lie on the spur of the moment and replied, "No, an applicant." Said he, "Card, I suppose." I truthfully replied that I had made an appointment, and he said, "No you don't old man, I'm married," so a card had to be sent and I never saw the fair writers.

Amongst the equipment were two tractors for hauling sledges, one driven by an aero propeller and the other a caterpillar. Shackleton had also devised a new type of tent and made considerable alterations in the foodstuffs for sledging parties. These were all taken to Finse in the mountainous part of Norway, between Bergen and Oslo. Here a party of us spent a very interesting time testing the tractors, tents and food. For the tent and food test, I was put in charge of six men to camp out and make sledge journeys daily over the mountains in the vicinity, the conditions being similar to what we could expect in summer in the Antarctic. We left the hotel after lunch one day and camped about five miles away. The following morning, Sir Harry Britten, a volunteer member, deserted and went back to the hotel saying "your beds are too hard." At the end of three days, the party was reduced to two; Dobbs and myself, and we stuck it out until recalled by Shackleton. Both the sledge tractors proved satisfactory in their trial runs on a frozen lake near the hotel and altogether the trip was both successful and enjoyable.

We returned to England on the SS "Eskimo" and one London newspaper said, "Sir Ernest Shackleton has returned from Norway bringing with him an Eskimo dog driver."

Shackleton purchased 70 dogs from the Hudson Bay Company and engaged an experienced driver to bring them to England and to accompany the Expedition. Shortly after this man's arrival, he was asking us all about conditions in the Antarctic. When he learnt there were no trees, no moss, no grass, he asked in a surprised tone, "What do the moose live on?" and when I told him there were no moose or any other animals, he said, "Hell, I'm off back North", and he went.

Shortly before the "Endurance" left London, we were honored by a visit and inspection by Queen Alexandra, accompanied by Lady Knollys, Lord Fisher and several other distinguished people. Shackleton very kindly allotted to me the duty of guide to the Queen. After the inspection, Her Majesty told Lady Knollys to take a photograph. Everybody fell in on either side and behind the Queen, Shackleton on her right and Lord Fisher on her left, when, just as the picture was about to be taken, Her Majesty called out, "Where is Mr Wild?" I was at the back and replied, and the Queen said, "Come here beside me," and pushing Lord Fisher away, she took my arm and then commanded the photo to be taken. I felt seven feet tall.

Everything was ready at the end of July and it was arranged for the "Endurance" to proceed to Cowes where His Majesty King George would pay a visit of inspection. These arrangements were upset by the imminence of war. The ship left London on August 1st and put in at Margate. There Sir Ernest heard of the order for general mobilization. He mustered all hands and said that he proposed to send a wire to the Admiralty offering the ship, stores and our own services. This message was sent and within an hour, a reply from the Admiralty arrived with the one word, "Proceed". A little later, Mr Winston Churchill wired thanking Shackleton for his offer and saying that the authorities desired the expedition to go on.

The "Endurance" then sailed to Plymouth and the King sent for Shackleton and gave him a Union Jack to carry on the expedition, and on Saturday, August 8th, the "Endurance" left Plymouth obeying the direct orders of the Admiralty and the King's Command.

To save the dogs a long sea voyage in cramped quarters on the "Endurance",

Shackleton arranged that they should go to Buenos Aires on the "La Negra", a 12,000 ton cargo ship, carrying a few passengers.

I travelled in charge, having with me as assistants Sir Daniel Gooch - an old friend of Shackleton's, Wordie - Geologist and James - Physicist, of the Expedition and one of the staff from Hackbridge Dogs' Home, where the dogs had been lodged during their stay in England. We all signed on as ABs, at a shilling a month, but our duties on board were confined to looking after the dogs and our accommodation was the best on the ship. When we arrived at Buenos Aires, Sir Daniel Gooch insisted on receiving his discharge and shilling, both of which he had framed.

These dogs, huskies, are of great variety, both in appearance and character. They are a mixture of wolf and almost any kind of big dog, Collie, Mastiff, Great Dane, Bloodhound, Newfoundland, Retriever, Airedale, Boarhound etc. Very few of them are dangerous to man if properly handled, but fight fiercely among themselves. When they were embarked in Liverpool, the stevedores would not go near them, and Gooch and the dog-man (I forget his name) and I had to take them all out of their crates to their kennels on the after well deck of the "La Negra".

The care of the dogs was almost a whole time job. At 6am, the stewards served us with tea and at 6.10am, I gave the order to "turn to". The sailors objected to washing down the dog deck, so that was our first duty; then the dogs were fed and watered, by which time our own breakfast time had arrived. On the second morning after leaving port, the two Scientists did not make an appearance and at 6.30am, I went to their cabin to enquire the reason. One of them said, "We have not had our tea yet." This being strictly against discipline, I put the hose through their port and washed them out and had no subsequent trouble.

After breakfast, sick dogs were attended to and each day, a few were combed and brushed, then a few at a time were allowed an exercise run. This usually ended in having to separate a mound of fighting dogs.

I remember one day all the passengers, about 15, were assembled at the rail overlooking the after well deck when a particularly bad fight occurred, in which at least a dozen dogs were involved. The Scientists were no good in a fight and Sir Daniel, the dog-man and I were struggling desperately for more than half an hour before we got them all separated and kenneled up. Gasping for breath, I happened to look up and saw no passengers. The Chief Engineer was standing there grinning and I asked, "Where are all the passengers?" He replied, "If you could have heard your own and Sir Daniel's language, you wouldn't ask."

At 11am, I gave the order "pipe down" and no more work was done until 5pm when the dogs were watered and fed. Occasionally one or more dogs got loose, when a fight inevitably started. If only one dog was loose, the dog-man attended to it, his cabin being conveniently situated, but if more than one, he blew his whistle and Gooch and I would go and give a hand. The sailors and firemen prudently gave them a wide berth.

There never was a better disciplined AB afloat than Sir Daniel Gooch, either in the Royal Navy or the Merchant Service. When I called "turn to" in the morning, he always replied, "Aye aye Sir," and was the first on duty. He obeyed all orders promptly and cheerfully and some of our work was too filthy to write about. When dogs escaped at night, he generally heard the dog-man's whistle and was on the spot wrestling with the snarling, fighting demons before I was. He was possessed of a keen sense of humour and was a delightful companion. When I gave the 11am order "pipe down", he usually came to me and saluting asked, "Are we off duty now Sir?" I would reply in the affirmative when he would bang me on the shoulder and shout "Righto you old blighter, come and have a spot." As we were generally very dirty at that time, the "spot" was taken in the Chief Engineer's cabin, he almost without fail having one waiting on the ice.

Sir Daniel made his final voyage over the Styx some eight years ago, and Moore, the Chief Engineer, was on the "Belgian Prince" during the Great War when she was torpedoed by an enemy submarine. As the ship was sinking and all hands had taken to the boats, the submarine came up and ordered everybody to come aboard. The boats were then stove in, the life belts taken away, the submarine's crew went below and then they submerged. The third engineer happened to be a very powerful swimmer and was picked up many hours after, or the fate of the "Belgian Prince" would never have been known.

There is a large, fairly wealthy and very friendly British community in Buenos Aires and during the short time we stayed there, we received considerable entertainment. Our officers and Scientists played a cricket match against the Burlingham Sports Club and beat them by one run, but I have always suspected the score was faked in our favour.

The voyage to South Georgia was very pleasant, good weather all the way. We anchored near the wharf of the whaling station in Cumberland Bay and made quite a long stay there, Shackleton having important structural alterations made to the main deck accommodation which greatly added to our comfort. The dogs were landed and tethered on the side of a hill to a long wire hawmer which was stretched in lines up and down the hill. Each dog was given room enough to allow him a good run, but not long enough to enable him to fight with his neighbours; the 70 dogs therefore covered a large area. There were numbers of rats on the island and these gave the dogs much sport and excitement, but alas, we later found the rats had communicated to the dogs a horrible intestinal worm, which proved fatal to several of them.

It was essential for some of us to be near the dogs all the time in case any get loose and six of us were allowed the use of the station hospital which was fairly close to the dog lines and was at the time empty. Two men were on watch day and night using a small shelter built in the lines, but the whole party worked together at feeding time. The dogs were fed principally on whale meat and enjoyed it exceedingly. The flesh of the whale forms a large proportion of the diet of the men at these whaling stations. In appearance, it is like beef but has a slightly coarser grain and is much more tender. The Norwegians use a lot of it and I have often wondered why other nations do not follow their example.

The island of South Georgia is mountainous, many peaks rising four to five thousand feet. It is always heavily snow-clad and glaciated, the lower slopes only becoming free of snow in the summer months, and these are covered with tussock grass. A stream of thaw water ran past the hospital and Dr Macklin took a bath in it each morning. I took the temperature of the water which was just below 32°F. What hardy people these Scots are!

Sir Daniel Gooch returned to England from here and we were all exceedingly sorry to lose him.

When the "Endurance" sailed from South Georgia on December 5th, she was very heavily laden and had a deck cargo of coal and several tons of whale meat hanging in the rigging for dog food. The weather favoured us and on the 7th, we met our first pack ice, close to the Sandwich Islands. This ice was particularly heavy and gave the ship some severe bumps. Clearing this we had two days good travelling before again encountering ice. Loose pack kept the officer of the watch on the alert and the man at the wheel busy and on the 14th, we ran into heavy pack again, and a heavy gale sprang up and made the ship unmanageable, so we hove to under the lee of a very large floe.

All members of the landing party took part in the general working of the ship and some of them made really good sailors. When I was on watch, I always liked to have Marston or Macklin at the wheel.

I have not yet introduced the party and will do so now:-

Sir Ernest Shackleton Leader

F Wild	Second in Command
Crean	In charge of all sledging gear. Crean was on both of Scott's Expeditions and is spoken of very highly by Scott. On the last of these expeditions, he and Lashley saved the life of Commander Evans (now Admiral).
Clark	Biologist
Hussey	Meteorologist
Hurley	Photographer (was on Mawson's Expedition)
Wordie	Geologist
James	Physicist

Lees   In charge of motors and stores
Macklin   Doctor and Bacteriologist
Marston   Artist
McIlroy   Surgeon

The above comprised the Landing Party

Worsley   Captain
Hudson   Navigator
Greenstreet First Officer
Cheetham   Second Officer
Rickenson   Chief Engineer
Kerr   Second Engineer
McNeish   Carpenter
Green   Cook

The above comprised the Ship's Crew

There were also eight sailors and firemen, Blackborrow the youngest man aboard, being a stowaway.

We found the Weddell Sea to be much more difficult for navigation than the Ross Sea. A great detail of the pack ice through which we had to force our way, was many years old and from 20 feet to 60 feet thick.

On Christmas Day, we were held up by a gale and impenetrable pack, but Crean put up a very fine dinner and in the evening, we had a concert. On New Year's Day, we had penetrated well into the Weddell Sea and had worked through nearly 500 miles of pack ice.

On January 10th, Coats Land, discovered by Dr William Bruce in 1904 on the "Scotia" Expedition, was sighted and a possible landing place was seen, but this was only 78° 18'S latitude and Shackleton was desirous to make a base in Luitpold Land, discovered by Fitchner in 1912 and nearly 300 miles further south. New land was seen and named by Shackleton "Caird Coast".

Blizzards and exceedingly heavy pack ice made our progress very slow and on several days when we were hopelessly jammed up, we took the opportunity of exercising the dogs, taking in ice for fresh water and a number of the party had a game of football on the level floe. Seals and penguins were often seen and a number were killed for food for men and dogs. At this time many of the dogs were ailing and one had to be shot.

There was no summer that year in the Weddell Sea, even in January when temperatures up to and above freezing point may be expected, the thermometer was frequently below zero, our lowest being -17°F.

On January 20th, we were so firmly enclosed by the pack that no movement was possible and from the mast head not a sign of open water could be seen. We could see the land we were making for about 40 miles away, but so far as affecting a landing was concerned; it might as well have been 4,000. Shackleton was, of course, bitterly disappointed at this check to his plans, but for several weeks, he was optimistic about being able to get free and I encouraged this feeling as much as possible. Worsley was not always as tactful as might be and one day, early in February, Shackleton, Worsley and I were walking around near the ship and coming to a large level floe several hundred yards square, Worsley stopped and said, "Oh boys, what a jolly fine football ground this will make." Shackleton said, "Well Wuzzles, I have about given up hope of getting out this year but you needn't rub it in so cheerfully."

As we could do nothing to help ourselves, fires were drawn to save coal and on February 24th, the ordinary ship routine ceased and the "Endurance" became a winter station. For the past month, whenever seals or penguins were seen, parties had been sent out to despatch them and bring them in; Worsley usually guiding the parties by signals from the mast head, the ice hummocks being too high to see any distance on the surface.

The dogs were put on the ice, their kennels being built in a circle a few yards away from the ship so that they might be easily found in bad weather. They were divided into six teams which were handled by Crean, Macklin, McIlroy, Marston, Hurley and myself. By this time, we had lost 15 dogs and post mortems showed that the cause of death was, in most cases, the worms with which they had been infected from the rats on South Georgia.

The cabins under the poop, which were occupied by the Officers and Scientists, were too cold to live in, so all stores were taken from the 'tween decks, which were made into a living and dining room. The stove, which had been intended for the landing party, was erected, cubicles built on each side and the place made quite snug. All meals were taken thereafter in "The Ritz" instead of the wardroom, this being fitted up into four cubicles and occupied by myself, Worsley, Crean and Marston. Shackleton alone retained his cabin right aft.

Time was found for recreation as well as work and many a good game of hockey and football was contested before the sun left us and a few games of football were played by moonlight. During the winter, we had chess, draughts, cards, dominoes etc and it was a rule to hold a concert on Saturday nights and this rule was very seldom broken.

Observations were taken for position as regularly as possible which showed our drift to be North West. Many icebergs were in sight at all times and some of these were a frequent source of anxiety. The pack ice drifts with the wind, but an iceberg 250 feet high, which is quite common, goes down to a depth of 2,000 feet. With all this bulk under water, the berg is more affected by currents than by the wind, and often travels in a totally different direction from that taken by the pack ice, and tears its way through the latter at a great rate, at times throwing up a churning wave of ice 60 feet high and creating a disturbance for miles. If a ship happened to be in track of one of these monsters, she would, of course, be crushed like an eggshell. Several of them came within a few miles of the "Endurance" whilst she was frozen in, so close that we could hear the thunderous roar of the crushing pack ice and sometimes feel a tremor.

After the dogs were trained, trips were made to icebergs that were within easy distance, for the sake of the geologist and the photographer. The training of a team of dogs requires much patience. I was nearly three months training my own team, but at the end of that time, I could sit on the sledge and drive in any direction by word of mouth and for days at a time, had no occasion to use a whip. My leader was a bloodhound and wolf cross, named Soldier because of his red coat, and he could follow a month old track with a foot of snow over it. Numbers of times I have taken the team out seven or eight miles, then given the order "Home Soldier" and have actually gone to sleep on the sledge and wakened up to find myself alongside the ship. The dogs loved these trips and when they saw their drivers approaching with the harness, they would jump around and yelp and tremble with excitement.

On May 1st, the sun left us and at that time, Shackleton wrote in his diary, "One feels our helplessness as the long winter night closes on us. By this time, if fortunate had smiled on the Expedition, we would have been comfortably and securely established on a shore base, with depots laid to the south and plans made for the long march in the spring and summer. Where will we make a landing now? Time alone will tell. I do not think any member of the Expedition is disheartened by our disappointment. All hands are cheery and busy and will do their best when the time for acting comes."

On May 15th, we held our "Antarctic Derby" in which all dog teams took part. The course was under half a mile and was run against time, so it was impossible to find a course free enough of pressure and hummocks for the teams to run abreast. Mine was the lightest team but was the favourite and the bookies had a bad day, as my time - two minutes nineteen seconds - was ten seconds better than any others. Hurley had a heavy team and challenged me to another race with seven dogs and a load of 910 lbs, or 150 lbs a dog, this to include a passenger. Again I was the favourite and this time my time was two minutes nine seconds against Hurley's two minutes thirty seconds, but I was disqualified as my passenger, Shackleton, fell off 10 yards from the winning post. He was most disgusted with himself and insisted on paying all bets.

During the winter, we were frequently visited by blizzards which kept us aboard, the worst one lasting from the 15th to 18th July, with a low temperature

-21°F to 35°F. During the blow, we had our first serious alarm from pressure. Many times in the past, we had heard the roar of distant pressure, and had seen ridges formed of huge blocks, 10 feet to 30 feet thick, thrown up to a height of 50 feet to 60 feet, but none nearer than a mile until now, when a huge ridge formed 300 yards away and the ship was severely shaken.

The break-up of the actual floe in which we were embedded came exactly a year after the "Endurance" left London, August 1st. Shackleton ordered all dogs and sledges to be brought on board as the ice was cracking close to the ship and masses were being driven under the keel, giving the ship a heavy list to starboard. The turmoil continued all day, the ship lifting several feet at times and listing over one way after the other.

The sight of this ice battle around us was most impressive, huge blocks as big as houses squeaked slowly into the air and sometimes giving a jump like an orange pip or cherry stone squeezed between thumb and finger. We knew that if we got actually in the line of pressure, nothing could save us. A heavy gale was blowing from the south and on August 3rd, an observation showed that we had made a good drift to the north.

By this time, the pressure had quietened down and we were able to see that the rudder was seriously damaged.

During the month of August, we drifted close past the charted position of Morell Land but saw no sign of it and soundings showed a fairly uniform depth of nearly 2,000 fathoms. The sun had now returned and as we had no pressure alarms for some time, the training and exercising of the dogs was resumed.

September was almost gone before another serious upheaval, though towards the end of the month we could see and hear approaching pressure, and on the 30th, we found ourselves badly caught. The ship shuddered, bent and groaned like a living thing and just when it seemed she must be crushed, she lifted and for some hours rode on top of the ice, until the pressure eased and allowed her to settle back into the water.

All through October these attacks were frequent and on one occasion, the "Endurance" was lifted 12 feet and thrown on to her side on the top of the ice, all within five seconds. She remained high and dry at an angle of about 40° for eight hours. Dinner was amusing, the diners sitting on deck with their feet against the bulkheads. At 8pm the ice opened and the ship settled back into the water, having suffered no damage.

On the 24th, the ship was again very roughly handled and it was evident that the end was not far distant, a bad leak had started and was barely kept under by the bilge pumps, steam had been raised that morning.

Shackleton writes, "I scarcely dared to hope any longer that the "Endurance" would live and during that anxious day, I revived all my plans for the sledging journey which we should have to make if we had to take to the ice. Stores, dogs, sledges and equipment were ready to be moved from the ship at a moment's notice.

The morning of the 26th was bright and clear, but the roar of the pressure continued. At 7pm, very heavy pressure developed, with twisting strains which racked the ship fore and aft. The planking was opened four to five inches on the starboard side and at the same time, we could see the ship bending like a bow under titanic pressure. Almost like a living creature, she resisted the forces which would crush her; but it was a one-sided battle. Millions of tons of ice pressed inexorably upon her. She was now leaking badly and at 9pm, I gave the order to lower boats, gear, provisions and sledges to the floe and move them to the flat ice a little way from the ship."

"The attack of the ice reached its climax at 4pm on the 27th. The ship was hove up by the pressure and the driving floe, moving literally across the stern, split the rudder and tore out the rudder post and stern post. Then, while we watched, the ice loosened and the "Endurance" sank a little. The decks were breaking upwards and the water was pouring in below and I ordered all hands on to the ice. At last the twisting, grinding floes were working their will on the ship. It was a sickening sensation to feel the decks breaking up under one's feet, the great beams bending and snapping with a noise of heavy gun fire."

"The "Endurance" sunk until her upper deck was two feet under water and then the ice pierced her sides and held her from sinking further. Masses of ice then rode over the decks carrying away the bulwarks and rigging and down came the masts. By this time, all stores had been taken to flat ice about 100 yards from the ship and as we started to pitch a camp, the ice commenced to split and crush under us and all gear had to be rushed across heaving ice to a bigger floe a quarter of a mile away. Here the tents were erected, but at midnight had to be hurriedly taken down and everything moved again as the ice had broken under us. At daybreak, about 2am, Shackleton, who had been pacing up and down all night, called Hurley and myself and we went over to the wreck and secured a tin of petrol, which we used to make a hot drink for all hands; this was passed into the various tents. It is to be supposed the men were all cold and miserable and perhaps might be excused, but the fact remains that no one said "Thank you", so I called "Now if any of you gentlemen would like your boots cleaned, pass them outside."

Our position at this time was 89° 5' S latitude and 51° 30' W longitude. We were nearly 600 miles from where we first became frozen in, but had drifted probably nearer 1,500 miles. Paulet Island was the nearest point where we could find food and shelter, a small hut having been left there by a Swedish Expedition in 1902. This was 346 miles from the position of the "Endurance" when she was crushed.

Shackleton mustered all hands and explained the position and stated that he intended to march to Paulet Island and then gave orders to move the camp to a larger and stronger floe where all preparations for the long trek were made. Shackleton and I went out to pioneer a road and at 8pm on October 30th, a start was made. One small party had to go ahead with picks and shovels to break a road through the pressure ridges and also frequently fill in cracks or small leads. The boats were the main trouble, each one with its gear and sledge weighing over a ton. The sledges were the point of weakness and they had to be very carefully handled to prevent them smashing up over the rough ice. On their account much more road making had to be done then would have been necessary for ordinary sledge loads.

With three boats and ten sledge loads of provisions and stores, it was impossible to take everything on at once, and relay work was the only thing possible. Hurley and I harnessed over two teams of dogs to the heaviest boat, and with the assistance of four men to steer the sledge and prevent capsizing, we got on better than the 18 men who were hauling the other boats. Our 14 dogs worked splendidly. Worsley was in charge of the party hauling the second and third boat, bringing them along a few hundred yards one at a time. The other dog teams relayed the ordinary sledges.

Our net gain on that first day's march was one mile, but the necessary deviations made the distance travelled nearly two miles and relay work brought this up to six miles. The ice on which we camped that night was not more than two feet thick, but was the only smooth unbroken patch to be found. Killer whales were blowing in the cracks all around, but fortunately did not attempt to attack us.

The next day again we only made one mile to the good. The snow was very soft and at times we sank to the hips. The pressure ridges were more frequent and at 5pm all hands and the dogs were played out and Shackleton decided to find a solid floe and camp there until conditions were more favourable. A suitable heavy floe was found the following day and all our gear was moved on to it.

This floe was from twenty to thirty feet in thickness and nearly a mile square when we pitched camp upon it, but during the two months we stayed there, it split up into a much smaller span. This camp received the name of "Ocean Camp".

When this sledging started, we were only carrying valuable sledging rations and Shackleton decided to save these for the boat journey that would inevitably have to be made and live as much as possible on seals and penguins. He also sent me with a party to the ship to endeavour to retrieve more food from her.

I found the "Endurance" in the same position, with the upper deck two feet under water. A fireman's slice, a heavy iron bar with a flat end three inches broad, had luckily been left on the prop which was above water. The flat end was sharpened and we rigged a small derrick over that part of the deck which covered the store room and then drove this weighty chisel up and down until a hole was made through the deck large enough for food cases to be extracted.

As we were striking blind through two feet of ice and water, this took many hours and after a whole day's work, we only retrieved about half a dozen cases. Light cases, such as biscuits and flour floated up, the first to appear being Callard & Bowser's butter scotch.

Day after day I returned to the ship and altogether calved over two tons of food stuff. Those cases which were too heavy to float were brought up by stabbing them with a boat hook and as nearly all the contents were in tins inside the wooden box, only a small portion of the contents were damaged by the salt water.

When abandoning ship and selecting stores, I asked the doctors if it was necessary to take any alcohol for medicinal purposes; they assured me that they had drugs in the medicine chest for all purposes and consulting with Shackleton, it was thought advisable to leave it behind. I knew that McIlroy's birthday was on October 3rd so I smuggled one bottle of whiskey amongst my kit and on that night arranged for a select party in my tent and triumphantly produced the prize.

Many other useful loads of material were taken over to Ocean Camp, amongst these was an ash shoot which Hurley converted into a blubber stove and all food was cooked on this during the whole of our stay on the ice. The wheel house was taken away almost intact and made an excellent shelter for the cook. A quantity of timber and spurs were used to build a lookout platform about 25 feet high and this proved most useful for spotting seals and penguins.

As the amount of food saved from the wreck would only last about three months even on very short rations, every seal or penguin that we sighted was killed. Worsley had wonderful eyesight and spent many hours on the lookout. Whenever he reported a seal or seals, one or more sledges were immediately sent out. If the seals were crab-eaters, I shot them as they are very lively, but if Weddell seals, they were clubbed, this kind being very tame and sluggish. The crab-eaters average about 8'6" in length and weigh about 500 pounds, and the Weddell from 9-11' and from 600-800 pounds. On these hunting trips, two sledges were usually man-hauled as there were many open cracks and unsafe places for dogs.

Shackleton personally supervised the issuing of food and was remarkably clever in devising varieties in these days. Later on, when there was nothing but flesh to eat, little variations was possible. The carving of food to the different messes was done by the cook for some time, but there were complaints made that he was not impartial, so Shackleton gave me that duty. There were five tents:

No 1 - Shackleton, Hudson, Hurley and James

No 2 - Wild, Wordie, McNeish and McIlroy

No 3 - the eight forward hands

No 4 - Crean, Hussey, Warston and Cheatham

No 5 - Worsley, Greenstreet, Lees, Clark, Rickenson, Kerr, Macklin and Blackborrow, the last named being the stowaway and the youngest man of the party.

Every man, Shackleton included, took his turn of messman for the day, his duty being to keep the tent swept, bring in food and wash up the one pot which was used for carrying in the food. No water being available, the pots were scoured out with snow. Each man had an aluminium mug, spoon and sheath knife, but no plates had been saved. These were improvised from empty tins or pieces of venesta wood.

Hunting parties went out every day except when blizzards were blowing. When confined to our tents, we occupied ourselves in mending clothes or books and playing cards. Cards were only popular when the temperature was fairly high, as it is almost impossible to deal and handle them with gloves on. A few books had been saved including a portion of the "Encyclopaedia Britannica". Hussey had managed to save his banjo upon which he was a very good performer and on Saturday nights, we continued to hold the usual concert, unaccompanied now by liquid refreshment.

On very clear day, Worsley took observations for position and it was soon conclusively proved that the drift of the ice was due almost entirely to the wind. For this reason, strong southerly winds were welcomed although they frequently brought snow and low temperatures.

The first few days at Ocean Camp were cold and miserable and on November 6th, no one left the shelter of the tents unless compelled to do so. The drift was so thick that it was difficult to find one's way from the tents to the cookhouse. Green, the cook, proved himself a real hero and never failed to have a meal ready on time. When this blow was over, Worsley informed us that we had travelled 22 miles north in three days; this announcement was greeted with loud cheers.

All hands were soon aware of the fact that our drift was dependent upon the wind and Hussey, the meteorologist, was constantly pestered for a weather forecast.

On November 21st, Shackleton was on the lookout platform and everybody else in the tents when we heard him shout "She's going boys!" Running out, we were just in time to see the stern of the "Endurance" rise and then a quick dive and all was over. Shackleton told me later it was the saddest moment of his life, but none of that showed in his demeanour and to all appearance, he was his usual cheery self. I felt as though I had lost an old friend and I think all hands had a similar feeling.

The end of November and nearly the whole of December were bad days. The temperature was so high, frequently only just below freezing point, that our sleeping bags were soaked and the snow surface was so soft that walking was difficult, every step being knee deep and frequently thigh deep. Many of the party showed signs of depression and Shackleton increased the food rations, which had a good effect. He also asked me what I thought of another attempt at sledging and I agreed with him that a spell of hard work would do everybody good.

Accordingly, on December 20th, Shackleton announced that he meant to try another march to the west to reduce the distance from Paulet Island. This caused quite a lot of excitement, everybody being anxious to move. The next day, Shackleton, Crean, Hurley and I, with dog teams, went out to survey a road. We found it difficult but possible, and marking out the easiest route for seven miles, we returned to camp.

December 22nd was kept as Christmas Day, and all non-essential foodstuffs were apportioned out by lot to the different tents. I well remember that amongst other things, our tent received a bottle of Heinz pearl onions. We had a real solid blow out, little dreaming that our next really good meal was eight months' distant.

There is no darkness in those latitudes at this time of the year, and a start was made the next day at 3am and afterwards, we travelled at night instead of in the daytime, as the sun being lower at night, the surface was harder. Each morning, after all hands had turned in, Shackleton and I went ahead for two miles to reconnoitre the best route.

On Christmas Day, we wished each other a Merry Christmas as we ate our dinner of seal meat and blubber and some stale thin damper made of flour and water and fried in blubber.

After seven days of the hardest imaginable labour, nearly always sinking knee deep in the soft snow, cutting away hummocks and ridges to make it possible to get the boats and sledges along, we were stopped by ice so terribly broken and pressed up that it was impossible to proceed any further. The total result of this killing work was an advance in a straight line of seven and a half miles, and as the nearest land was over 200 miles distant, and Worsley's observations showed that the drift had carried us further away than when we started, it was no use continuing the struggle. A strong old floe was chosen and a camp made which was named "Patience Camp", an appropriate name it proved as we had to remain there for three and a half months.

During one march, Crean fell into a crack that was snow covered and was totally immersed. There was a keen wind and 10° of frost and the water temperature was about 30°F (salt water freezes at 28.3°F). He stripped under the lee of a boat, a very poor shelter and we hastily unpacked some of our kit bags and fitted him out as quickly as possible from various members' spares, but he was almost paralysed before he was reclothed and was some time before he recovered from the shock.

By this time our supply of food was very short and our meals had to consist mainly of seals and penguins and except when the weather prevented it, parties were sent out daily. There were many blank days and our rations were cut down until just sufficient to keep us alive and very much against his feelings, Shackleton ordered the dogs to be shot. This duty fell upon me and was the worst job I ever had in my life; I have known many men I would rather shoot than the worst of the dogs. I knew everyone of them well and though some were much more lovable characters than others, I had a great affection for every one. These dogs vary in disposition as much as men do. A few had to be whipped to work and some must not be whipped or they would lie down and cry. Some would make the most delighted pets, but petting is taboo, as if one is made any fuss of, the remainder become jealous and will kill him at the first opportunity. When a fight starts, they must be separated as they always fight to a finish and the loser is killed and torn to pieces. They seldom attack men, but if they do, they must be hit hard and quickly, as many of them weigh well over 100 pounds; our heaviest was 138 pounds and a fight with a dog of that size is a very serious matter. Dr Macklin was bitten in the arm by one of his team but this was the only serious injury.

The shortage of seals and penguins meant not only an inefficiency of food, but as the only fuel was blubber and penguin skins, there were many days when we were unable to afford more than one hot drink a day. Some of the dogs were eaten and though far from fastidious, I think their flesh was the nastiest I have ever tasted and the toughest.

One day I heard Lees yelling for help and running out from the tent, saw he was being chased by a huge sea leopard and seizing the rifle, I shot it. When it was cut up, there were 22 undigested fish inside it which gave us the only fish dinner we had for many months.

When open lands occurred near Patience Camp, sea leopards were sometimes seen swimming about and I got three on different occasions by pretending to be a penguin. I stooped down near the water waving my arms up and down like flippers and the sea leopard came charging at a terrific rate through the water and shot out on to the ice. I ran back a few yards so that if the first shot was not fatal, I would have time for another before the beast could escape, but on each occasion, the first shot was successful. One of these was 16 feet in length and had the remains of 13 Adelie penguins inside him. These penguins weigh about 12 pounds, which will give some idea of the enormous appetite of a sea leopard.

On January 13th, a heavy blizzard came up from the south-west and lasted six days. We were terribly uncomfortable in our wet sleeping bags and flimsy tents, but no one grumbled as everyone knew the wind was driving us rapidly north. When the next observations were taken, we found this storm had carried us 84 miles. The great drawback of the frequent blizzards and thick weather was the impossibility of hunting and our food ration was woefully inadequate.

One morning, Crean called me to say he had seen a seal only about 150 yards away and I pushed out with the rifle ordering some of the others to bring a sledge. Visibility was bad, at most 50 yards, but presently Crean pointed out the seal, partially hidden behind some ice hummocks and not more than 30 yards distant. I leveled the rifle, a 44 Winchester, carrying a flat nosed soft bullet, and was actually pressing the trigger when the seal rose upright and to our horror, proved to be one of the Scientists who, being of a modest nature had chosen this spot instead of our retiring shelter.

By February 22nd, we were 80 miles from Paulet Island and praying that the ice would carry us there as we knew that a hut and provisions had been placed there in 1904 by a party in search of the Nordenskjöld Expedition. Strangely enough Shackleton had fitted out this expedition. However, the fates willed otherwise and by the middle of March, we were level with the island but 60 miles east and for all the chance we had of reaching it over that tumbled sea of ice, it might as well have been 1,000 miles away.

Practically the whole of March was stormy and miserable. For days at a time, it was impossible to move from our tents, and our floe, which had been nearly a mile square when we first made our camp on it, had gradually cracked up until only about 200 yards across. Several times we had to scramble out when a crack appeared through the camp and in the darkness shift tents and haul boats over the crack in order to keep everything together. It was a remarkable thing that these alarms always occurred at night. There is no meteorological, scientific or any other reason for this; it was just sheer cursedness.

During this period, Shackleton had a severe attack of sciatica and for several days could not leave his sleeping bag without assistance. This was the only time whilst we were on the floe that he failed to visit each tent, even during blizzards, to make enquiries as to every man's health and comfort.

After our disappointment in passing so far from Paulet Island, we began to look out for Clarence or Elephant Islands, about 100 miles north and on April 7th, the former came into view. By this time, a distinct swell was running through the pack ice and our camping site was becoming rapidly smaller and on Sunday April

8th, the end came. I had a much greater knowledge of the ways and vagaries of pack ice than any other member of the party and for months, I had been actually dreading the time coming when we would have to take to the boats, but I did not, of course, communicate my fears to anyone else. Almost every time I had entered or left pack ice, the outer edge was in the utmost confusion, masses of ice weighing hundreds to thousands of tons, heaving up and down and churning against each other with a continuous thundering roar, making it exceedingly dangerous to enter or leave, even with a well built wooden ship specially constructed for the purpose. How much more hazardous then to escape with three frail boats, the largest of which was only 21 feet long, the other two being 18' 6".

However, as it turned out, my fears were groundless. At one o'clock that day, our floe cracked across again right through our camp and then slowly opened up, leaving us sufficient room to launch the boats and row through lanes to a pool of open water about a mile distant. By this time, darkness was setting in and we set about looking for a camping place, and soon found a large flat piece, probably 20 feet thick and roughly 50 yards square. The boats were hauled up and tents pitched and soon the blubber stove was going. After our meal, watches were set and the remainder of the party turned in.

Shackleton was unable to sleep and after an hour or so in his sleeping bag, went out to have a look round and as he was approaching the men's tent, an extra heavy swell split the floe under the tent. Before the tent was down and all the men clear, the crack had widened to four feet and it was then found that one man was in the water. Being fastened up in his sleeping bag, he was helpless. Shackleton threw himself down at the ice edge and was able to grasp the bag and hauled bag and man on to the floe just as the crack closed again. As the man, McIness, was being helped out of his bag, he was asked was he alright; he replied, "Yes, but I lost a _____ tin of tobacco." When told he ought to be thankful to be alive, he said, "So I am but that doesn't bring the tobacco back." The crack again opened, dividing the camp and when all tents and boats had been hauled over on to one place, it was found that Shackleton had been left on the wrong side of the crack, which was now so wide that he was out of sight. I at once ordered the lightest boat to be launched and in a few minutes, rescued Shackleton and brought him back. He said afterwards he had never felt so lonely in his life. Further sleep was out of the question and immediately there was sufficient daylight, the boats were launched and we pulled away to the north through the leads to open water.

The boats were named after some of the principal supporters of the expedition. In the "James Caird", which was the largest, were Shackleton, myself and nine others. Worsley was in charge of the "Dudley Docker" with eight others; and the

"Stancomb Wills" carried the remaining eight, Hudson and Crean in charge.

When we left the shelter of the pack, we found a strong breeze blowing and heavy spray came aboard. The spray froze as it fell and in a very short time, men and gear were covered with a thick coating of ice. Baling was impossible and the ice had to be chipped off with knives and ice axes. It was plain that in a few hours, we should founder, as Shackleton gave the order to return to the pack. Soon after arriving in comparatively smooth water, a small iceberg was seen with a slope running down on one side to sea level. This one was evidently several hundreds of years old so Shackleton decided, as all hands were cold, tired and sorely in need of sleep, to haul up the boats and camp. He said to me, "It would be too unkind if that thing chose this particular night to break up." It did not break up, but during the night, the swell increased and the berg began to rock like a cradle and the fear that it might capsize drove away all thought of sleep. When daylight came, it was seen that the pack had closed around us, huge pieces dashing and grinding against the berg, making it quite impossible to launch the boats. Late in the afternoon, an opening occurred and the boats were rushed into the water. There were several narrow escapes from being crushed before we finally emerged into more open water, by which time darkness had again fallen, heavy snow squalls limiting our vision to a few yards.

This was a bad night; we could not find a suitable floe on to which we might safely haul the boats and as we were afraid we might lose each other in the darkness, the boats were made fast to each other by the painters and drifted all night about 20 yards apart. Every few minutes, lumps of ice had to be poled off and killer whales were blowing all around. These beasts were the cause of great anxiety, as they might have come up under one of the boats, or have gone over one of the painters, in the latter case their 20 - 30 tons weight would have pulled two boats under water; so one man in each boat was standing by all night with an axe ready to cut the painter.

At dawn, the wind dropped and we commenced rowing to the westward, our object at this time being Deception Island, where there was a food depot. There was also a church built of wood, which we thought might be used to build a more seaworthy craft than our tiny boats. There was also a chance that one or more whalers might still be there. At 8am, the boats were made fast to a solid flat floe and the cook and cooker put on it. In a short time a meal was prepared. In the meantime, all hands were able to run round and ease their cramped limbs, with the exception of one in each boat to prevent them bumping against the floe or each other.

It was amazing how this hot meal improved the condition of all. Several of the party had to be helped out of the boats but the hot soup and seal meat soon put new life into them.

The sun was now up and partially dried our outer garments and melted the ice from our beards. After breakfast, all sails were set and the westerly course resumed. For three days now the wind had been easterly and the general opinion was that at last 50 miles of westing had been made. At noon, Worsley got a sight and Shackleton told me to take our boat over to him. The result was most disappointing. Instead of making west, the observation showed that we were 30 miles east of our position on the 9th when we first launched the boats. Shackleton did not announce this bad news to the party but simply said we had not made such good progress as expected.

The nearest land now was Hope Bay at the northern end of Graham Land, 80 miles distant and as the wind was foul for Elephant Island, it was decided to try for Hope Bay. At dusk, the boats were made fast to a floe but a nasty choppy sea was running and it was impossible to effect a landing with the blubber stove, and a make shift meal was made in each boat over the primus lamps. During the night, a sudden shift of wind forced us to cast off and until dawn, the boats were kept together by means of the painters, some of the men in each boat rowing to keep head on to the sea. The temperature was 36°F below freezing point and every few minutes the oars had to be hauled in to chip off the accumulation of ice which made them too heavy to handle. Our outer clothing was like a heavy suit of armour with no joints.

The sky was clear at dawn on April 13th and it was evident that the pack was too heavy to penetrate in the direction of Hope Bay. The wind had shifted and was now fair for Elephant Island, which was about 100 miles distant, and Worsley and I agreed with Shackleton that this was our best hope, the majority of the party looking seriously exhausted and several becoming light headed.

The sea was too rough for a hot breakfast to be prepared, but Shackleton gave permission for all hands to eat as much as possible; many of the party were unable to take advantage of this owing to seasickness.

With a fair wind, we made good progress through the pack and at noon, we suddenly found ourselves in the open sea, but by no means more comfortable, the sea rapidly becoming more rough as the shelter of the ice was left behind and more and more water coming aboard. I had early discovered that I had no one in my boat except Shackleton who could be trusted at the tiller, and as he was fully occupied by the general supervision of the fleet, I was at the tiller the whole time we were moving.

That night a sea anchor was made with oars and a sail and the boats were kept together by the painters and a dreadful night it was. At least half of the party were insane, fortunately not violent, simply helpless and hopeless. Again Shackleton's marvellous powers of fortitude, unselfishness and consideration for others were shown. From this time until our landing, he looked after these helpless men, just as though they were babes in arms, and all mothers will understand what I mean.

Our worst privation was the lack of water; we had left the ice unexpectedly suddenly and had neglected to take a stock on board and without ice, we could have no hot food or drink. We tried eating raw frozen seal meat but this was so salt that it increased our thirst. When daylight came, we saw Elephant Island on the bearings worked out by Worsley but still a long 40 miles distant. McIlroy reported from "Stancomb Wills" that Blackborrow's feet were badly frost-bitten. All that day we battled on through a heavy sea and my boat made much worse weather of it as the "Stancomb Wills" was so slow that she had to be taken in tow. For two nights and two days, I sat at the tiller and I cannot help quoting from Shackleton's book where he says, "Always, while I attended to the other boats, signaling and ordering, Wild sat at the tiller of the "James Caird". "He seemed unmoved by fatigue and unshaken by privation." The night of the 14th was the worst I have ever known. A heavy sea was running and spray after spray flew over the boats, driven by a gale with cutting force. In addition to the spray, there was almost constant snow which hid the land for which we were making, and as I could not see the compass, steering had to be done by the wind. As hour after hour passed, I began to fear the wind had changed and we were sailing in the wrong direction. About 3am, Shackleton was attending to one of the semi-conscious men and asked me some question. Bearing ahead through my sore and bloodshot eyes, I had just at that moment caught a glimpse of a moonlit glacier on Elephant Island, and instead of replying to the question, I said as plainly as I was able with swollen and aching tongue and throat, "I can see it! I can see it!" By the time Shackleton turned, the island was obscured again and he afterwards told me he had a momentary dread that "poor old Wild's gone off his head". Shortly after this, I told the carpenter, who was attending to the sheet, to take the tiller for a while so that I could rest my eyes. We changed places, but in less than two minutes, the boat broached to and a heavy sea came aboard, the ice cold water giving another shock to our already soaked and shivering bodies, and I had to resume my place at the tiller. The boat towing astern also had suffered, but the shouts of alarm from her were really a relief to me as they proved that at least some of her crew were still alive. Nothing had been seen for many hours of the "Dudley Docker" and we could only hope she was still afloat.

At 7am, just as the first sign of dawn appeared, I felt the sea become much less heavy and guessed we had got under the lee of the land or an iceberg, when suddenly the snow cleared and right ahead, apparently only a few hundred yards distant, appeared an enormous cliff, thousands of feet high, the top invisible in the clouds. I immediately altered course to starboard, let go the painter of the "Stancomb Wills" and yelled to them to take the oars and follow us. It was soon obvious that the cliffs were at least a mile distant, and the boats were headed closer to try to find a landing place. Shackleton's tongue and throat were so swollen that he could only whisper and his orders were passed on either by Hurley or myself, when joy of joys, the boats ran into a field of ice fragments which had fallen from a glacier; millions of pieces from the size of marbles or footballs. All the sick men came to life and eager hands were thrust over the side. I don't remember ever tasting anything more delicious than that first piece of ice.

For 12 miles the coast proved to be impossible for a landing, cliffs and glacier faces rising perpendicularly from the sea for many hundreds of feet. At 9am at the north-east end of the island, a narrow beach was sighted at the foot of the cliffs, partially sheltered from the sea by an outlying fringe of rocks. Not an ideal landing place but it was land and, as another 12 hours at sea would most certainly have killed at least half the party, the boats were headed in.

Shackleton called the "Stancomb Wills" alongside and boarded her as she was the lightest boat and ran her on the rocky beach; and just then the "Dudley Docker" was sighted, which was a great relief to our leader. With great difficulty, largely owing to the extreme weakness of the men, the boats were hauled above high water mark, oars being used as rollers. When I was satisfied the tide was ebbing and the boats were safe, I went to join Shackleton and found him standing looking at a most pathetic sight. Many of the men were reeling about exactly as though under the influence of alcohol, roaring with laughter, filling their pockets with stones, and some of them rolling amongst the shingle, burying their faces in it and pouring handfuls over themselves. Here I feel I must quote from Shackleton's account: "I remember that Wild came ashore as I was looking at the men and stood beside me as easy and unconcerned as if he had stepped out of his car for a stroll in the park."

The first thing to be landed was the blubber stove; an unfortunate seal was lying near, and in a very short time a hot drink was ready. The effect was wonderful. When we landed not more than six out of the 28 were able to do much in the way of work, but after the drink and a meal of seal meat, all except two were fit to take part in landing stores, hauling up boats and erecting tents etc.

It was not until 3pm that all this was done and the men able to turn in and all this time good old Green was kept busy at the stove. Before we turned in Shackleton, Worsley, Hurley and I inspected the beach and found that at spring tides and in heavy gales, the whole place would be under water. However, a sleep was imperative and it was decided to spend at least the one night here. This was April 15th and since the breakup of the ice on the 8th, Shackleton had not attempted to close his eyes. I had a few minutes doze on the night of the 9th before the floe split up on which we were camped and Worsley admitted to a few hours' sleep during that nightmare of a week.

The next day broke bright and clear and all hands were soon busy spreading sleeping bags and clothing to dry. Shackleton ordered me to pick a boat's crew to explore to the west in the hope of finding a safer camping ground. I chose Marston, Crean, Vincent and McCarthy and we got away in the "Stancomb Wills" at 11am. The coast line was indented by many fairly deep bays and as it was necessary to examine all of them, our progress was slow. No possible abiding place was seen until we were seven miles to the west, when we found a spit of land running out from the cliffs. It was something like Chisel Beach at Portland on a smaller scale; 200 yards long and 70 yards wide and at the outer end, a piece of land 100 feet high. This had steep cliffs except in one spot where a well worn path wound to the top. There was probably half an acre of moderately level stony ground, used by the Gentoo penguins as a rookery, several hundred birds were still there although so late in the season. In comparison with our present site, this looked a paradise, especially as a few seals and young sea elephants were basking on the beach, and after a hasty meal we started on the return journey. The tide was evidently against us and it was 8pm when we sighted a blubber flare which Shackleton had ordered to be lit for our guidance.

The breaking up of the camp, re-storing and launching the boats the following morning took a long time and some of the men were inclined to grumble at leaving the safety of solid land to face the horrors of another boat journey; it was near noon when a start was made. Almost immediately a strong gale sprang up and I am certain no man of the party will ever forget that trip. Although we kept as near in shore as possible, all hands were quickly soaked to the skin by the flying spray and even the men at the oars felt the cold severely. The "Dudley Docker" was pulling only three oars, as we had unfortunately broken several when using them as rollers to haul up and launch the boats, and she was driven out to sea.

It was getting dark when the beach we were making for suddenly loomed ahead out of the driving spume and a few minutes later, my boat and the "Stancomb Wills" were driven up on to the beach. It was not possible to haul them high enough until they were unloaded and to do this, we had to stand from thigh to waist deep in the surf, the temperature of the water being well below freezing point for fresh water. Rickenson, the Chief Engineer, fainted before this work was finished and others were almost too exhausted to stand. Just as the last boat had been hauled clear of high water mark, the "Dudley Docker" struggled in. Worsley had been fortunate enough to gain the shelter of an outlying rock, where his crew rested until their aching arms had recovered sufficiently to make another attempt. Without this temporary relief that boat's crew would assuredly have been lost.

In this raging storm and darkness, this spit of land (afterwards named Cape

Wild) did not look half so hospitable as when I had seen it in bright sunshine the day before. However, we succeeded in getting the blubber stove lit, partially sheltered behind some large rocks, and after a hot meal, decided it was not such a bad place after all.

In the "Sailing Directions", a book carried by all marines, Elephant Island was described as "An island 30 miles by 12 miles rising precipitously to a height of 8,000 feet but with many low lying beaches covered with tussock grass and swarming with seals, sea elephants, penguins and sea birds". No one had ever landed on it before us and we had found the beaches and tussock grass conspicuous by their absence, and before we were rescued, we were to go very hungry for many weeks on account of the scarcity of seals, sea elephants or any other form of life.

The gale increased that night to hurricane force and the tents, which had been hurriedly erected in the darkness, were all flattened out, the pole of Shackleton's tent striking Hudson a heavy blow on the hip. Though he said little about it at the time, this was the cause of much suffering to him later on. Hudson was the navigating officer and was familiarly called "Buddha", as he had served in the B.I. boats and spent a lot of time in India. Another catastrophe that night was the complete destruction of the eight-man tent, and when daylight appeared, it was found that two bags of spare clothing had been left too near the sea and an extra large wave had carried them away; a most serious loss.

The gale continued with thick driving snow and some shelter had to be found for the men who had lost their tent. It was too badly ripped up for repairs so the "Dudley Docker" was turned upside down and lashed to rocks to prevent it being blown away. One side propped up on boulders and then the opening closed with rocks and snow until only a hole large enough for ingress and egress remained.

This day, April 18th, was my birthday and though I have spent many tough ones in my life, this was without doubt the worst ever. Almost the whole day was spent under our flattened tents, in soaking clothing and sleeping bags. Shackleton got the cook out and the two of them, with great difficulty, made a rough shelter for the blubber stove, cooked a hot stew and passed it round to each tent. This was entirely unexpected, but all the more appreciated, and this time the recipients did not neglect to say "thank you".

Although the gale continued the following day, much necessary work had to be done. Some sort of shelter had to be made for the cook, Crean, who cannot be praised too highly. A circle of rocks was built as much under the lee of the cliff as possible and a sail secured over the top. This did not prevent swirling eddies of snow finding the way in. then the boats had to be hauled farther up the beach and the tents re-erected, oars and masts being used for this purpose, and sorry enough habitations they were. Whilst these tasks were being accomplished, several men were knocked down by the wind and some were cut and bruised by flying lumps of hard snow and small stones.

Blackborrow could not stand on his swollen frost-bitten feet and was in dreadful pain. Hudson was lame through the blow on the hip and Rickenson too weak to be of any service. Some of the party, not many I am pleased to say, had become despondent and were in a "what's the use" sort of mood and had to be driven to work, none too gently either.

On this day, Shackleton took Worsley and me apart from the others to discuss plans for the future. We knew that no search party would ever dream of looking for us on Elephant Island and also that no whaler would approach near enough to sight us, as the island is surrounded by submerged reefs and half tide rocks, usually also by heavy pack ice and grounded bergs, making navigation exceedingly dangerous.

The nearest point of civilization was Port Stanley in the Falkland Islands, 540 miles distant, but the prevailing winds made a boat trip in that direction impossible. South Georgia, on the other hand, was in the right direction for the wind, but 800 miles distant, and there is no place in the world where such a heavy sea runs.

We all agreed that an attempt to take the whole party would certainly mean the loss of all hands and Shackleton decided to take the "James Caird" and with five others try to bring assistance. Worsley and I at once volunteered to go with him, but he said, "Sorry Wild, you must stay to look after the party here". We then returned to the party and Shackleton announced his decision and asked for volunteers. Quite a number asked to be taken, but many of the poor fellows wished never to see a boat again as long as they lived and kept mum. Worsley was a certainty; I think I have mentioned earlier that he was the quickest and most reliable navigator I have ever sailed with. For the others, Crean, McNeish, McCarthy and Vincent were chosen. The two doctors, McIlroy and Macklin, volunteered, but Shackleton said they must remain to look after the sick men, much to my relief as I did not wish to lose either of them. I also asked for Crean, but he begged so hard to go that I said no more about it. McNeish was the carpenter, McCarthy and Vincent very capable and willing sailors, and Crean had been on both Scott's expeditions. It will be remembered that Crean and Lashley saved the life of Admiral Evans, then Commander, on Scott's last expedition.

On the 20th, the weather was too bad to allow us any outdoor work and the tents began to show signs of disintegration through the constant buffeting. On this day, the cook's duties proved too much for him and he had to be relieved - on e of the grumblers being told off for the job.

The weather improved the next day and a start was made on making the

"James Caird" as seaworthy as possible for the hazardous journey. Shackleton and I went through our small supply of stores and a month's supply of provisions for six men was apportioned out. The temporary cook was kept busy for several days frying seal steak and Greenstreet and Cheatham were kept occupied in thawing out a belt of frozen canvas and rending it into the shape of a deck cover for the boat. This was to fit over a deck framework which was made by the carpenter from sledge runners and box lids. When completed it had rather a Heath Robinson appearance, but, as it turned out, it undoubtedly saved the lives of the party, as without it the boat could not have lived through the terrific seas which were encountered.

A strong back was also made from the mast of the "Dudley Docker" and fitted to the keel. The ice had to be melted to fill the two 18 gallon water breakers; this alone meant many hours work for the cook and night watchman. Little could be done on the 22nd as another blizzard was raging and Shackleton was getting worried because, during lulls in the storm, heavy masses of pack ice were seen about two miles to the north.

In the hope of finding better shelter, some of the men were employed in digging a hole in a steep snow slope at the landward end of the spit, but this had soon to be abandoned, as every snow squall filled the hole up again.

The 23rd broke fine and clear and all preparations being completed before the end of the day, Shackleton decided to make a start the following morning. The launching the next day was a difficult and, to many, a painful operation. The "James Caird" could not be launched with her load aboard, so she was pushed off empty with Vincent and McNeish to hold her off in deep water. As she floated, a wave caught her broadside on and she rolled so heavily the two men were thrown into the water. The Stancomb Wills" had already been launched and her crew rescued the men and towed the larger boat out and anchored her clear of the breakers.

Besides stores and equipment, it was necessary to carry ballast, and a half a ton of round boulders were placed in the bottom of the "James Caird", the "Stancomb Wills" being used as a ferry. All of us where were engaged in the task of loading up were soaked to the waist and it was to be several weeks before we experienced the comfort of dry clothes.

After the last load had been taken off, Shackleton came ashore to say goodbye to the party. His only order to me was that I should make an attempt to reach Deception Island the following spring in the event of his failure to return.

He was then ferried on board, the sails were set and the momentous voyage began. We gave them three hearty cheers and watched the boat getting smaller and smaller in the distance; then, seeing some of the party in tears, I immediately set them all to work. My own heart was very full. I heard one of the few pessimists remark, "That's the last of them", and almost knocked him down with a rock, but satisfied myself by addressing a few remarks to him in real lower deck language.

At 4pm, I climbed the rocks and through the binoculars caught a last glimpse of the boat just as she disappeared amongst pack ice to the north east. Shackleton afterwards said we looked a most pathetic group on the beach, little realizing how much more pathetic his tiny craft looked as it slowly dwindled from our sight.

My first consideration was the matter of adequate shelter. All hands were in bad condition and suffering from exhaustion due to long exposure to the wet and cold. Many had salt water boils and three were confined to their sleeping bags; Hudson was lame through the blow on the hip from the tent pole; Rickenson had collapsed from heart trouble, and Blackborrow could not stand on his frost-bitten feet. Blackborrow was a stowaway and the youngest member of the party. He had come aboard in Buenos Aires on our outward journey. Three days after leaving Buenos Aires, one of the sailors came rushing along to Shackleton's cabin in a state of great excitement. It was rather bad weather and a lot of water was coming aboard and it appeared this man had gone to the locker in the fo'c'sle, where sea boots and oilskins were kept. When he took hold of one of the boots, he found a man's leg in it and Blackborrow stepped out of the locker, scaring the sailor stiff. Shackleton asked, "What kind of a man is he?" "Oh, a great big ugly fellow, sir, bigger than any man aboard, and looks real dangerous, sir!" Shackleton said, "Come on, Frank, let's have a look at him."

When we got down into the fo'c'sle, there was a very harmless-looking lad who tried to stand to attention when Shackleton spoke to him. He was evidently weak from seasickness and hunger and Shackleton ordered him to sit down, and asked, "Why are you here?" He replied, "I want to go with you, sir".

"You will now have to work and you will be sent back from South Georgia" said Shackleton. The lad said, "I want to work, but please don't send me back." Shackleton said, "Do you know that on these expeditions, we often get very hungry, and if there is a stowaway available, he is the first to be eaten?" Shackleton was not fat but fairly heavily built and the boy looked him over and said, "They'd get a lot more meat off you, sir!"

The boss turned away to hid a grin and told me to turn the lad over to the boson, but added, "Introduce him to the cook first." Blackborrow turned out to be a good sailor and all-round handyman and was duly signed on in South Georgia as a member of the crew. He almost worshipped Shackleton and kept his cabin in such a polished condition as to put the rest of the ship to shame.

All the tents were badly torn by the heavy wind, which was again sweeping the beach, and I tried once more to dig a cave into the snow slope. After penetrating some eight or ten feet, we came to solid ice and we quickly found that as a dwelling, it would be impossible as streams of water were running down on all sides. I then gave orders to the party to collect quantities of flat stones and with those, two walls were built 16 feet apart and 4 feet high; the two boats were then turned upside down alongside each other on top of the walls, the few pieces of wood we had were nailed across from keel to keel and one of the sails stretched over them to form a roof. The side walls were made by Marston from the torn tents.

The site was chosen where some protection was given by two large rocks, to which the boats were lashed to prevent the wind blowing them away. Although far from weather-proof, that night was the most comfortable we had experienced for a long time. When we got up in the morning, our sleeping bags were covered by several inches of snow which had found its way through numerous holes. These were later plugged up with rocks, snow and cast-off clothing.

All this took a long time, carrying the rocks for the walls proving most exhausting and it was noticeable that the big men suffered more than the little ones. I have found this to be the case on all my expeditions. It is naturally impossible to apportion food in ratio with the size of a man; the small man is expected to do as much work as the big man, and usually does so.

The size of our new abode was 16 feet x 10 feet and the height from ground to thwarts four-and-a-half feet. Accommodation was made for six men to sleep on the thwarts by using the stern and bow gratings as a platform. Marston fashioned a hammock which he slung under the thwarts and had decidedly the most comfortable bed. The rest slept on the ground, taking their places under my directions. The space was small for 15 men and they had to be carefully arranged. Almost every night during the four and a half months of our stay there, disputes would arise.

"Hi, so-and-so, you've pinched six inches of my space."

"I haven't, I was here last night." and I had to go along and tell one or other to move over, and could not turn in myself until all the naughty children were nicely tucked up.

The floor was shingle, the stones varying in size from pigeon's eggs to cricket balls and mixed up with ice and penguin droppings. In the next few days, the upper surface was removed and fresh clean stones brought in. At first the stench of melting guano was appalling and even after the new floor was laid, it was still very strong. Later, it either got better, or we became used to it.

For some time the interior was pitch dark and blubber lamps were contrived from old tins, the wicks being made from used surgical dressings. The wicks required frequent sniffing or the lamps would go out and our supply of matches was very short. So long as we had tobacco all pipes and cigarettes were lit at the lamps, but, alas, the tobacco all gave out long before we were rescued and many weird substitutes were experimented with. On previous expeditions, I have found dried tea leaves quite a good smoke, but on Elephant Island we had no tea. Seaweed was tried, but could not be kept alight. Our sleeping bags were moulting and the reindeer hair as put into the pipes, also some grass which had been in our boots for months, but the most hardened smokers soon gave them up and the non-smokers complained bitterly against the noxious fumes.

In the middle of winter, I was walking round the camp by moonlight and found Bakewell, one of the sailors, digging a tunnel in a huge snow drift which had formed at the base of the high cliffs near our hut. I asked what he was doing and he replied, "When we landed here, sir, I threw a coat down at the foot of these rocks and it had half a plug of tobacco in the pocket." He had to tunnel 30 feet before he got to the rock face and then 12 feet to one side where he was lucky enough to find the coat. No one offered to help him and Bakewell shoveled many tons of snow in the four days he was working. The tunnel was so long, the snow had to be shifted three times.

After the prize was secured, it was found to be so wet that it took three days to dry by the stove whilst meals were being cooked. Bakewell then cut a portion into very fine shreds and made a cigarette, giving me the first puff on it. I was standing up outside and that one whiff made me so giddy I had to sit down or I would have fallen. Although I expostulated with Bakewell and pointed out that no one had helped him with his digging, he insisted on sharing all round. Very few owned pipes at this time, so cigarettes were made using pages of the Encyclopaedia Britannica. I had a pipe given to me by Rudyard Kipling, on which he himself carved "F.W. from R.K.". I lost it amongst the stones on the hut floor and although I spent many hours searching for it, I never found it.

ELEPHANT ISLAND

It is generally believed that there was an understanding between the men on Elephant Island not to expound on their time there. 'The less said the better,' would have been a typical attitude of the period, and to make public any behaviour of men driven to the limit of survival would have been seen as disloyal. It is only now as diaries and letters come into the public realm that something can be discovered of those dreadful three and half months.

The objective of Shackleton's Imperial Trans-Antarctic Expedition was to traverse Antarctica. This could only be achieved with depot-laying by two parties starting from either end of the proposed journey. One group of men was delivered by the ship *Aurora* to Ross Island next to the Great Ice Barrier with orders to lay depots across the Barrier and to the foot of the Beardmore Glacier. This group included Wild's brother Ernest, and its story stands out as one of the most horrifying and courageous of the Heroic Age. Shackleton's men, including Wild, in the ship *Endurance*, were to commence their journey from the Weddell Sea side of the continent.

Endurance set sail for Buenos Aires from Plymouth on 8 August 1914. In late October, she departed from Buenos Aires, and three days later Perce Blackborow a stowaway was discovered. He was allowed to remain on board but was warned by Shackleton that if anyone needed to be eaten it would be him! After a month's

The men on Elephant Island. Wild with pipe

stay at South Georgia they headed into the ice-laden Weddell Sea but in January, a hundred miles from its destination, the ship lost its battle with the ice and became trapped.

The 28 men on board were at the mercy of the ice and the ocean currents, which carried them on a circuit of the Weddell Sea. By spring, it was obvious that the ship would not be released from the ice, so Shackleton ordered the men to decamp with the dogs onto the ice flows and used the ship as a store cupboard.

Walter How recounted an incident: 'The morning after we left the ship (for the ice) we were under our tents roughing it for the time being and about a hundred yards away from the ship. And Shacks, Cmd Worsley and Frank Wild, they'd been up all night long, round and round, seeing that everything was OK. And about 5 in the morning Frank Wild came to the tent; he went to every tent – there were 4 or 5 tents – various members in the crew in each "Here you are boys, show a leg" and a beautiful jug of hot coffee. Nobody had the common decency to say thank you. And Frank Wild's remark was "would any gentleman like his boots cleaned?" Never forget it. They had been out all night long, below zero, and we were tucked up in our bags or blankets or whatever we'd got and then this jug of hot sea [sic] came in.'

Slowly and inexorably the sheer force of the ice buckled and snapped the ship, and on 21 November 1915, 15 months and 13 days after leaving England, it sank,

Wild watching the end of the Endurance

taking with Shackleton's hopes and dreams. Shackleton wrote: 'At last the twisting grinding floes were working their will on the ship. It was a sickening sensation to feel the decks breaking up under ones feet the beams bend and snapping with a noise of heavy gunfire. At 5pm she went down. I cannot write about it.'

Some provisions were saved, as were the three lifeboats, *James Caird*, *Dudley Docker* and *Stancomb Wills*. The plan was to drag the boats northwest across the ice to Snow Hill Island, where supplies had been left in a hut during a Swedish expedition in 1901–04. Huge hummocks of ice made the journey impossible and they had no option but to make camp on the drifting ice as it heaved and cracked beneath them. The first camp, Ocean Camp, sustained them for two months before they moved on and set up Patience Camp.

When it was obvious the splintering ice flow could carry them no farther they took to the boats and made for Elephant Island.

Their predicament had lasted for five agonising months, during which the hateful job of shooting the dogs fell to Wild. The job was made worse by the affection he felt for his own team, which he had trained to follow simply his voice commands.

The six-day boat journey to Elephant Island was nearly one challenge too many. Some of the men, virtually comatose due to the cold and seasickness, were too weak to row. Meanwhile, their mouths were cracked with thirst, while waves constantly crashed over them, soaking them to the skin. Except for a handful of men, including Shackleton and Wild, who were together in *James Caird*, nearly all suffered frostbite. Shackleton later wrote: 'Wild sat at the rudder with the same calm, confident expression that he would have worn under happier conditions; his steel-blue eyes looked out to the day ahead.'

By the time they reached the first landing – called Cape Valentine – most of the men had broken down both mentally and physically. Blackborow, wishing no doubt that he had resisted the temptation to stow away, was now unable to stand due to frostbite. He was given the dubious title of the first man to set foot on Elephant Island. As *Stancomb Wills* beached, he was ordered by Shackleton to jump ashore but he simply fell into the surf. Realizing he could not walk, some of the men climbed off the boat and dragged him bodily on to the land.

'Some of the men were reeling about the beach as if they had found an unlimited supply of alcoholic liquor on the desolate shore. They were laughing uproariously, picking up stones and letting handfuls of pebbles trickle between their fingers like misers gloating over hoarded gold.....Wild, who always rose superior to fortune, bad and good, came ashore as I was looking at the men and stood beside me as easy and unconcerned as if he had stepped out of his car for a stroll in the Park.'

They called the beach on which they landed Cape Valentine, but it was deemed unsuitable; if a northeasterly gale were to blow, the men on the narrow beach would be swamped by the sea. Elephant Island was no more than a series of submerged mountaintops protruding from the ferocious ocean and battered remorsefully by the elements.

The following day, Wild and four men set out in *Stancomb Wills* to look for another site. He arrived back that evening with the news that he had found a finger of land, roughly 100 by 30 yards, which he believed could support them. It jutted out at right angles from the coastline with a backdrop of cliffs and a glacier.

The stores were repacked and the reluctant men ordered back into the boats for the seven-mile journey along the coast to 'Cape Wild.'

Lacking the luxury of radio communication, no one knew of their plight. Shackleton was left with no choice but to set out across the Southern Ocean on an 800-nautical-mile voyage to South Georgia, taking five men with him. The 22-foot *James Caird* – little more than a rowing boat with a sail – was made seaworthy for what would be perhaps the most dangerous open-boat journey undertaken in modern history.

It was Wild's onerous duty to be left in command of the remaining 21 men. The tents, shredded by wind and weather, were useless. For living quarters, they turned the two remaining boats upside down on a four-foot wall constructed with stones found on the beach, over which the broken tents were stretched. It was just high enough to sit under.

Although they had some supplies brought from *Endurance*, they mostly relied on seal and penguin for their diet. The relentless cold, the gloomy half-light of winter, the constant food rationing and the fear of abandonment drove them into despondency. Each day it was Wild's job to pull the members of the party back from the brink of despair by exerting both encouragement and discipline, which started with the command 'Roll up and stow, the Boss is coming today!'

Salvation came from the large colony of gentoo penguins roosting on the headland at the end of the spit, and sometimes 40 could be shot or clubbed to death in a day. Luckily, there was something of a beach that enabled seals to come ashore, and they, too, were swiftly disposed of. The meat of these mammals was mostly eaten raw.

In the less-than-sterile conditions under the upturned boats, Blackborow's foot, now gangrenous from frostbite sustained on the boat journey, had the toes amputated by the two doctors, Macklin and McIlroy.

The sleeping bags of reindeer skins were rarely dry, and shed their hair onto and into everything, including the food. Gallons of 'liquid filth' had to be continuously bailed out from the shingled floor of the 'hovel.' A blubber stove, belched out black smoke until a chimney made from a biscuit tin and passed through the 'roof' improved conditions considerably.

To keep spirits up, Saturday night concerts were organized, in which they all took part. Miraculously Hussey's banjo had survived and his playing became the centre piece of every show, along with Wild's baritone voice, which his brother Stanley likened to that of to Paul Robeson. Wild had a seven-inch chest expansion, measured by Stanley himself who claimed, 'on a calm day in the Antarctic he could call the men in to dinner from half a mile away.'

Reginald James composed a song entitled 'Antarctic Architecture,' which caused much hilarity amongst the men. The first two verses of the six-verse ditty were:

> My name is Frankie Wild-o! and my
>   huts on Elephant Isle,
> The most expert of architects could
>   hardly name its style.
> But as I sit all snug inside while
>   outside blows the gale,
> I think the pride is pardonable with
>   which I tell my tale.
>   O Frankly Wild-o Wild-o tra-la-la-la
> Mr.Franky Wild-o tra-la-la-la-la-la-la.
> My name is Franky Wild-o and
>   my hut's on Elephant Isle
> The wall's without a single brick,
>   and the roof without a tile,
> But nevertheless you must confess,
>   for many and many a mile
> It is the most palatial dwelling place
>   you'll find on Elephant Isle.

Thomas Orde Lees, who was given the difficult job of being in charge of stores, was the least popular man on Elephant Island. According to polar historian A.G.E. Jones, Orde Lees had shown himself to be cowardly and lazy during the boat journey to Elephant Island and was accused of engaging in a system of swaps and sales of food until Wild put a stop to it.

John Thomson, Orde Lees' biographer, wrote that 'he was a disciplined man and any food he put aside to consume at a later time, I believe, was from his own ration. Shackleton recognised this quality in Lees early on when he made him supply officer, and he was right to do so. Lees of course cared little for what the men thought of him, and really invited the type of petty denigration that was often delivered to him.'

Orde Lees wrote, 'there is a clique up against me to whom Wild gives too much head. I am called a Jew.' A few months later, he wrote again in his diary: 'strong cliques are now formed. This is bad.'

As the weeks grew into months and inertia set in, along with the anxiety over rescue and lack of food, it was Wild's iron discipline tempered with encouragement that stopped the situation developing into anarchy. Macklin recounted many years later that 'His resourcefulness, efficiency, absolute fairness and his quiet discipline and particularly his optimism kept everybody contented and satisfied that the best was being made of a pretty bad situation.'

One of the main causes of contention between Orde Lees and Wild was Orde Lees' assumption that Wild was not laying in enough stock of seals and penguins. Whether Wild believed that by overstocking he would be sending out the wrong message to the men or that he believed penguins and seals would continue to come on shore, he stuck to his plan. His intransigence drove Orde Lees to nag relentlessly. Macklin did not share Orde Lees' misgivings. 'I do not think it could be said that we were starving on Elephant Island, but we were often very hungry. We still had some odds and ends – nut-food, milk powder, biscuit, sugar and if I remember a few dried peas and some tapioca. Wild controlled the issue of these things very skillfully so as to maintain a feeling of anticipation, but there was so little of them that they were more of token value than real food value. As time went on supplies of extras petered out altogether. Wild was inclined to go on the principle of "when we have it we'll eat it; when its gone we'll go without," so the diet fluctuated considerably. This pleased most of us.'

According to Orde Lees' daughter, Zoe, she and her mother were told by him that a ballot took place in order to choose a victim to be killed and eaten and his name was drawn. Another report suggests there was a plot to fake a shooting accident on the Island and he would be the casualty.

Purportedly, Orde Lees learnt of this in the 1950s in a letter written by a fellow shipmate who did not want to go to his grave carrying the burden of such a ghastly plot. John Thomson, his biographer, thought it was possibly Frank Hurley, the photographer, who had written to him. However, according to James Fisher, Shackleton's biographer, Orde Lees wrote in a letter: 'As a matter of fact they i.e. Wild and perhaps Hussey, had planned to kill me as being the most active of all, merely because I was a tea totaller, in order to feed my comrades. I have retained Dr Hussey's letter on the subject.'

Further evidence of this is a quote by Hussey: 'Wild didn't like him he disobeyed orders it was his entire behavior. He was the one who was going to be killed and eaten, if we……..oh we were terribly short you know a few days before we were rescued, and we'd very little food for some days and Wild said to me, as he and I were walking up and down the shore of Elephant Island. Well, if we don't get food soon, we'll take that so and so out on the hill and we'll kill and eat him. It wasn't merely the state of the time, but I felt at the time and I feel now, that he really meant it. I've seen Wild sit down and eat a piece of raw seal or raw penguin just killed, and I felt that he would be quite capable of anything.'

Orde Lees lived with this morbid knowledge for the rest of his life, although by the time he died on 1 December 1958, he had lived a full and successful life. Thomson describes him as a man 'who was adored by his daughter, useful to Shackleton and ...... bore no malice of his adversaries.'

After more than three months, even the most optimistic of the men began to question the chance of rescue, but Wild had discussed a plan of action with Shackleton when they first landed on Elephant Island. Four members of the party, including Wild, would set out for Deception Island in *Dudley Docker* in the hope of meeting up with whalers returning for the spring.

As it turned out, this alternative was never needed. Due to the extraordinary seamanship of the navigator Worsley, Shackleton and his men reached South Georgia, although on the wrong side of the island. After making landfall, they spent four days recuperating and feeding off albatross chicks to regain their strength. They then sailed down an inlet and set up camp on a beach nicknamed Peggotty Camp.

Two of the men, McNish and Vincent, were too exhausted to continue, so were left on the beach with McCarthy to take care of them, while Shackleton, Worsley, and Tom Crean set out to scale on foot the vast Allardyce mountain range and make for the Stromness whaling station.

The three men, in feeble condition and wearing not much more than rags, scaled Alpine peaks and crossed glaciers and crevasses with nothing more than an ice pick and a length of rope, eventually arriving at Stromness 36 hours later to the total astonishment of everyone at the whaling station.

It took Shackleton four attempts to rescue the men from Elephant Island. With the continuing war in Europe it was impossible to secure a rescue ship, and when he finally succeeded in finding one, two attempts were thwarted by barricades of sea ice and a third when the ship developed engine trouble.

In the end it was thanks to the Chilean government – which offered Shackleton the small naval vessel, *Yelcho* – that he succeeded in reaching the island. It must have been a glorious sight when, after 105 days on the island, the men blackened by blubber smoke, and with hair wild and matted, were greeted by the sight of a small wooden ship appearing out of the mist on the horizon. From it a boat was lowered and the figure of 'the Boss' could be seen coming down the ladder and stepping into it. As he came within hearing distance he called out: 'Are you all well?' Wild, hoarse with emotion, called back, 'All safe, all well, Boss.' Shackleton, attentive as ever towards his men, approached the shore and threw tobacco and cigarettes at them.

It was a mad dash to get the bedraggled group of castaways safely off the island before the ice could ensnare them. Just as the last boatload headed for the ship, Orde Lees, who was wanting to show Shackleton their living quarters, somehow failed to be on it. He could be seen running across the beach waving and screaming frantically, undoubtedly to the jeers of the men. Shackleton turned back and the straggler dived into the boat to be met with a curt reproach from Shackleton. Finally, they were on their way back to the welcoming crowds of Punta Arenas. 'It was not until we were safe aboard the ship, and well under way, that one had time to offer up a prayer of thanksgiving for this timely deliverance from a living death.' wrote Orde Lees.

A month later, via Argentina, most of the men left for England although Shackleton and Worsely left for New Zealand to help with the rescue of the Ross Sea Party. The men who had been completely out of touch with civilization were now suddenly confronted with the horrors of the First World War. Putting aside all that they had endured, the majority of them rushed to enlist in Europe's deadliest conflict.

Frank Wild's five Antarctic Expeditions

British National Antarctic Expedition	Robert Falcon Scott	DISCOVERY 1901–04
British Antarctic Expedition	Ernest Shackleton	NIMROD 1907–09
Australasian Antarctic Expedition	Douglas Mawson	AURORA 1911–14
Imperial Trans-Antarctic Expedition	Ernest Shackleton	ENDURANCE 1914–16
Shackleton-Rowett Expedition	Ernest Shackleton	QUEST 1921–22

L-R: Back: Laurie, Rupert, Mabel (holding Renee), Kubie (holding Nancy), Ethel
Front: Wild & Joy — Wild's niece who is in her nineties.

THE WILD FAMILY

Benjamin Wild born 1846 died 1915 married 1870 **Mary Cook** born died 1909

The 13 Wild siblings

Sarah Ann Margaret born 1871 died 1914 - married **Thomas Harry Bryant** – two children – **Ernest** & **Beatrice**

John Robert Francis born 1973 died 1939 - married **Vera Altman** 1921, **Beatrice Rowbotham** 1931

Charles William born 1874 died 1897

Mary Elizabeth (Cissie) born 1876 died 1962

Minnie Rosetta born 1877 died 1877

Rosetta Blanche born 1878 died 1878

Henry (Harry) Ernest born 1879 died 1918

Benjamin Eustace born 1880 died 1900

Valentine Rupert born 1883 died 1973 married Mabel Russel – one daughter **Renée**

Laurence Cook born 1884 died 1983 married Ethel Mary Grose - two daughters **Joyce Edith** & **Annie Mary Cook**

Percy Hutchinson born 1886 died 1953

Christine Constance born 1887 died 1978 married **Rowland James Garratt**

Stanley Oscar born 1891 died 1984 married Rosie Rigby one daughter **Josephine**

ACKNOWLEDGEMENTS.

To thank everyone who has helped me during the past seven years is an impossible task.

I am deeply grateful to June Rowbotham who entrusted me with Beatrice Wild's papers that became the cornerstone of my research into Wild's life in South Africa. I am very grateful to her for the copy of the Memoirs and her encouragement to publish them. Luigi Caseleggio's passion for polar history and dogged research of Wild were key to me fulfilling this project. I am grateful to have had time with Brian Frost before he died and for his generosity in sharing memories and photographs and I thank his wife Colleen for her kind hospitality each time I visited Cape Town. I thank Shaughn Frost for his genuine interest in Wild and his co-operation in piecing together many fragments of the story. I am indebted to Joan Provis, besides remaining my ally throughout, played a truly significant role in this project and gave up much of her time helping me trace Wild's footsteps. I thank Mike Rattray who owned Quest Estate for his contribution and the historian Professor John Lambert of Pretoria University, who generously gave me much of his time and access to his invaluable paper "Maintaining a British Way of Life". I must acknowledge Peter Baker, whose irrepressible enthusiasm for the Wild story led to the setting up a plaque in his pub in the village of Richmond in the Karoo, South Africa, It reads, 'To all who read this plaque it is hereby dictated that you lift your glass and/or light up a cigar to one of the greatest polar explorers of all time'.

I am most grateful to the English descendents of the Wild family. The late Anne Fright, Wild's niece who encouraged me at the very start of the project and I thank her daughter Judy Corfield, Wild's great niece for her permissions, interest and support. Tim Fright who recently sledge-hauled the final 97 miles to the South Pole in honour of his great- great uncle's uncompleted 1909 mission has added considerably to my mission. I am grateful to his father Nicholas for introducing me to their cousins, the Australian branch of the Wild family, Julie George and Richard Francis. Their unstinting generosity in giving me material and photographs, many unseen, has been incalculable; Julie undertook the mammoth task of re-typing the Memoirs and Richard's help with the family tree and much else cannot be overstated. Their mother Joy Francis, Wild's niece, an indomitable lady in her 90's has supported my endeavours unstintingly.

Staying with the Antipodeans I am indebted to the author John Thomson for sharing with me some insightful material relating to Wild's time on Elephant Island.

I thank Yorkshireman Tony Wright, a distant cousin of Wild's, for bringing to my attention all sorts of genealogical material including that of Captain Cook.

Piecing together the journey of Wild's medals has been central to this book, an arduous task made easier by my 'co-sleuther' the American medal expert Glenn Stein FRGS. I have relied heavily on his inexhaustible expertise. John MacKenzie the son of Don MacKenzie who handled the Polar medal in its early days in South Africa has been an immense help as has Michael Naxton formerly of Sotheby's. I thank too, David Erskine-Hill of Dix Noonan Webb, medal auctioneers, for his assistance. Unbounded thanks go to Dr Mike Wain, custodian of the Wild medals, and co-devotee of Wild.

I have been very fortunate to have had the notable Polar authority Robert Stephenson of the Antarctic-circle.org website in my corner, especially sharing with me his limitless knowledge of Aurora Australis books.

Some of my happiest times were spent in Kwazulu Natal with Peter and Susan Rutherfoord of Ghost Mountain Lodge that overlooks Wild's former Quest farm. They gave me full access to their ancient shop ledgers as well as driving me around the area. The Rutherfoord's introduced me to Ron Selley's book 'West of the Moon' which in turn led to a meeting with Ron Selley on the west coast of the Cape. He generously gave me unlimited access to his grandmother Milly's diary which brought to life Wild's time in Mkuze.

Jeni Ingram of Mpumalanga introduced me to her father Bjorn Behr who remembered Wild. Behr kindly gave me a copy of a treasured photograph of Wild and sent me the paper clipping stating the ashes were in a chapel. A thoughtful gesture that changed the course of my book.

Alkis Dukakis, the Johannesburg historian, never faltered as I bombarded him with requests for information of South Africa's history and particular its mining industry. I thank Meg Jordi for the copies of her father's letters to Trix and John Lambert Professor for his insight into early South African history.

I am grateful to Lesley Venn who has worked tirelessly in helping me locate Vera Bogosoff's family. I thank Alexandra Shackleton for permission to quote from her grandfather, Sir Ernest Shackleton's work and I thank Richard Macklin for allowing me to quote extensively from his father's material. Jean Burnham generously lent me valuable material relating to Dr James McIlroy. I appreciate the support and friendship given to me by Wild's former biographer, Leif Mills.

So much of my research has depended on the goodwill, patience and erudition of the Scott Polar Research Institute of Cambridge University and I thank in particular, Heather Lane (Librarian and Keeper of Collections), Naomi Boneham (Archivist) and Lucy Martin (Picture Library Manager). I thank the Mitchell Library of the State Library of New South Wales for their goodwill and support regarding the Memoirs.

My gratitude goes to Alan Buff whose crucial role in the story – led me to

Wild's ashes. Heartfelt thanks go to my Ice Tracks business partner Carolina Mantella whose love of Antarctica is inimitable. She was not only the driving force behind Wild's commemoration in South Georgia but ran our business single handed as I strove to finish the book.

I offer my sincere thanks to Mike Cable's inexhaustible determination to bring out the best in the book and his patience with my intransigence. Sincere thanks are due to book designers Robin Ollington and Frank Lee of Lodge Graphics and Derek Caudwell for his indexing.

I owe an incalculable debt to Barbara Kinghorn, whose steely determination fortunately rubs off. For many years she has cast a gimlet eye over my scribblings and the thrust of her pen pared the original Wild manuscript into shape.

Innumerable authors are indebted to the historian Dr Beau Riffenburgh for his expertise, astounding knowledge and skilful editing of polar works. I am no different. As I was flagging, his unstinting generosity, praise and encouragement and undeniable skill saw me over the last hurdle.

Biographers become possessed – for a time we have only one real interest and we are unsympathetic to the ennui our narrowing world and contracting conversations cause.

My large family, friends and siblings have had many demands placed upon them during the research and writing of this book. I have called for their undivided attention while endlessly holding court on my subject. Thank you.

The Butler daughters' bountiful encouragement and advice in my somewhat belated writing career has been phenomenal. A final and heartfelt thank you is for Jim, who for the past seven years has had to share me with another man, and has done so with grace.

NOTES

EARLY LIFE
Page
5 'Nothing gave me more pleasure': Stanley Wild letter to Julie George 25 February 1973)
7 'Frank was always climbing': Letter to K.G. Thomson SPRI Ms 1078/2/D
7 'He was a little terror': Letter to K.G. Thomson 1957 SPRI Ms1078/2/D
7 'As a boy': SPRI Ms 1078/2/2D
8 'We had to steam': Ms SPRI 944/5/1-8
9 'The King gave the Victorian Order': Diary of Edward Wilson.
9 'As Frank got down': The homecoming as described by Stanley Wild letter to his niece Julie George 25 February 1977
9 'Frank loved to come and confess': SPRI Ms1078/2/22
9 'There are some things': Polar Record Vol 18, No 112, 1976 page 43-45

THE WARS YEARS AND NYASALAND
11 'Highly interested and amused': Letter to Julie George Stanley Wild 1 November 1973
11 'Commander Wild I believe?': Letter to Julie George Stanley Wild 1 November 1973
13 'Sheer good luck': The Arrow Magazine
14 'Wonderous accounts': SPRI Ms/3/4/D
14 'Wonderful country': SPRI Ms/3/4/D

QUEST EXPEDITION
17 'Worsley, who is a fine seaman': SPRI Ms1591/1/7/1/D 16 June1921
18 'On Christmas day a whole gale': Macklin SPRI Ms1591/25/1
18 'good night boys': Macklin SPRI Ms1591/25/1
18 'You are always wanting me': Shackleton's Last Voyage Frank Wild
18 'Wild was most extraordinary': SPRI Ms1078/2/8/D
19 'I assembled each mess': Shackleton's Last Voyage Frank Wild.

19 'So we said good-bye': Shackleton's Last Voyage Frank Wild
22 'He didn't tell me about it': Conversation between James Fisher and McIlroy 26 August 1955 transcript Mrs Jean Burnham
22 'I have his photograph': SPRI Ms 1078/5/5/D
22 'it is hardly necessary': letter to E.A. Perris, news editor, Daily Chronicle, 23 October 1916

SOUTH AFRICA
23 'I saw Vera in Durban': Smuts letters UCT BC 714
23 'Presented by humble duty': SPRI Ms 944/2/1-5
23 'I should hate to settle': SPRI Ms 944/5/1-8
24 'Do I long for the sea': SPRI Ms 944/5/1-8
24 'I do long for the sight' SPRI Ms 944/5/1-8
25 'as the little man' :SPRI Ms 1078/5/D
26 'was not very favourable….I was very sorry to hear': Smuts letters UCT Smuts papers BC 714
26 'You are lucky' Bigelow Poultney SPRI Ms 1688 not fully catalogued
27 'I watched pumkins' Milly's diary, West of the Moon Ron Selley
27 'in the remote parts of': Zululand Times 2 April 1925
27 'the ten historical plagues': Zululand Times 15 March 1928
27 'most of us are ex-servicemen': "Hluhluwe Cotton Settlement," African Sugar and Cotton Planter 1, no. 8 June 1925
28 'none of us had much money': Milly's diary, West of the Moon Ron Selley
28 'We danced to the music': Milly's diary, West of the Moon Ron Selley
28 'Spry, Nick and I': Milly's diary, West of the Moon Ron Selley

30 '*on fare that the poorest of the poor would have scorned*': Press Cuttings SPRI Ms 1078/5/
30 '*The first time I set my eyes*': West of the Moon Ron Selley
37 '*I always feel very grateful*': Ms 1078/2/11D
37 '*I was sorely tempted to part*': SPRI Ms 100/117D 24 August 1932
37 '*It is not a very*': SPRI Ms 944/9/D
43 '*Why dammit, the man*': SPRI Ms 1078/5/D
44 '*like two excited schoolboys*': Letter to Julie George 25 Feb 1977.

BRIEFLY BETTER TIMES
40 '*So long as a man*': SPRI Ms 944/5/5
42 '*to have Frank there*': SPRI Ms 1688 (not fully catalogued)
43 '*I managed to make*': Letter from Jack Scott SPRI
43 '*I am still blasting*': SPRI Ms1078/3/5/2 letter to Rupert 28/11/38
44 '*we are all on*': SPRI Ms 1688 (not fully catalogued)
44 '*we are all on*': SPRI Ms 1688 (not fully catalogued)
44 '*the civil list pension*': SPRI Ms 1688 (not fully catalogued)
45 '*if only I had*': Trix Wild letter Dora Poultney SPRI Ms 1688 (not fully catalogued)
47 '*I have lost my grip*': SPRI Ms 1688 (not fully catalogued)
48 '*I doubt if Wild*': obituary Polar Record 1940 3 (19): P 280–281

WHY THE MEMOIRS WERE NEVER PUBLISHED
67 '*that he did not die*': SPRI Ms 1078/2/14/D
67 '*such a notable and gallant*': SPRI Ms 1078/2/14/D
67 '*the only Diary I have*': SPRI Ms 1078/2/14/D

67 '*dependent on us*': SPRI Ms1078/2/14/D
68 '*I should be very willing*': SPRI Ms 1078/2/14/D
68 '*I do hope your writing*': SPRI Ms 1078/2/14/D
68 '*to give me full*': SPRI Ms 1078/2/15/D
68 '*I have not received*': SPRI Ms 1078/2/14/D
69 '*is she middle aged*': SPRI Ms 1078/2/15/D
69 '*The book would not*': SPRI Ms 1078/2/15/D
69 '*First he (Thomson) must have*': Letters in possession of Meg Jordi, Cape Town
70 '*Does not the fact*': SPRI Ms 1078/2/14/D
70 '*to see myself deprived*': SPRI Ms 1078/2/5/D

MY QUEST
74 '*over boasted and over run*': SPRI Ms 1078/3/6

ELEPHANT ISLAND
190 '*the morning after*': Walter E. How Seaman SPRI Ms 1078/2/22
191 '*at the last twisting*': Shackleton's Diary
191 '*Wild sat at the rudder*': South by Sir Ernest Shackleton
191 '*Some of the men were reeling*': South by Ernest Shackleton
193 '*On a calm day*': Stanley Wild
193 '*there is a clique*' Orde Lees Diary
194 '*His resourcefulness, efficiency*' SPRI Ms 1078/2/8/D
194 '*Wild didn't like him*' SPRI Ms 1078/2/22
194 '*Macklin recounted*': SPRI Ms 1688
194 '*I do not think it*': SPRI Ms 1078/2/8/D
194 '*As a matter of fact*': SPRI Ms 1078/2/5/D

BIBLIOGRAPHY

Bickel, Lennard. In search of Frank Hurley, Macmillan 1980

Brown, A. Golden Heritage, Stilfontein, Transvaal 1983

Cartwright A P Valley of Gold Howard Timmins Publishers 1961

Cartwright A P Golden Age Purnell 1968

Doorly, Gerald S E. Voyages of the Morning. Bluntisham 1994

Emden, P H Randlords Hodder & Stoughton, 1935Haddelsey, Stephen. Born Adventurer – The life of Frank Bickerton, Sutton Publishing, 2005

Hayes, James Gordon. Conquest of the South Pole, Thornton Butterworth, London, 1932

Huntford, Roland. Shackleton. Hodder & Stoughton Ltd, 1985

Hurley ,Frank. Argonauts of the South

Letcher, O. The Gold Mines of Southern Africa, Waterlow, 1936

Marr J W S. Into the Frozen South, Cassell & Co Ltd, 1923

Mawon, Douglas. The Home of the Blizzard

Mill, Hugh Robert. The Life of Sir Ernest Shackleton

Mills, Leif. Frank Wild. Caedemon of Whitby, 1999

Poulsom, Neville. The White Ribbon. Seaby 1968

Riffenburgh, Beau. Racing with Death: Douglas Mawson – Antarctic Explorer, Bloomsbury 2008

Riffenburgh, Beau. Nimrod Bloomsbury 2005

Scott, Robert Falcon. The Voyage of the Discovery 1905

Selley, Ron. West of the Moon, 30° South Publishers (Pty) Ltd, 2009

Shackleton, Ernest. South 1919

Shackleton, Ernest. The Heart of the Antarctic

Shorten, J.R. The Johannesburg Saga: the author, 1970

Thomson, John. Elephant Island and Beyond The Life and Diaries of Thomas Orde-Lees.

Thomson, John. Shackleton's Captain, A biography of Frank Worsley, Mosaic Press, 1999

Tyler-Lewis, Kelly. The Lost Men, Bloomsbury 2006

Wild, Frank. Shackleton's Last Voyage, Cassell & Co, Ltd, 1923

Worsley, FA. Shackleton's Boat Journey

Seaver George. Edward Wilson of the Antarctic. Naturalist and Friend

Seaver, George. Scott of the Antarctic: A Study of Character

Newspapers

The Star South Africa

Bedford Guardian England

Rand Daily Mail

Published papers

J Lambert, '"Maintaining a British Way of LIfe": English-speaking South Africa's Patriotic, Cultural and Charitable Associations' Historia: Journal of the Historical Association of South Africa, vol 54, no 2, pp 55-76.

Aurora Australis Penguins Watched these Polar Printer (John Feely (State library of Victoria) Melbourne

Matthew A Schnurr Loweveld Cotton: A political ecology of agricultural failure in Natal and Zululand, 1844-1948

Matthew A Schnurr "Hluhluwe Cotton Settlement," African Sugar and Cotton Planter 1, no. 8 (June 1925):

Unpublished sources

National Archives London (F0610/190, F0917/2049)

Singapore National library (NL501)

University of Cape Town Library (BC 714 Smuts letters)

The Alexander Turnbull Library New Zealand

Mitchell Library Sydney (ML MSS 2198)

The Royal Geographic Society

The Scott Polar Research Institute Cambridge

207

Illustrations

Front Cover Frank Wild courtesy of Scott Polar Research Institurte SPRI

Robert Falcon Scott, Ernest Shackleton, Douglas Mawson, Roald Amundsen Courtesy of SPRI

Mary Wild with Frank's brother, Laurie courtesy of Julie George & Richard Francis & Joy Francis

Benjamin Wild courtesy of Julie George & Richard Francis & Joy Francis

Wild family group courtesy of Judy Corfield

Shackleton and Wild on Quest courtesy of SPRI

Shackleton's burial on South Georgia courtesy of SPRI

Cairn overlooking Cumberland Bay author

Shackleton's grave today author

Wild's step son Valor courtesy of June Rowbotham

Wild (right) with his trusted houseboy Dick in white apron courtesy of June Rowbotham

Wild in front of the South African Railway hut courtesy of June Rowbotham

Wild (centre)working on railway on Mkuze River courtesy of June Rowbotham

Wild in front of the South African Railway hut courtesy of June Rowbotham

Nick Selley and Frank (right) with the notorious 'coffin' courtesy of June Rowbotham

Tented camp near Pongola River courtesy of June Rowbotham

Illustration of Wild in ox cart courtesy of Robin Ollington

Ghost Mountain standing proud above the Umbombo mountains courtesy of Bob Rayner

Lecture notes courtesy of SPRI

Wild with nephew Brian at the Great Zimbabwe ruins courtesy of Brian Frost

Trix with nephew Brian and the Wolseley courtesy of Brian Frost

Trix's notes of Wild's death courtesy of June Rowbotham

Transvaal Sea Cadets marching in Wild's funeral cortege through the centre of Johannesburg courtesy of the Star

Family group, Trix second from left courtesy of June Rowbotham

Medal courtesy of Dr Mike Wain

Ledger at Braamfontein Cemetery author

Memorial Plaque courtesy of James Butler

The Nimrod Expediton 1907 -1909. L-R Wild, Shackleton, Marshall and Adams courtesy of SPRI

Wild at Mkuze with Ghost Mountain in the background courtesy of June Rowbotham

Kloof Ridge, the house that Wild built for Frost author

The Columbarium at Braamfontein cemetery author

Portrait taken of Frank Wild taken for his Memoirs during the 1930's.

The Men on Elephant Island. Wild with pipe courtesy of SPRI

Wild watching the end of the Endurance courtesy of SPRI

The hotel in Gollel where Wild worked behind the bar author

Portrait taken of Frank Wild for his Memoirs during the 1930's courtesy Bjorn Behr

A hand written page from the Memoirs courtesy Mitchell Library, State Library of New South Wales

Back Cover Frank Wild in winter gear courtesy of SPRI

INDEX

THE FRANK WILD MEMOIRS